A Good Investment?

A Good Investment?

Philanthropy and the Marketing of Race in an Urban Public School

Amy Brown

 University of Minnesota Press
Minneapolis
London

An earlier version of chapter 4 appeared as "Waiting for Superwoman: White Female Teachers and the Construction of the 'Neoliberal Savior' in a New York City Public School," *Journal for Critical Education Policy Studies* 11, no. 2 (2013): 123–64; reprinted with permission. An earlier version of chapter 6 appeared as "Consciousness-Raising or Eyebrow-Raising? Reading Urban Fiction with High School Students in Freirean Cultural Circles," *Penn GSE Perspectives on Urban Education* 9, no. 1; reprinted with permission. Sections of chapters 1 and 3 were published in "A Good Investment? Race, Philanthrocapitalism, and Performative Professionalism in a New York City Small School of Choice," *International Journal of Qualitative Studies in Education* 25, no. 4; and in Denise Blum and Char Ullman, eds., *The Globalization and Corporatization of Education: Limits and Liminality of the Market Mantra*, 9–30 (New York: Routledge, 2013); reprinted with permission. Sections of chapters 1 and 2 were published in "Philanthrocapitalism: Race, Political Spectacle, and the Marketplace of Beneficence in a New York City School," in Bree Pickower and Edwin Mayorga, eds., *What's Race Got to Do with It? How Current School Reform Policy Maintains Racial and Economic Inequality*, 147–66 (New York: Peter Lang, 2015); reprinted with permission.

Published by the University of Minnesota Press
111 Third Avenue South, Suite 290
Minneapolis, MN 55401–2520
http://www.upress.umn.edu

Library of Congress Cataloging-in-Publication Data
Brown, Amy.
A good investment? : philanthropy and the marketing of race in an urban public school / Amy Brown.
Includes bibliographical references and index.
ISBN 978-0-8166-9112-8 (hc)—ISBN 978-0-8166-9114-2 (pb)
1. Public schools—New York (State)—New York. 2. Educational fund raising—New York (State)—New York. 3. Education—Social aspects—New York (State)—New York. 4. African Americans—Education—New York (State)—New York. 5. Academic achievement—New York (State)—New York. I. Title.
LA339.N5B76 2015
373.09173'2097471—dc23   2014047948

Printed in the United States of America on acid-free paper

The University of Minnesota is an equal-opportunity educator and employer.

21 20 19 18 17 16 15   10 9 8 7 6 5 4 3 2 1

For Victor

If I am not what I've been told I am, then it means that you're not what you thought you were either! And that is the crisis.

— JAMES BALDWIN, "A TALK TO TEACHERS"

Unto whomsoever much is given, of him shall be much required.

— LUKE 12:48

Contents

Preface and Acknowledgments

Although my research officially began in 2008, when I was hired to teach tenth-grade English at College Prep, this project really began in 2003, when I started teaching public middle school in New York City. I began to question how my, and my students', presence in our English classroom articulated with politics of class, race, and place in the United States and globally. I looked for answers not only in my classroom but also in the graduate-level classes I was taking toward my master's degree. I became enthralled with the critical and exploratory work that qualitative researchers were doing in order to expose how, when, and why people's consent is shaped to accept inequality as both legitimate and natural (Hebdige 1979, 15). This work embodied a certain kind of possibility, and thus, after teaching for three years in New York City's public schools, I went to graduate school to study social anthropology.

From the beginning, I knew that I would return to New York City schools for my fieldwork. As I took classes at the University of Texas at Austin that focused on feminist and critical race theory, as well as on African diaspora and activist anthropology, I thought more deeply about my own identity politics, as well as the politics involved in being a teacher and a researcher. I remained fascinated with the construction and consequences of race, and became more interested in the intersectional ways in which privilege and oppression operate. I also became interested in the ways in which qualitative research could lend power and voice to lesser-heard stories. Beginning my teaching at College Prep, I knew I wanted to focus on the ways that people were rearticulating or resisting prescribed social categories, but I was unaware when I started of the impact that the school's reliance on private funding would have on the ways that people managed their performances and constructed their ideas about themselves and the world.

In addition to learning about the intersection between privatization of public schools and the construction of race, class, and gender, embarking on this project helped me to deepen my relationships with students, parents, and colleagues at College Prep and thus to improve my teaching practice. It also led me to a deeper awareness of my own identity as an educator, an anthropologist, and a White woman. In other words, qualitative research helped me to hold up a mirror not only to College Prep but also to myself and to the world beyond College Prep.

It is for this reason that I owe my biggest thanks to the College Prep community. Officially, I was a teacher and anthropologist there, but to this day I still count many College Prep community members, including former students, parents, and colleagues, as dear friends. To preserve their anonymity, I cannot name them here, but for their trust, openness, patience, humor, courage, and love in some of the most important moments over the past seven years, I am eternally grateful.

Outside College Prep, my teachers, mentors, and colleagues provided the questions, challenges, support, and guidance that helped me to stick through this project, even when it seemed most muddy and murky. My "coach," Doug Foley, oversaw this manuscript through and beyond the dissertation stage; Doug, I can't thank you enough for your unflinching honesty and overarching support for my scholarship. I'm lucky to call you my mentor and friend, and couldn't have asked for a better advisor. I thank Nadine Bryce for the brilliant teaching and mentorship that inspired me to explore anthropology and for reminding me that it is never too early to begin the thinking/writing process.

To some of my earliest teachers, Dorothy Habecker, Anne Riley, Josephine Pirrone, Rachel Crawford, Robert Makus, and James Taylor, I thank you for providing me with a crucial foundation for critical thinking, reading, and writing. Ted Gordon, João Costa Vargas, Keffrelyn Brown, Jemima Pierre, Kevin Foster, Maria Franklin, Pauline Strong, Martha Menchaca, John Hartigan, Suzy Seriff, Laura Lein, and Luis Urrieta were also incredible teachers and fabulous models of what it means to be politicized and publicly engaged intellectuals, and I'm grateful for their deep engagement with me and with my work. Peter Demerath has also, over the years, offered invaluable guidance, as have Brad Porfilio, E. Wayne Ross, Maia Cucchiara, Eli Goldblatt, and David Hursh. I am deeply grateful to Jill Koyama and Tom Pedroni for their commitment to improving this manuscript. I thank Pieter Martin, John Donohue, Ana Bichanich, and the incredible editing team at the University of Minnesota

Press for their patient and essential direction through the publication process.

Thanks to Orson Robbins-Pianka and Lane Stilson at the Stern School of Business for valuable statistical guidance, and to Sharon Givens for helpful editing of a first version of this manuscript. I benefited greatly from the advice and support of many of my other colleagues affiliated with the Council on Anthropology and Education, including, but not limited to, Bryan McKinley Jones Brayboy, Greg Tanaka (who so aptly suggested the title of chapter 4 during a CAE Works in Progress Session; thank you, Greg!), Christina Convertino, Wes Shumar, Carol Brandt, Kathryn Hayes, Marguerite Wilson, Denise Blum, Stephanie Daza, Marta Baltodano, Bradley Levinson, Rolf Straubhaar, Ted Hamann, Kathy Schultz, and Janet Hecsh. Thanks to Jane Gordon and Tricia Way, who gave me valuable feedback on this work when I presented it at Temple University's Workshop on Political Theory.

I thank my colleagues in the Critical Writing Program at the University of Pennsylvania, especially Valerie Ross, Patrick Wehner, Rodger LeGrand, Doug Paletta, Brighid Kelley, Mingo Reynolds, R. J. Bernocco, Matthew Johnson, Carol Kalin, Rafael Walker, Miriam Clinton, Dana Walker, Jacqueline Sadashige, Shaleigh Kwok, and Durba Chattaraj, for their energy and for their ongoing support of my teaching and scholarship. From the Graduate School of Education, I thank Kathy Hall, Alex Posecznick, Francisco Ramos, Lauren Scicluna, Susan Thomas, and Chezare Warren for their guidance and support, and I thank the graduate students in my 2012 Qualitative Modes of Inquiry course, especially Liu Jiang and Jonathan Tam, for their valuable insight and questions. I'm fortunate to be an honorary member of the GSE family. In the Department of Anthropology and the School of Social Policy and Practice, I thank John Jackson and Deb Thomas; it's been a pleasure to connect with and learn from you both. At the Wharton School, I thank Anne Greenhalgh, Derek Newberry, Madeline Boyer, Mario Moussa, Joanne Baron, Pete Fader, Michael Joiner, Annette Mattei, Renee Torchia, Lauren Hirshon, Vishal Bhatia, Todd Norris, Aviva Leggatt, and Dave Heckman; I'm lucky to be a part of the Executive Education HPT observer team with you all. To my friend and colleague Mark Stern, it's been an adventure working with you, and I look forward to continuing to learn and write together. To Bree Picower and Edwin Mayorga, I'm honored to collaborate with you on activist and academic work. Jamie Thomas, I foresee great fun and great work ahead! To the members of the Philadelphia Teacher Action Group, the Caucus of Working Educators, and the Philadelphia Teaching and Research in Support of Public Education Organizing Committee, especially Kelley Collings, Rhiannon Maton, Dan Symonds, Shaw MacQueen, Larissa Pahomov, Shira Cohen, Pamela Roy, Ismael Jimenez, Sheila Myers, Eileen Duffey, Peggy Savage, Kathleen Riley, Kristin Luebbert, Ron Whitehorne, Anissa Weinraub, David Hensel, Tatiana Olmedo, Paul Prescod, Chris Rogers, Diane Payne, Tamara Anderson, Tom Hladczuk, Alison McDowell, Jaimie Stevenson, Max Rosen-Long, Luigi Borda, Nat Bartels, Sarah Burgess, Karel Kilimnik, Kristin Combs, Madeleine Nist, Hanako Franz, Amy Roat, Nora Kerrich, Nick Palazzolo, Barbara Ferman, Encarna Rodriguez, Jerusha Conner, Sonia Rosen, and Barbara Ferman, your drive, determination, and energy continue to feed my own. It is a privilege to be a part of our important and ongoing struggle for educational equity.

I also owe a huge thanks to my family: to David, Laura, and Sarah Brown, I wouldn't be me, nor would this book be a book, without you. Thanks for your unwavering belief in me, even through the times I doubted myself. To my bubby, Sarah Shumofsky, who taught me to tell it like it is, thank you. To the Browns (and the Andersons, the Strickers, the Christies, the Thompsons, the Brookinses, and the Cosgrays), to the Shumofskys (and the Chivos and the Meuses), to Sr. Teresa Kennedy, Rob Whitcher, Tracy Adams, Frank Alagna and John Meehan, the Cavanaughs, and the Franeks, and to the Bellantis, the Pilatos, the Keats, Barbara Marder, the Klevanses, the Macdonalds, and the Bartsches, your love and care over the years have made all the difference.

To my closest friends from the University of Texas at Austin, Roger Reeves, Monica Jimenez, Courtney Morris, Martin Perna, Chris Loperena, Mohan and Briana Ambikaipaker, Raja Swamy, Tifani Blakes, and Naomi Reed, thank you for your brilliance and for your inspiration. The coffees, dinners, late-night writing "seshes," wine/beer, and running/swimming dates with all of you helped to make Austin a home away from home. I thank Rene Valdez and the Fulmore Middle School Young COBRAs for many stimulating conversations and for basketball and soccer games that kept my head clear as I wrote a first version of this manuscript in 2010–11. Thanks to supportive colleagues in anthropology and education at UT Austin, who helped to push my thinking further in both academic and social settings: Emmet Campos, Alysia Childs, Alix Chapman, Gwendolyn

Ferretti, Hafeez Jamali, Nedra Lee, Elvia Mendoza, Mubbashir Rizvi, Lynn Selby, Tane Ward, Mitsy Chanel-Blot, Chris Milk Bonilla, Maribel Garza, and Gabby Yearwood. I owe much gratitude to my partner, my lifelong friends, and my loved ones. Bo Blizard, your love, support, intellect, and humor continue to make my work infinitely better. Thank you to all of my chosen family members in the United States and abroad, for helping me to maintain focus, for challenging me, for helping me to keep my mind and heart open, for helping me make meaning of the world, and also for reminding me to laugh through both the easy and tough times: Teresa von Fuchs, Kerrie Mitchell, Liz Knauer, Rachel Ciporen, Tommy Crowley, Sam Adewumi, Lourdes Cardriche, Katey Metzroth, Emil Nassar, Amaryllis Rivera Nassar, Lauren Ball, Kareema Nunley, Hollis Holmes, Jess Hsia, Kap Rapoza, Asher Vance, Melissa Fernando, Charles Harrison, Michal Greenberg, Celine and Paco Nassar, Ricky Borges, Melissa Mendez, Jermar Perry, Stephen Elliott, Karen Linton, Lewis Marcel Hughes, Alisha Ebling, Mike Washington (a.k.a. Bear), Wale and Kaya Oyejide, Tim Blackwell, Sharif Lacey, Paul Rutherford, Rugigana Kavamahanga, Matt Brennan, Jared Matthews, Beth Bour, Jody Agostinelli, Alex Argo, Anouk and Hugo Bidot, Marie-Stephanie Lohner, Ka'shaundra Fortsch, Sarah and Kevin Bunch, Dayo Adeyemi, Cristal Williams, Phil Asbury, Nyasha George, Edgardo Vasquez, Nada and Geoff Stevens, Cliff Colmon, Case Dorkey, Lanaya Irvin, Imani Bossier, Panch Nishan Khalsa, Joel Kretschman, Olivia Foschi, Christopher Orr, Sarah Scherer, Joel Brandon, Paul Taormina, the Léon-Bejarano family, Claire Pelham, Linda and Mason O'Neal, Toreono Thomas (a.k.a. Pax), Kofi Ofori, Lucia Cantero, Justine Welch and Eli Mastin, Matt White, Halima Cassells, Jessica Yamasaki, and David and Margaret Blizard.

Finally, thanks to my past, present, and future students, who are always my best teachers.

Privatization and Political Spectacle in Education

It was April of 2010, and I was in my second year of ethnographic teacher research at the small, unscreened New York City public high school of choice that I call the College Preparatory Academy (hereafter, College Prep).

On that spring day, as usual, I dismissed my students, and sat down at my desk to check my e-mail. I noticed that one had just arrived from Sebastian Thomas, the director of the school's in-house nonprofit organization, which read:

> The College Prep Spring Benefit is on Thursday, April 29 from 6pm to 8pm at The Firm. Present will be 100–150 of the school's most generous supporters, and approximately 8–10 student ambassadors. I would like to invite one member of every grade team to attend, with the understanding that this is a work event. Per session pay is not available. We will be responsible for mingling and talking up the school and our respective roles to guests . . . you should take into account what the evening calls for: energy, positivity, relentless conversation-starting . . . essentially, sales. Not everyone on the team may enjoy or feel that he/she is good at that.
>
> Thanks,
> Sebastian

Curious, I volunteered, and was approved by Mr. Thomas to attend.

College Prep created its own in-house nonprofit organization, which I call "the Foundation," in 2008, in order to solicit funds from the private sector, most notably a corporate law firm in midtown Manhattan, which I call "the Firm." Because of the Foundation, College Prep's website thanks five foundations, seven elected officials, and thirty-four companies and organizations for their charitable donations, and also thanks more than three hundred individuals who have each donated five thousand dollars or more to the school. It is important to note that of the 458 students enrolled in the school, grades 9–12, 81 percent identify as Black, 17 percent as Hispanic, 1 percent as Asian / Pacific Islander, and fewer than 1 percent as White or American Indian[1] (nysed.gov 2008–9). Of the school's thirty-five teachers, twenty-three identify as White, seven as African American or Black, three as biracial or mixed race, and two as Latino.[2] While these statistics are typical of New York City schools, College Prep's 93 percent graduation rate and 97 percent college acceptance rate for seniors stand out as atypical, compared to New York City's average graduation rate of 62.7 percent (schools.nyc.gov 2010). With its high graduation and college matriculation rates for Black and Brown urban students, College Prep markets itself through advertising, media, and benefits as both needy and deserving of funders' generosity.

Before the benefit, Mr. Thomas sent out memos and held meetings with the teachers and students whom he had chosen to attend. As expressed in the e-mail, staff and students were carefully selected to properly represent College Prep. We had "the look": teachers were young, articulate, energetic, and predominantly (except for one) White. Students were Black and Latino, spoke in Standard English, consistently came to school on time and in uniform, could talk about being college bound, despite the hardships or challenges in their lives, and would be sure to say great things about College Prep. It was important to perform both neediness and deservedness in our solicitation of funders' help and to make funders feel generous, important, appreciated, and not threatened. Despite the fact that teachers and students were not paid for attending the event and were coached beforehand by Mr. Thomas to talk up the school, to "dress like teachers" or "dress like students" (in school uniform, with dress shoes), to not walk around the room in groups larger than two, and to refrain from eating (or, for teachers, partaking in any liquor from the open bar at the event), the College Prep community was well aware that it was the money from these funders that provided the copy machines, paper, LCD projectors, interactive whiteboards, food at weekly staff meetings, mobile computer labs, and well-staffed college advising office. Many of us (including me) had been affiliated previously with other New York City schools where the only resource freely available to teachers was chalk. While we knew that we had to play up racialized and classed stereotypes of "at-risk" urban youth and "savior" teachers, we were also grateful for the resources that were made available by our "sales" techniques.

So at the benefit, I played my part. I avoided the tables of chocolate-covered strawberries, napoleons, cream puffs, pot stickers, sushi, and crudités that lined the edges of the room. Shirley Temple in hand, I circulated through the room, talked up the school, and actually enjoyed the conversations with the potential funders. Many seemed to be genuinely interested in my perspective on education and in my role and experience at College Prep, and were happy to drop checks made out to the Foundation in the designated box as they left the room. At one point, I checked in with two of my students who were walking around together. They said they were doing well, then walked away, saying, "we are going to keep circulating." They seemed to have taken Mr. Thomas's advice at the brief pre-benefit coaching huddle to heart: "Remember," he said, "whatever you do, you don't need to be nervous; this is what you do. You are good at this."

And we were. After the benefit, Mr. Thomas sent out a thank-you e-mail that expressed that revenue accrued from the benefit made up 34 percent of the Foundation's annual budget, and was the school's second biggest source of funding behind the Robin Hood Foundation.[3] For the fourth year in a row, he had been successful in choosing and coaching just the right students and teachers on the art of selling an image. But to what degree was the College Prep community aware that this image, while easy for funders to digest, was based on a hierarchy of need and privilege that placed our students at the bottom and funders at the top? While some of our students came from low-income families, others came from middle-class ones. While some of our students would be the first in their families to attend college, others had parents with college and graduate degrees. While some of our students were homeless or lived in shelters, others went home every day to traditional two-parent nuclear families. Yet in the keynote speech at the event, the narrative about College Prep students was not one that allowed for diversity of experience. Rather, it was one that constructed College Prep as a miracle, a school that worked with kids who, despite coming from the most challenging of circumstances, were set up for college matriculation and success due to their hardworking teachers and the generosity of funders.

According to Cucchiara and colleagues, school *privatization* refers to the policies and practices that bring the power of the private sector to bear on public institutions, while *marketization* refers to a broader phenomenon and indexes a more general shift toward embracing business-oriented principles. Marketization highlights the fact that the shift occurs both in education policy and in the discourse around the operation of schools and the purpose of education (Cucchiara, Gold, and Simon 2011). Social change in education policy and practice is thus aligned with social entrepreneurship and an education market that prioritizes freedom, choice, and competition in the name of social justice.

While education may be the path to upward class mobility in the United States, to what degree does competition for private funding in urban public schools depend on marketing and perpetuating poverty in order to thrive? How do actors in educational institutions author their identities in the context of marketization? How are need, privilege, and deservedness racialized in the context of marketization in education, and how does this impact the agency of people who teach and learn in urban schools? This ethnography portrays the complex ways students, teachers, parents, and administrators at College Prep navigated the complicated current of private-sector involvement in public education. It portrays, as Anne Ferguson so aptly states, "the processes by which well-intentioned individuals actually and actively reproduce systems of oppression through institutional practices and symbolic forms of violence" (2001, 73). It also argues, along the same lines as Mary Smith and her colleagues (who draw, as I do, on Murray Edelman's theories of political spectacle), that sometimes the appearance of "success," equity, or justice in education can actually function to maintain stark inequalities and inhibit democracy (Edelman 1988; Smith et al. 2004). Edelman argues that what the public sees as political problems are always constructions that are reinforcements of dominant ideologies. Treating political news as spectacle, his text demonstrates the ways mainstream media shape what counts as a "problem" and what counts as a "solution," upholding dominant structures of power.

Building on Edelman's theories, however, I argue that actors—students, teachers, families, and administrators at College Prep—knowingly participate in the political spectacle in ways that both enable and constrain them. Their performance "in front of the curtain" enables them in terms of material resources and (maybe) life chances, but at the same time, "behind the curtain," these same actors are deeply and troublingly aware that the spectacle subjugates them through furthering problematic and oppressive narratives about their identities and communities.

This awareness was evident in the inner conflict that Mr. Thomas conveyed months after the benefit, when I sat down to interview him for this book.[4] The conversation turned to the idea that the school has to be intentional about the story it tells in order to convince funders that it is worthwhile for them to invest their money in it. This demonstrates, as Mr. Thomas described, the qualitative effect of school reform that is shaped by the fact that

> [Former] Mayor Bloomberg and [former] Chancellor Klein are businesspeople at heart. And what are the principles of business? We're going to give you the freedom to do your work, but that means at the end of the day that you need to come up with results . . . test scores are going to be high; there's going to be evidence of real learning.

Mr. Thomas believes that by facilitating private and public partnerships through the Bloomberg/Klein model, he is "effecting change." Yet he expressed his ambivalence, stating that he has to "constantly work with people so that the messaging about the school is not exploitative." While he believed that this was important, he asked,

> If some rich, important person has his or her heartstrings tugged by the story of so-and-so, and that person writes us a check for like thirty thousand dollars and then we are able to do all this stuff with it, is that okay? I don't know. I am still asking myself that question. I don't know.

Mr. Thomas shared an anecdote about NBC wanting to film a show that would feature Sarah Ferguson, the Duchess of York, giving a college scholarship to a student with a "big sob story." Mr. Thomas pulled aside one student, Kadeem, who had been raised by his grandmother in an impoverished section of the city, and asked him if he was interested. But, he advised Kadeem, he should only agree to this if he was comfortable. Mr. Thomas explained to Kadeem, "TV producers are always looking for the human-interest story, even if ironically it takes the humanity out of the person who they are interviewing." He advised Kadeem not to sell himself out, but told him: "sometimes we buy ourselves opportunity by telling people what they want to hear." In sharing this information both with

Kadeem and again with me in the interview, Mr. Thomas expressed his ambivalence about his work. On the one hand, College Prep is served well by access to important private-sector resources. On the other hand, in order to access the resources, the institution has to conform to, and in fact rely on, a very specific image that both conflates and reifies problematic stereotypes about race, class, and place (Gregory 1998; Haymes 1995). This dehumanizes teachers, students, and their communities. Mr. Thomas's participation in the spectacle helps to construct a problem: scarcity of resources and opportunities for "needy" and "at-risk" Black and Brown urban students, and then to construct a solution: philanthropic investment by funders. Rather than participating in a spectacle that constructs capitalism, racism, competition, or inequity as the problem, Mr. Thomas ambivalently participates in one that makes funders comfortable and garners resources and support for some of (but not all of) New York City's public school students and teachers.

The Story of College Prep

Claire Cohen, the founding principal of the school, often tells the story of how and why she became a teacher, and how College Prep was created in 2004. I heard her tell it when she was the keynote speaker for the school's homecoming event in 2009.

A White woman who was twenty-nine years old when she became founding principal of the school, Ms. Cohen grew up in Brooklyn, and attended public school. The day after she graduated from college, she was called to jury duty on a murder trial. The victims were twelve- and thirteen-year-old boys from Bedford-Stuyvesant, a predominantly Black neighborhood in Brooklyn. The defendant, she said, was thirteen years old. As she sat in the trial, she was deeply disturbed by the directions that she saw these children's lives were taking. She was aware that one in three Black men will be incarcerated at some point in their lives. She decided in court that day that she wanted to make an impact on these lives, and that in order to do this she would become a teacher. "Together," she said to the audience of school alumni who had gathered for homecoming that day, "we can prove that demographics are not destiny, and I have made it my career to make sure that Students of Color in New York City have access to the same opportunities that their more affluent peers have."

Ms. Cohen began her career as an English teacher and later started working for the New York City Board of Education as a literacy consultant. At a meeting with principals, a regional superintendent announced that a new small, themed high school would be opening in the region the following year. Ms. Cohen e-mailed the superintendent and told her that she was interested in being the principal of that school because she was interested in empowering public school students. The superintendent told her that she had potential, and Ms. Cohen started her training to lead College Prep the following year by becoming principal of a different public high school.

College Prep opened in 2004 and shared a building with an elementary school for four years. Many of the founding ideas and ideals for the school were created by Ms. Cohen along with some of the other staff members who still worked there when I arrived in 2008, including Mr. Thomas (the director of the Foundation), Mr. Battle (a Black teacher who was certified to teach English, but started at the school as a science teacher, and then by 2008 was teaching physical education), Mr. Davis (the parent coordinator, who is African American), and Mr. McGinnis (a White math teacher).

The school was in a part of town where much of the commerce was fast food, takeout Chinese restaurants, liquor stores with bulletproof glass between the customers and the owners, and bodegas. Classroom windows looked out on a large public housing project and on the raised expressway that cut through the neighborhood. The school started with a class of ninth graders and added a new class every year. By 2008, it had outgrown its first building. At that point, there had been several articles published in the *New York Times* as well as in journals popular in the corporate world about the school's size, hardworking staff, needy but college-bound students, and social-justice theme. College Prep was making a name for itself, and in 2008, the school formally created an office for the Foundation.

College Prep subsequently moved to a six-story, newly renovated building in a central area of the borough close to several subway trains, commerce buildings, corporate offices, shops, cafés, and restaurants. The school still shared its building (and thus the cafeteria, gym, and library), this time with two other schools: a middle school and a special education school, but there seemed to be ample room for all the students. The outside of the building was freshly painted in bright primary colors. The front boasted large plateglass windows, so that pedestrians could walk by and see into the building's lobby, as well as into the main office of the Foundation. Banners listing the colleges that some of the school's alumni were accepted into adorned the glass.

Unlike in the previous building, there were elevators for teachers and staff, and lockers lined the walls for students' use. There was also a dance studio for students who took classes in ballet, modern dance, and jazz, a college office, and an office that specialized in extracurricular activities and programs. Classrooms were painted a cheerful yellow, and the "gymatorium," where basketball games, assemblies, and performances were held, took up the entire top floor of the building. A computer lab with up-to-date equipment was available to students. Teachers had four copy machines and unlimited paper at their disposal, and each teacher had access to an LCD projector and an interactive whiteboard for use with working classroom desktop computers. Unlike at many other New York City public schools, students were not scanned for weapons when they entered the building. They were expected to adhere to dress code when they entered, which was a white- or blue-collared shirt, khaki or black pants, or skirt for girls, and solid-colored black shoes. Hoodies were explicitly forbidden; students were allowed to layer with a blue or black cardigan. The school appeared a warm and welcoming place to its visitors. Parents whom I talked to often mentioned that when they first walked in, they felt like they were in a private or charter school. Some commented on the corporate feel of the building. I agreed that there seemed a stark difference between College Prep and other public schools I had taught in or visited in the past, both in terms of tone and resources.

This Study: An Overview

To write this ethnography, I gathered data during two years of fieldwork and deep engagement in the College Prep community. My selectivity in choosing particular pieces of data to highlight out of thousands of pages of field notes, journals, school memos, documents, and interview transcripts reflects my partial views and particular agenda.[5] The stories that I choose to tell constitute a purposeful form of social critique, for ethnographic writing is a political process of telling stories about how people engage with one another in the context of structures that regulate power and privilege (Fine et al. 2003). These structures sometimes inhibit and sometimes facilitate human agency. In this case, social structures form the basis for how people engage with an educational institution. As a White, straight, middle-class woman trained as both a teacher and an anthropologist, my positionality provides me with a unique but always partial view into the "stories we tell ourselves about ourselves" (Geertz 1973). I tell these stories about College Prep because it is both politically engaging and important to me to expose and critique those forms of power that continue to structure intersectional inequalities of White supremacy, patriarchy, and class inequity, often through the misleading guise of "social justice" or "color blindness" (Bonilla-Silva 2014). I "speak" my own "truth to power" here. This is never a neutral enterprise, and my views do not represent those of all College Prep community members, although I do my best to represent the voices, stories, and perspectives of some, as I saw and heard them. This particular exercise, or form of storytelling, informs how I see myself within the context of the community I study, and informs a larger project of troubling dehumanizing forms of domination that too often go unmarked or unnamed in educational institutions, and beyond.

College Prep's marketing and image management, including at the benefit, demonstrates the contested terrain of social justice in education, especially in an era that emphasizes policies of accountability and reliance on private-sector philanthropy to move toward upward mobility and social equity for urban students (Saltman 2010), often through the language of "college or career readiness" (Dillon 2010). In a political spectacle furthered by mainstream academic and popular discourse that problematically conflates race, class, and place,[6] urban students are often portrayed as poor, Black or Brown, at risk of academic failure, and in need of "help" from philanthropic outsiders in order to succeed economically according to mainstream standards. Sanctioned federally and at the state level, standards-based educational "reforms" treat the process of teaching and learning as methodologically universal and measurable through assessments like school graduation rates and high-stakes test scores. The existence of—and our experience at—the benefit demonstrate the racial politics that can undergird public schools' dependence on private or corporate philanthropy (even in those schools that realize ideals of college readiness or matriculation for students), and our strategic complacence in (and simultaneous critique of) this spectacle.

The conflict over what *social justice* and *good education* mean forms the foundation for many of the everyday interactions at College Prep between staff, students, and parents/guardians, because College Prep's discipline policies prioritize the performance of corporate *professionalism* for its students, and the school's mission statement prioritizes college matriculation and social justice. Additionally, the school depends on private funding for its resources. While these are the "official" politics of the school, the everyday interactions, and the awareness that students, staff, and families have of their use as "props," demonstrate the racialized tension that can arise when well-intentioned, liberal individuals believe so strongly in their own versions of social justice that they speak for or silence those who are oppressed (Dyrness 2011; hooks 1990). This can lead to what Smith et al. (2004) call a "political spectacle" in education, where the language of ideals like justice or equality often ironically serves to mask growing injustice or inequality. Smith et al. argue that political spectacle can serve to pacify people and to mute critique or resistance. College Prep demonstrates a racial project and a political spectacle that are particularly insidious as the political economy of urban education in the United States becomes more dependent on the private sector for resources (Burch 2006, 2009; Lipman 2011); they reify the very social hierarchies College Prep purports to alleviate.

A General Outline

In chapter 1, I place the ethnography into the context of a political economy of urban school reform in New York City. I critique the popular documentaries *Waiting for "Superman"* (Guggenheim 2010) and *The Lottery* (Sackler 2010), and look not only at key figures and movements in urban education reform and the school choice movement since 2000, but also at corporate philanthropists whose financial altruism contributes to a market-based logic in education. I analyze how these reforms articulate with the construction and contestation of racial meaning at College Prep. At the end of the chapter I revisit some of the school's image management and marketing practices, highlighting the importance that is necessarily placed on corporatization and image management in order to maintain needed resources in the context of New York City education reform. Those who are more interested in the ethnographic portrayal of College Prep may wish to skip this chapter, since it functions to provide a more macro-level sociohistorical context for what I observed at the school.

Upholding what many students and staff called "the College Prep look" was a strong underlying value of the institution, with race, class, and gender implications. Chapter 2 profiles the school's image management project from the perspective of school staff and administrators. The chapter opens with a description of a professional development meeting where staff viewed College Prep's promotional film, used to advertise to potential funders, for the first time. I describe and analyze the film, the students who were selected to appear in it, and teachers' reactions to it. I turn then to an ethnographic documentation of the everyday at College Prep. While the school "markets miracles" through its promotional materials, I focus here on the tensions between what lies behind and in front of "the curtain" in the context of College Prep's political spectacle.

College Prep teachers evaluate and grade students on their "professionalism" in each class using a point-based metric. Chapter 3 examines how the school normalizes the discourse of professionalism in order to make college-bound students more marketable to the private sector. I analyze how the agency of College Prep community members furthers or contests the school's public image, and look at the school's discourse of professionalism through the lens of the "political spectacle" of education policy (Edelman 1988; Smith et al. 2004). Based on school discipline records, as well as extensive participant observation, a student questionnaire (appendix B), and interview data, this chapter centralizes the voices of students who resist the school's version of performed professionalism. The chapter analyzes the race, gender, and class implications of College Prep professionalism, and looks at the ways some students and staff members enact a critique. I place the curricula of professionalism into the context of the school's image management project by arguing that professionalism silences critical conversations about racism, classism, or sexism because it furthers a meritocratic ideology that is grounded both in color blindness and in a deficit view of students. The chapter concludes by suggesting an alternative curricular model of professionalism, inspired by student and staff resistance.

Chapter 4 looks at how the figure of the White female "savior" teacher fits into school privatization and marketization. College Prep's teaching staff is predominantly White and female. The trope of the White female "savior" teacher is popular in contemporary film and literature, and much of the school's image management strategies are structured around selling raced and gendered images of the "ideal type" savior teacher. Grounded in extensive participant observation and interviews, I closely profile three White female teachers at College Prep who are seen as excellent educators by colleagues, students, and parents. I then compare these cases to their "ideal types" in literature and film. Each of the teachers profiled in this chapter sees herself as a social justice educator, yet each enacts a different praxis of social justice in interviews and in her class-room. I examine these women's identities and roles within larger social structures of race and neoliberalism. I contend that, despite the best of intentions, one teacher embodies a "White neoliberal" model of social justice, and sees her role in the classroom as giving students the tools to enhance their marketability. The others embody a model of social jus-tice that is based on what media scholar and political scientist Lilie Chouliaraki (drawing on Hannah Arendt) names "agonistic solidarity" (2011). These teachers enact a critique of the school's emphasis on corpo-ratization, and argue for a form of social justice based on a systemic cri-tique of structural inequity. They problematize human vulnerability (in this case, the marketing of students as racialized "others") as a question of global injustice, collective responsibility, and social change, and see students as diverse, historical agents. The chapter argues for remaining continually critical about the use of the term "social justice" in leftist edu-cational discourse, and demonstrates how the figure of the White female teacher fits into school privatization, marketization, and the encourage-ment of students' "professional" performance.

Chapter 5 discusses another well-known trope: the urban, Black, ado-lescent girl, as portrayed both in teacher narratives and films, as well as in mainstream College Prep discourse. At College Prep, the student population is primarily female (72 percent) and African American (81 percent). This chapter profiles three students whose circumstances, his-tories, personalities, and aspirations complicate mainstream ideas of the at-risk urban student. The school's heavy-handed image management, "professionalization," and marketing of its students not only furthers many of the deficit-based stereotypes found in mainstream films and teacher narratives; its marketing techniques depend upon and further social inequality by promising opportunities for students' upward mobil-ity with the help of a sufficient amount of private funding. This chapter shows how students' perspectives and experience trouble this trope. It begins with a critique of the "ideal-type" African American, urban, ado-lescent girl in movies and literature, and uses the case studies of College Prep students to critique the abstracted models of Black, urban, adoles-cent girls that are perpetuated both by College Prep's marketing and by mainstream narratives about urban schools, like *Freedom Writers* (LaGravenese 2007) and *Dangerous Minds* (J. Smith 1995).

Chapter 6 details my attempt at an activist intervention during the summer following my first year of teacher-research at College Prep. I explored my ideas for humanizing pedagogy in resistance to the school's participation in a troubling political spectacle. Drawing on Paulo Freire's methods (1970), I held a weekly "cultural circle" book club that met outside of the school with four former students, all young women who identify as African American. Students chose reading materials in the cultural circles (all urban fiction books) and chose to critically read the texts by looking at how race, gender, and power operated in the books. Students found the cultural circles to be an engaging experience, but were wary of a model of teaching and learning that was outside of school-sanctioned models of success—ostensibly color-blind meritocracy and upward mobility. This has important implications for teachers and researchers who attempt to find the contemporary relevance of critical pedagogy in an era of standards, accountability, privatization, and corporatization of schools.

Chapter 7, based on interviews conducted in 2011–14, details student, parent, and staff reactions to reading the ethnography. Participants were given a copy of the manuscript, and after several weeks were asked, in semistructured one-on-one interviews or focus groups, to detail their critiques. This section brings together the threads of my main argument, examines the various stances participants took on my critique of the school's model, and analyzes how students and staff construct their identities in relation to the study.

In the afterword, I use my findings to make recommendations for education policy and teaching practice. Given our entrenchment in competition and marketization of schools, and given the way in which racial meaning is tied into this, what are we to do besides critique the status quo? The political spectacle in which staff, students, families, and parents participate at College Prep is undergirded by the requirements of federal and local accountability mandates. These mandates often dictate the ways in which funds are transferred from the government and other public institutions to private organizations, or vice versa (Burch 2006, 2009; Koyama 2010). In this educational climate and current, what are the opportunities for reworking these relationships that allow for the possibility of democratic and equitable education, antiracism, and the strengthening of civil society (C. Katz 2004)?

Appendix A outlines more specifically the methods used in gathering data for this study. All in all, over two years of teacher-research at College Prep, I served as an English teacher, mentor teacher, and cheerleading coach. I interviewed forty-five members of the school staff (including administrators, security guards, guidance / college office staff, and deans of discipline), fourteen alumni, fourteen parents/guardians, and ten students. I shadowed eight students throughout their school day over the course of my research, and conducted hundreds of hours of participant observation in classrooms, at fund-raising events, at field trips, and at staff meetings. I collaborated with teachers and students on authoring and disseminating a school-wide questionnaire (see appendix B) about students' home life, school life, personal interests, and aspirations. At the invitation of the administration, I returned to the school in October 2010 to present the questionnaire results and facilitate a community dialogue with teachers, students, and parents/guardians about what students' feedback means for teaching and learning at College Prep. Appendix A details more specifically the benefits and challenges of this form of insider ethnographic research.

Cultural critics (Giroux 2004; Macrine, McLaren, and Hill 2009) and educational researchers (Apple 2006; Hursh 2009) critique market-based reforms in education for excluding the possibility of democracy and critical thinking in schools, but their critiques remain predominantly on a macro, theoretical, or policy level.[7] Meanwhile, contemporary liberal patrons of education, like Bill and Melinda Gates, Mark Zuckerberg, Eli Broad, Sam Walton, and the Robin Hood Foundation donate to U.S. urban public schools in the name of preparing students to become college or career ready in a market-driven, consumer-based economy.[8] I contend, along with Baltodano (2012), that there are fundamental conflicts between the aims of philanthropy and the aims of democratic, public education. By documenting the ways students and teachers in this community both reproduce and contest the school's norms, I interrogate the place of democracy, humanization, and character education in U.S. public schools, informing both pedagogy and policy. It is my hope that this work is useful for funders, teachers, students, families, scholars, and education policymakers in the context of great changes and increasingly heated debates about the purposes and goals of U.S. schools.

1

A Mind Is a Wonderful Thing to Invest In

Philanthropy and the New York City Public Schools

> *The problem of our age is the proper administration of wealth, so that the ties of brotherhood may still bind together the rich and the poor in harmonious relationship.*
>
> —Andrew Carnegie, *The Gospel of Wealth* (1889)

> *I can conceive of no greater mistake, more disastrous in the end to religion if not to society, than that of trying to make charity do the work of justice.*
>
> —William Jewett Tucker, liberal theologian, in response to Carnegie

In a meeting held in June of 2013, the head of the United Negro College Fund (UNCF) reported that the organization would be updating its slogan from "A Mind Is a Terrible Thing to Waste" to "A Mind Is a Terrible Thing to Waste but a Wonderful Thing to Invest In" (Demby 2013). Each ad would include the new tagline, "Invest in Better Futures." Several undergraduates spoke at the meeting, each ending their story with the phrase "I am your dividend." The journalist who wrote the story points out that the change represents a clear shift from language grounded in community activism to one situated in markets, investment, and economic value creation. What are the implications of profiling Black students as "dividends" that are needy and deserving of charity only if they are able to demonstrate the ability to become entrepreneurs within a neoliberal and profit-oriented context? In other words, as economies of need become economies of profit in education, how does the categorization of Black students as representative of fiscal potential in an "affect economy" (Adams 2012) intersect with the maintenance of inequality and White supremacy? This discursive shift toward profit, strategic investment, and empowerment of the private sector in shaping educational philosophy and policy, I demonstrate, is evident not only in philanthropic organizations like the UNCF, but also increasingly in public educational institutions like College Prep.

While many scholars have focused on the insidious ways philanthropists can influence the formation of public policy in education (Baltodano 2012; Ravitch 2011a; Saltman 2010), this book qualitatively documents the ways in which the lived experience of privatization in urban education rearticulates race, class, and gender inequalities, thus undermining the aims of democratic teaching and learning (Lipman 2011; Shiller 2011). My findings at College Prep demonstrate a clear relation between philanthrocapitalism, White supremacy, and economic inequity, and I argue for critical awareness of and resistance to this problematic trend. In this chapter, I trace a brief history of what Ealy (2014) calls the "problem industrial complex" and connect this to a racialized political economy of education in New York City under former mayor Michael Bloomberg. This lays the foundation for subsequent ethnographic chapters, which demonstrate how the problem industrial complex intersects with the experience of College Prep teachers and students, and how some teachers and students resist.

Philanthropy, Race, and Education: A Brief History

The ways in which we understand social problems—and their remedies— are influenced by structures of power. According to Edelman, political developments are always creations of the publics concerned with them (1988). He argues that political media use various tactics in order to entertain, distort, or shock a largely nonvoting public. These tactics are what he calls a "political spectacle." Explanations of problems, he argues, are always constructions that are likely to reinforce dominant ideology. "The spectacle," he writes, "carries no meaning in itself. It is always a gloss on the phenomenal worlds of individuals and groups" (93). In addition to political media, the ways in which philanthropists in education and those who must cater to them construct a political spectacle of social justice maintain White hegemony, both in the past and through the present.

White, wealthy men have historically had a role in constructing and solving educational problems (and furthering educational inequities). In fact, in the late nineteenth century, industrialists like Andrew Carnegie, John D. Rockefeller, and Julius Rosenwald invested in primary and secondary schooling as well as college education in order to ensure that semiskilled and often African American workers were well trained (Gasman 2012). James Anderson (1988) notes that these philanthropists laid the groundwork for the development of Black education in the United States: by and large, corporate philanthropic foundations favored industrial training and the maintenance of racial inequality. Watkins (2001) argues that the philanthropic architects of many educational institutions were faced with the same dilemma that many philanthropists are faced with today: how to ideologically reconcile great wealth with social altruism (181). The way they did this was through a financial and political project of accommodationist education, teaching the values of conformity, obedience, sobriety, piety, and enterprise for Black people, thus combining constitutional ideals of freedom with social subservience (182). In other words, after the Civil War, states Watkins, "America's apartheid had to be made workable. It needed to appear natural and ordained. Beyond that, Blacks needed to be convinced that their lot was improving" (182). According to Edelman (1988), "ideology and material conditions are part of the same transaction" (3). White philanthropists had to create an ideology—a political spectacle—that could justify their privilege in the context of racialized material conditions of great inequity. They did this through systematic construction of benevolence and charity that continues through the present.

While the Carnegies and the Rockefellers of their day were known for their level of philanthropic giving, Hay (2013) argues that today, we appear to be entering a new "golden age of philanthropy" because of philanthropists' power in shaping public policy, and because of unprecedented emphasis on "impact" and "measurable goals." Ealy (2014) marks the late 1960s as the beginning of today's "big philanthropy," with the publication of Cornuelle's *Reclaiming the American Dream* (1965), and the subsequent publication of *Healing America* (1983), both of which asserted that it was not up to "big government" to solve social problems. Rather, it should be the "task of philanthropy to support anew the 'vast, idle capacities of individuals and institutions to act freely and directly on public problems'" (89). Others trace the beginning of this "golden age" to a 2009 meeting between a select group of the super wealthy dubbed the "Good Club" (Rogers 2011). Predominantly White men,[1] the attendees included Bill Gates, Warren Buffett, David Rockefeller, Ted Turner, Michael Bloomberg, and George Soros. At that meeting, the Good Club chose global population growth as the problem to target. As Rogers (2011) aptly states, "this is not a choice of a group concerned with public opinion. It veers into the murky waters of women's reproductive rights and religious, cultural and ethnic politics and not least, eugenics" (376). A year later, in 2010, Bill and Melinda Gates and Warren Buffet announced the Giving Pledge (Rogers 2011, 376). As of September 2014, 127 billionaires have pledged to give at least half of their wealth to charity either during their lifetime or after their death (givingpledge.org). Philanthropists such as the Gates family began to take on other "challenges," for example, "extreme poverty and poor health in developing countries, and the failures of the American education system" (Gates and Gates 2014). While the intentions of Gates, Buffett, Bloomberg, and others may be framed as benevolent, it is also important to point out that in addition to increased political power and influence, the philanthropic sector enjoys a financial reward: tax-exempt status and sometimes charitable deductions for donors (Ealy 2014). In fact, as Saltman (2011) points out,

> although roughly half of wealth given to foundations comes in the form of small donations, the real financial benefits principally go to the big givers at the top of the economy who are able to significantly reduce their tax burdens. For every ten dollars given by the Gates Foundation, four dollars is lost from the public wealth in taxes. The philanthropist would otherwise give his money to the public in the form of taxes. (8)

In this way, the construction of social problems and the political spectacle involved in solving them reinforces the class privilege of the elite and undercuts the possibility of equity in public education.

Today's big philanthropists are popularly known as "philanthrocapitalists." *Philanthrocapitalism* is a more advanced version of venture philanthropy. It is loosely based on the practices of venture capital investing, and is often focused on achieving measurable results. It is often characterized by a high degree of involvement by donors with grantees (Jenkins 2011). Philanthrocapitalism, then, is a form of wealth transfer, often from a wealthy individual through a foundation or to an organization, so as to affect some kind of "social justice" (Lorenzi and Hilton 2011). It rests upon an ethic of neoliberalism, that is, an adherence to classic liberal economic values of deregulation, competition, free markets, and the entrepreneurial self (Friedman 1962). Neoliberalism is more than just the laissez-faire capitalism espoused by Adam Smith ([1776] 2010). Rather, according to Baltodano (2012), neoliberalism as a political rationale implies active political intervention and the manipulation of social institutions, including the media, the law, universities, and the state. It is a form of state-enabled capitalism that seeks to intensify the alliances between corporations and cultural institutions. As Baltodano explains, neoliberal economics become a political rationale because the needs of government are subsumed by—and often support—the needs of the market. This occurs through a political spectacle of choice as justice, and innovation through market competition. As my findings at College Prep show, students and teachers are often aware that they are used as "props" to uphold this performance.

Philanthrocapitalists do not enjoy only a financial benefit. They also enjoy political benefit. This is especially evident through what Rogers (2011) has named "philanthropolicymaking," as philanthrocapitalists such as Bill and Melinda Gates, Sam Walton, and Eli Broad demonstrate a plutocratic (and often experimental) influence over the formation of public policy. Some scholars critique "philanthropolicymaking" (Rogers 2011; Williamson 2012) and warn against the strong alliances between philanthrocapitalists and the state (Keohane 2013); others advocate for critiquing the movement in general (Edwards 2011; Husock 2011). Even some who seem to be in favor of schools raising supplementary funds through partnerships with nonprofits or corporations admit that it is systemically problematic (D. Green 2012), and that philanthropy may serve to justify extreme inequality (Thorup 2013). The private sector has such an impact on social policy because it is not democratic—in other words, philanthropic foundations are not elected by anyone, but yield tremendous power in defining social and educational policy. Philanthropic foundations can completely fund and administer projects; thus, their power has an effect similar to law, brokering ideas and making culture (Watkins 2001, 20).

Major philanthrocapitalists are involved in public schools (Ravitch 2011a), but as Saltman (2011) argues, their involvement is both racially and class coded:

> The neoliberal declaration of a "failed system" . . . is not leveled
> explicitly against rich, predominantly white communities and
> public schools for whom high levels of historical investment
> and the benefits of cultural capital have resulted in high achievement, traditionally defined. Rather, the declaration of "system

failure" is leveled against working-class and poor, predominantly nonwhite communities and schools. (5)

He argues that this tends to place blame on the public (rather than the private sector) for educational inequalities. While educational funding is linked to wealth through property taxes and local funding, he explains, the private sector has continually played a role in creating and continuing inequality (5–6). Connecting failure to poor and working class non-White communities, and subsequently entrusting the private sector for solutions, is a process that serves to insulate White middle-class and elite privilege. "Failing" schools, often Black and Brown, compete for finite resources that are allocated by the private sector, while those schools deemed as "succeeding," often White, continue to benefit from long-standing social and historical privilege. While it may seem as if "failing" students and schools need funders to "save" them, in a racialized political economy, funders depend on students in order to construct their own privileged identities. This is one facet of "racial philanthrocapitalism" (A. Brown 2012). Resources continue to be unevenly distributed, furthering problematic and pervasive narratives that connect success to Whiteness. Thus, systemic inequity does not change.

As Shiller (2012) points out, the experimental and plutocratic influence of philanthrocapitalists was especially evident in New York City when the Bill and Melinda Gates Foundation advocated in the early 2000s for moving to a system of small schools in order to foster competition and choice for parents. As a result, Shiller writes, today New York City has more than three hundred small schools, which were originally supposed to be based around innovative and unique themes, but were also still held accountable for improving their test scores. Despite the Gateses' wholehearted embrace of small themed schools in New York City, in 2008, their foundation announced that it planned to shift the focus of its education grant-making from the creation of small schools toward an effort to double the amount of low-income people who complete a college degree or certificate by age twenty-six (Jenkins 2011, 45; Naylor 2011). The Gates Foundation seems to make somewhat arbitrary and experimental decisions about when to invest in—and when to abandon—its policy experiments, often with little or limited data. In the context of White supremacy, these decisions are actually far from arbitrary. Despite discourse that masks the furthering of race and class inequality with the language of reform, increasing privatization and corporatization of public education has racial, political, and economic consequences (Fabricant and Fine 2012, 2013; Mora and Christianakis 2011).

While there have been some philanthropic initiatives to combat structural racism (HoSang, n.d.), race is often avoided in philanthropic conversations (Venkatesh 2002), which tend to focus on short-term deliverables and returns as well as simply reporting current disparities (HoSang, n.d.). More important, benevolent philanthropic discourses in the United States and globally function as "cultural scripts" that maintain and perpetuate power differentials, rearticulating Whiteness as associated with "progress, technology and civilization, while situating Blackness (and other marginalized identities) within the discourse of nature, primitivism and pre-modernity" (Zhang, Gajjala, and Watkins 2012, 205). For example, as Richey and Ponte (2011) point out, advertising for Bono's "Product Red" constructs a certain kind of AIDS victim (heterosexual, Black African women and children) as a racialized and gendered primitive "other" that consumers can help "save" through their purchases. Although they function at the policy or marketing level, these neocolonial and cultural scripts are often lived at a local level; they are attributable to the hegemonic influence of an ostensibly well-meaning private sector.

Watkins (2001) demonstrates the ways philanthropy became a science, rather than simply being based on an ethic of public charity; in other words, a rationality and a science of giving differentiate philanthropy from indiscriminate charity. This continues through the present, as evidenced by more recent publications, like Peter Frumkin's *The Essence of Strategic Giving* (2010). The science of giving that developed out of the charity movement was predicated on a key irony: those who give stand to profit from maintaining the inequities that are fundamental to capitalism, but construct their philanthropic models based on the rhetoric of social and economic justice. Indeed, Watkins reports that,

> as upper middle class and often wealthy reformers . . . adopted corporate philanthropy, the charity movement changed. Committed to concern for the downtrodden, their close associates were bankers and industrialists who profited greatly from those whose labor they expropriated yet whose causes they celebrated. An efficient society always provided the rationale for their charitable actions. (2001, 84)

This irony lies at the heart of contemporary corporate philanthropy—maintaining an efficient society comes about through maintaining current social structures, equitable or not. Reforms occur, yet only in ways that ensure the maintenance of America's existing political and economic systems. This is evident through the discourse around the contemporary school choice debate as well as on school models that are dependent on philanthropy. Reforms that construct justice based on a market model place emphasis in capitalism and competition as being the solution to, rather than the cause of social inequity.

Philanthropy and Education in New York City

Macedo (2003) points out that common schooling was an important tenet of the immigrant-heavy United States in the late nineteenth century, although the discourse of common schooling demonstrated a political spectacle that disguised maintenance of stark inequality. Ostensibly, common public schools were supposed to neutralize religious and class boundaries, but they also perpetuated rampant xenophobia, racism, and anti-Catholicism. Following this legacy, Americans still operate in the context of a political spectacle that emphasizes a good (but not necessarily an equal) education as more of a public than a private asset that should be available to all (Wolfe 2003). According to New York State's education clause, "the legislature shall provide for the maintenance and support of a system of free common schools, wherein all children of this state may be educated" (Schwartz and Steifel 2011). The Education Law Center (ELC) reports that the Campaign for Fiscal Equity (CFE) has engaged in courtroom battles about the meaning of this clause with New York State in 1995, 2001, 2002, 2003, and 2006 (Education Law Center 2013). In a landmark decision in 2001, the courts required New York State to provide the city with additional funds to fulfill its constitutional obligation of a "sound basic education" for all public school students (Schwartz and Steifel 2011), and the courts have upheld this decision since. Despite the courts' rulings, enacting these decisions has proven difficult.

In New York City, most financial support for public education is provided by federal, state, and local sources, but philanthropic support and voluntary contributions have become important as well, especially in the wake of the Bloomberg/Klein era.[2] In fact, in 2005, the *New York Times* ran an article entitled "New York City's Big Donors Find New Cause:

Public Schools" (Herszenhorn 2005). The article outlines how Bloomberg and Klein were in the process of forging a tight bond with the private sector and reports that they had already raised 311 million dollars, "turning public education into a darling cause of the corporate-philanthropic-society set." According to Schwartz and Steifel, in 1982, the New York City Board of Education created the Fund for Public Schools, a 501(c)(3) nonprofit that could accept donations on behalf of the school system. Bloomberg and Klein relaunched this fund with the objective of strengthening public/private partnerships and implementing systemwide reforms (ibid.). The total amount that the Fund for Public Schools raises (nearly 245 million between 2003 and 2009) is relatively small compared with the entire Department of Education (DOE) budget, but it is important because of its speed—in other words, the DOE can quickly and flexibly implement ideas and innovations that may not be funded through a public budget (ibid.). In fact, as the *Times* article mentioned above states, "in the context of the system's regular budget of about $15 billion a year, $311 million might seem insignificant. But tax dollars come with so many strings that the administration has viewed private money as crucial for research and development and an array of experimental programs." College Prep is an unscreened public school that is affiliated with an education-related nonprofit (in addition to the Foundation, the in-house nonprofit that the school created) that supports a consortium of public schools in the city. The nonprofit focuses on education and college readiness for underserved students, and receives direct public support (direct contributions from individuals and foundations) in addition to support from the Fund for Public Schools (Schwartz and Steifel 2011).

Schwartz and Steifel (2011) examine seven organizations in New York City that are dedicated to providing education-related services: Achievement First, Good Shepherd, the Harlem Children's Zone, New Visions for Public Schools, Outward Bound, The After-School Corporation, and the Urban Assembly. The authors state that between 2005 and 2007, these organizations received over 300 million dollars in direct public support (77). The authors also direct attention to a large donor—the Bill and Melinda Gates Foundation—which, between 2000 and 2009, gave over 112 million dollars in grants to education organizations. This figure does not include grants made to the Fund for Public Schools. "In the two years immediately following Bloomberg's inauguration," Schwartz and Steifel write, "the Gates Foundation's grants to NYC-based organizations increased dramatically: from more than $1.8 million in 2002 to more than $38 million in 2003" (77). Philanthropists continue to exert great influence over New York City public schools through their contributions to the Fund for Public Schools as well as through their contributions to other nonprofit organizations that fund education and education-related services.

Goldsmith and his colleagues (2010) cite Bloomberg's "entrepreneurial approach" to public school reform as particularly effective. Along with business executive Joel Klein (whom Bloomberg appointed as his first chancellor of schools), a former U.S. deputy attorney and antitrust lawyer, Bloomberg joined with civic entrepreneurs in order to inspire "innovation"; as Goldsmith, Georges, and Burke write, by partnering with nonprofits and the private sector, Bloomberg "infused the system with catalytic talent from nontraditional areas, partnered with private sector entrepreneurs to widen choice, disrupted traditional school management by developing new routes for advancement, and granted managers the authority and autonomy to innovate" (204). Through greatly expanding the number of privately run charter schools, revitalizing the Fund for Public Schools, and increasing the role of both nonprofit and for-profit intermediaries in the public school system, Bloomberg merged private interest with public good in an unprecedented fashion.

Bloomberg's favoritism of private interests and the city's financial elite came from his own background. A self-made multibillionaire, Bloomberg is a former bond trader and creator of Bloomberg L.P., the leading financial news and data company in the world (Weikart 2009). Throughout his term, Bloomberg awarded more than 900 million dollars in tax breaks to some of the city's largest corporations, including Bank of America, Pfizer, Hearst, Goldman Sachs, and the Bank of New York, in order to keep corporations in the city and subsidize further development (ibid.). Indeed, Weikart argues that part of Bloomberg's success as mayor came from the fact that he came from Wall Street, and that his clients were the financial elite; when he was elected, they had "one of their own" in power, and could impose their desires on public policy decisions.

The School Choice Debate

Many of Bloomberg's education reforms were in the interest of furthering the controversial argument for school choice. The current debate tends to fluctuate between market-based arguments that advocate for the advancement of the individual and arguments that advocate for equity of resources through increasing the likelihood that the most disadvantaged can receive a good education at no cost. Discourse around school choice began with a 1955 essay written by economist Milton Friedman, which proposed the idea of a voucher system, or a system where publicly subsidized funds would contribute toward private schools. Friedman believed that a voucher plan would end the government's monopoly over public education, and stimulate competition that would lead to greater economic efficiency as well as the elimination of failing public schools. If the United States could create a marketplace of education through publicly financed but privately run schools, then failing schools would be forced to either improve or close (Viteritti 2003).

In 1978, Harvard law professors John Coons and Stephen Sugarman shifted the conversation about school choice from one that glorified the market to one that glorified the pursuit of social justice through increased opportunity. Coons and Sugarman advocated a targeted school voucher system for the most socially and economically disadvantaged families, arguing that freedom is promoted through giving everyone (especially those who did not previously have it) access to the market (ibid.). The social justice argument for market access promoted a unique blend of political alliances between those on the left who advocated redistributive public policy and those on the right who advocated the market-based model of the liberal state (ibid.).

Neither Friedman's argument nor Coons and Sugarman's enjoyed much mainstream success until after the 1983 release of the U.S. Department of Education's report *A Nation at Risk,* which argued that "a rising tide of mediocrity" in public schools was threatening the country's competitiveness in the global marketplace. This seminal publication laid an important foundation for the school choice debate as well as for the political climate of President Obama's Race to the Top educational policies and their predecessor, President Bush's No Child Left Behind Act. Because U.S. schools were allegedly failing the economy, *A Nation at Risk* put pressure on schools to partner with corporations, who supposedly had expertise on how to improve education (Molnar 2005). Following *A Nation at Risk,* and the national education crisis of the 1980s, political scientists John Chubb and Terry Moe took up the school choice debate in their 1990 publication *Politics, Markets, and America's Schools,* bringing the conversation further into the mainstream (Viteritti 2003). Chubb and Moe did not endorse a fully privatized system, but provided empirical support for Friedman's original arguments, advocating for a system where public schools would compete with private schools. Some students were to be given publicly supported "scholarships" to private schools, and managerial autonomy would be maximized at the school level (ibid.). Chubb and Moe argued that the market could be the antidote to the problems and ineffectiveness caused by democratic control of public schools.

Yet, despite persuasive equity arguments, experiments with school voucher programs in the 1990s in Cleveland, Ohio, and Milwaukee, Wisconsin, inspired legal controversy. Parents were free to use publicly subsidized vouchers to send their children to private, faith-based schools, and this was the issue of contention. Critics argued that this was a violation of the First Amendment's separation of church and state (Molnar 2005). While high courts in Ohio and Wisconsin, as well as the U.S. Supreme Court, ruled in subsequent cases that giving vouchers directly to families and not to religious institutions does not violate First Amendment rights, supporters of voucher schools have been repeatedly defeated on ballot initiatives (ibid.). Charter schools have been a much less controversial and much more accepted form of choice in this debate (ibid.).

First popularized by former president of the American Federation of Teachers Albert Shanker, charter schools were originally conceived as independent, non-faith-based public schools that would be started by special interest groups. Charter schools operated under a "charter," or a contract between an "operator," such as a group of parents or a private school acting pro bono, and a sponsor, such as a local school authority. Once granted by a district or a state, charters were to be publicly funded and supported, but offered more freedom in how public money was spent (Kelly 2007; Molnar 2005). The advent of charter schools in the urban United States gave the movement for school choice more momentum as new political coalitions between traditionally left-leaning, Black and Latino, poor or working-class parents unified with traditionally right-leaning, White, elite social conservatives who favored market logic and competition as a means to social good (Pedroni 2007; Wolfe 2003). Both camps argued, for different reasons, the injustice of the discrepancy in educational opportunity between children of parents who have the option of choosing a school by paying for it or moving to a different school district and those who do not: urban parents fought for their children's education, and social conservatives fought against a government monopoly of public schools. This kind of coalition, argues Wolfe (2003), demonstrated a "new politics of race," which occurred largely (and more successfully) under the auspice of social equity arguments as opposed to arguments about individual freedom or competition.

Yet, underneath these new politics, publicly funded charter schools became a vehicle for privatization as for-profit education management corporations like Edison, National Heritage Academies, and White Hat made their way into running charter schools, sometimes, as in the case with Edison, to be met with great controversy and eventual failure to make a profit or to meet academic standards while providing adequate resources for students (see Molnar 2005, 91–119). Creating this kind of market in education does not necessarily grant parents more autonomy (see below for a discussion of the 2010 film *The Lottery*, in which there are insufficient spaces for children whose parents would opt out of the traditional public zoned schools in their Harlem neighborhood). Nor does the charter necessarily improve or enhance school performance and curricula (Kelly 2007; Molnar 2005). Instead, both charter and traditional public schools are under pressure to focus on exam results in the short term in an effort to avoid being labeled as "failing" (Kelly 2007) by the high-stakes assessments put into place by federal education policies like the No Child Left Behind Act and Race to the Top. Lipman (2004) argues that, in fact, federally sanctioned models of standards and accountability define a *good school* as a "high scoring" school. This definition individualizes failure and places blame on principals, teachers, students, and parents, thus negating the state's responsibility for the structural root of the problem. Many "failing" urban schools are located in some of the most impoverished communities in the United States, where capitalism and White supremacist racial structures have led to destitution, underdevelopment, and social crisis (Marable 2000). Allegedly color-blind high-stakes testing policies, where everyone is held to the same standards, cannot incorporate any discussion of these structural realities (Lipman 2004), nor can a market-based political spectacle of competition and innovation.

School Choice in New York City

In New York City, school choice began in the early twentieth century with the creation of selective specialized high schools such as Stuyvesant,

Brooklyn Technical High School, and The Bronx High School of Science (Corcoran and Levin 2011, 200). In the 1980s, the city began to downsize its large, factory-style schools. The beginning of small themed schools in New York City occurred under Chancellor Joseph Fernandez's tenure in 1990–93, when a number of smaller alternative schools were created (ibid.). The city's Small Schools of Choice (SSCs) evolved in the late 1980s from being an alternative to large high schools for unsuccessful students, often based in grassroots initiatives by teachers and administrators, to become the normative and widespread response to the failure (by state and national standards) of the city's large schools (Ancess and Allen 2006). When Fernandez was in office, New York City was the recipient of the Annenberg Challenge grant (Annenberg Institute 2011), a twenty-five-million-dollar, two-to-one matching challenge private grant from politically conservative publishing mogul and philanthropist Walter Annenberg. To utilize the money, Fernandez turned to the Fund for Public Schools to help him oversee proposal requests by community-based organizations and educators for small themed schools in the city (Domanico, Innerst, and Russo 2000). The Fund for Public Schools then combined the resources of four other intermediary nonprofit organizations—New Visions for Public Schools, the Center for Collaborative Education (CCE), the Center for Educational Innovation (CEI), and the New York Association of Community Organizations for Reform Now (ACORN)—to institutionalize development of small schools in order to provide choice to low-income communities (Annenberg Institute 2011). They also influenced the New York City Board of Education to create an Office of New and Charter School Development (ibid.).

Since 2002, New York City has implemented a centralized high school admissions process where eighty thousand students per year indicate their school preferences (Bloom, Thompson, and Unterman 2010; Corcoran and Levin 2011). In middle school, students (and parents) have the opportunity to rank their top twelve high school choices. Then, a centralized computer system matches students with schools (which have also entered their own preferences into the system). If students are not matched with a school in the first round, then there are subsequent selection rounds. If a student is never matched with a high school, then they attend an under-enrolled school in their neighborhood. School themes are supposed to connect to students' interests (Ancess and Allen 2006). The themes also, ideally, should provide students with a preview of sorts as to possibilities for their future careers, as well as provide a core curriculum for teachers in all subject areas to connect to their lessons. One critique of this model is that students are encouraged to consider schools that are not in their neighborhoods, making it more difficult for schools to partner with students' communities.

New York City's SSCs, including College Prep, are a direct outcome of the school choice movement, the "knowledge industry" that is a result of the increasing privatization and marketization of public education, and federally sanctioned support of high-stakes tests as a measure of "good" education. While the common threads of New York City's SSCs in the late 1980s and early 1990s were these grassroots initiatives, today the common thread of these schools (including College Prep) is that millions of private dollars in start-up grants are not given to school systems but to private, not-for-profit intermediaries such as Achievement First, Good Shepherd, New Visions for Public Schools, or the Robin Hood Foundation, the leaders of which are usually not educators (Ancess and Allen 2006; Schwartz and Steifel 2011). SSCs were created with the goal of preparing students for the competitive demands of the world economy (Ancess and Allen 2006), with a special emphasis (according to a report funded by the Gates Foundation) on disadvantaged students from historically underserved communities in the city (E. Foley 2010). In addition to providing students with more individualized attention, small themed schools were intended to guide students on a more focused path through a field of study or discipline such as nursing, teaching, law, literacy, or technology, and to foster the three core principles of academic rigor, personalization, and community partnerships (Bloom, Thompson, and Unterman 2010).

Small, themed public schools in New York City continue to be heavily influenced by philanthropic aid—and philanthropic agendas. In the same way that the Annenberg Challenge money was distributed to four nonprofits that acted as intermediaries in the 1990s, the Gates Foundation began investing funds in small school intermediaries in New York City in 2001, and with the Carnegie Corporation of New York and the Open Society Institute made a thirty-million-dollar grant to New Visions for Public Schools, New York City's largest school reform association, to establish seventy-five small schools by 2005 (E. Foley 2010). Deeper investments by the foundation came about as the state granted Mayor Bloomberg control of the New York City Department of Education's 1,400 schools. By the fall of 2003, the Gates Foundation committed fifty-one million dollars to ten intermediaries to establish sixty-seven new secondary schools in New York City (ibid.).

According to another Gates Foundation–funded report about graduation rates for New York City's SSCs (Bloom, Thompson, and Unterman 2010), beginning in 2002, the Bloomberg/Klein administration closed more than twenty underperforming high schools and opened more than two hundred charter and traditional public secondary schools. The report states that 123 academically nonselective SSCs have been created in the city since 2002. In total, Klein created 333 new public schools, and more than 80 charters between 2002 and 2009, using a total of seventy million dollars in outside funding from organizations like the Gates Foundation, the Carnegie Corporation, and the Open Society Institute, and relying heavily on New Visions for Public Schools as a developer (Bloom and Unterman 2012; Goldsmith, Georges, and Burke 2010). Bloomberg and Klein created the Center for Charter School Excellence, raised the number of allowable new charters from one hundred to two hundred statewide, and imposed no limits on the number of existing public schools that could turn into charters (Goldsmith, Georges, and Burke 2010), further merging private interests with public institutions.

Structured by New Visions for Public Schools, the process to start a small school was competitive, and was supposed to inspire creativity and innovation from prospective school starters. Getting funding for a small school was designed as a three-step process: First, prospective school planners received three thousand to five thousand dollars to outline a school concept. Second, if the concept was approved, planners received between sixty-five thousand to eighty-five thousand dollars to develop a formal school proposal, recruit staff, and begin professional development. Winning teams were granted four hundred thousand dollars (minus earlier grants) to ramp up their designs (E. Foley 2010).

Ancess and Allen (2006) explain that, according to market (Friedman-inspired) theory, creating small themed schools was supposed to encourage equity by stimulating competition among the schools, which would theoretically increase the number of good schools and decrease or eliminate the bad ones. They argue, however, that the themes tend to function as a sort of code (for example, "School for Math and Science" might attract high-achieving students, usually boys, while a "School for Social Justice" might attract poor or working-class students). Usually, they explain, more elite parents have the money and the insider knowledge to ensure advantage in the system; not all schools are equal, and many struggle with insufficient space, inexperienced teachers, new principals, and vulnerable or challenging students. Other scholars argue that this particular model of choice tends to exacerbate segregation as students tend to prefer high schools where the majority of the student population matches their own academic, racial, and socioeconomic backgrounds (Corcoran and Levin 2011). In other words, the model of smaller themed schools can function to perpetuate, rather than eradicate, inequity through ostensibly de-raced, de-classed, and de-gendered hidden tracking.

In March 2010, an article entitled "Pressed by Charters, Public Schools Try Marketing" appeared in the *New York Times* (Medina 2010b). The article discussed the methods used by public school principals in Harlem to recruit students (and their parents) to the school. The article explained that in Harlem, because there are so many charter schools, public school administrators must fight dropping enrollment rates that could lead to school closure. Another *Times* article, from 2012, entitled "Enrollment Off in Big Districts, Forcing Layoffs" (Rich 2012), demonstrated the problematic effects of this trend on public school teachers and students, especially those who were not lucky enough to be accepted into charter school lotteries. These competitive reforms communicate the illusion of innovation and improvement in education, but in reality cannot change the inequitable distribution of resources and opportunities. Even the schools that construct themselves as success stories must necessarily prioritize maintaining their image over empowering students and their communities, as I argue, is demonstrated at College Prep.

Medina's *Times* article illustrates that traditional public schools use some of the same marketing techniques that charter schools use to interest students and parents, including revamping school logos, making school T-shirts, emphasizing after-school programs, creating blogs and websites, and advertising through flyers and mailings to parents. This is controversial because good advertising comes at a cost. The article gives the example of the Harlem Success Academy, a charter school that spent 325 thousand dollars to recruit their 3,600 applicants. Charter schools are publicly funded but privately run. While charters are, ideally, through the choice that they give their consumers (students and their parents), supposed to create healthy competition, the article demonstrates that the logic of fair competition through choice is flawed. Eva Moscowitz, a former city councilwoman, founded the Harlem Success Academy. The school has a big board of trustees, many of whom are affiliated with private corporations like Goldman Sachs or Morgan Stanley. Connections like these give publicly funded charter schools quite an advantage in getting extra resources for advertising; they have significant financial support from both the public and the private sectors.

The *New York Times* documented another ugly side of private sector competition in an article on January 13, 2011, entitled "Charter School Cries Foul over Decision to Close It" (Chen 2011). The article profiles the story of the Ross Global Academy, a charter school that is closing. While the New York City Department of Education claims that the school was closing for poor performance, the article reveals the real reason why the charter will not survive: money. The school's building is promised to Girls Prep, another charter school, even though 3.5 million dollars were spent on renovations for Ross.

Courtney Sale Ross, the widow of Steven J. Ross, who was a Time Warner chairman, founded Ross Global Academy. Sarah Robertson, the daughter-in-law of financier Julian Robertson, founded Girls Prep. Her foundation, the Robertson Foundation, made twenty-five million dollars in contributions in recent years to three entities closely associated with former New York City school chancellor Joel Klein. While it's true that Ross Global struggled with unusually high teacher and principal turnover, violence in school, and low test scores, the *Times* (Chen 2011) writes: "The school's decision to publicize its fight throws into the open, in raw and awkward fashion, the tight relationship between the city, which has promoted the creation of charter schools, in general, and the wealthy patrons of some of these schools" (A27). Whether the charter school revolution in New York, and in many other urban areas of the country, has raised the bar for teaching and learning or for post-graduation opportunities is debatable (Kelly 2007; Molnar 2005; Spencer 2012). But many public schools, including College Prep, an unscreened public school, must draw in private money, or find other ways to stay on top if they are to remain competitive within the regulations of the new game. Indeed, this is the very logic of President Obama's Race to the Top educational policy move. In his State of the Union address on January 25, 2011, he summarized the policy, saying, "If you show us the most innovative plans to improve teacher quality and student achievement, we'll show you the money" (Obama 2011). Resources are finite, and the ideology is competitive.

School Choice, *The Lottery,* and *Waiting for "Superman"*

In relation to education under Bloomberg and Klein, "Schooling becomes one more consumer choice where one benefits by choosing wisely. Those who work hard are admitted to good schools and do well; those who do not work hard have only themselves to blame. Inequality is explained as differences in personal effort" (Hursh 2007, 26). The logic of competition in order to encourage innovation is especially evident in the discourse of proponents of school choice in a recent documentary film, *The Lottery* (Sackler 2010). The film portrays the struggles of four Black families in Washington Heights as they compete with their neighbors for coveted spots for their kindergarteners in Eva Moscowitz's Harlem Success Academy charter schools, as opposed to attending failing zoned schools in their neighborhood. Discourse in the film about school achievement and inequity is both racial and class-based; film clips cameo both former chancellor Klein and President Obama lamenting the racial achievement gap for African American and Latino students, while Moscowitz states that the real inequity is in the choices that middle- and upper middle-class parents have over which school their child will attend (as opposed to poorer parents who do not have these choices). A brief clip of President Obama, however, sums up the real problem with the outcome of insufficient schooling in the United States: "Jobs will not be done and purchases won't be made," he says. In other words, students who grow up with inadequate education are not marketable for jobs, and they will not be consumers. Ostensibly the lack of a "good" education in the United States, then, inhibits the growth of the free market and inhibits global competitiveness.

An irony of the film is that while it critiques educational inequity, it lionizes a system of competition that necessarily produces winners and losers: in the end, two of the students "win" spots at the school through a lottery system, and two do not. Additionally, the film profiles angry resistance from parents at the "underperforming" Public School 194 when Moscowitz, and parents whose children attend her Harlem Success Academy, fight to have another branch of their school take over PS 194's building. The conversation becomes one of respect and ownership of the community (from PS 194 parents) versus one of what children can "become" career-wise when they leave the Harlem Success Academy on the way to college readiness (from Harlem Success Academy parents). These competing ideals encapsulate an important facet of the debate around school choice, privatization, and the public good—that is, should U.S. schools foster community or competition? Who should be responsible for ensuring that children get a "good" education: communities, government, teachers' unions, corporations, philanthropic organizations, or individuals? Former chancellor Klein, an advocate of school choice, states in the film that with a system of school choice, "parents vote with their feet": in other words, they will opt out of "bad" schools by enrolling their children in "good" schools. Yet, if a good public education were free and universal, why would parents have to vote, or compete at all for their children's welfare?

The logic of school choice arguments demonstrates the value of markets and competition over teachers and students (Hursh 2007). This can especially be seen in widespread anti–teachers' union discourse from proponents of school choice (Compton and Weiner 2008), including Eva Moscowitz in *The Lottery* (Sackler 2010), where she repeatedly describes the teachers' union as "thuggish." Additionally, externally mandated systems of standards and accountability tend to see both schools and teachers as commodities: the end goal is for students to compete in the marketplace, but standards-based reforms give the appearance that the state takes an interest in education and in empowering students and their communities (Hursh 2007). This logic underlies a political spectacle wherein corporate and private philanthropy in education masquerade as justice. Because competitive reforms cannot be universal or systemic, educational inequalities are exacerbated while hegemony is maintained. Meanwhile, the state can increase its own capital by saying that schools do not need more money, they just need to compete with one another. This competition puts pressure on traditional public and charter schools to get money through private investors, rather than from the state (ibid.).

Similarly, in *Waiting for "Superman"* (Guggenheim 2010), five children compete for coveted places in charter schools with the goal of becoming college-ready. The film maligns public schools, public school teachers, and teachers' unions. It highlights Geoffrey Canada and Michelle Rhee, both of whom criticize the bureaucratic nature of the public school system. Yet the same irony lurks in *Waiting for "Superman"* as in *The Lottery;* while the films critique a flawed system at the hands of the failed state, the proposed solution—charter schools—doesn't lead to equity either.

Politicians and policymakers increasingly take advice from those in positions of corporate power in regard to public education. In his attempt to overhaul New York City schools, former chancellor Klein met with corporate consultants including Chris Cerf, the former president of controversial Edison schools and the commercial manager of public schools in twenty-five states; the consulting firm Alvarez & Marshal, which revamped the school system in St. Louis and is rebuilding the system in New Orleans; and Sir Michael Barber, a leading thinker on accountability and achievement for teachers and public officials. In his native England, Barber served on a committee nicknamed the "hit squad," which closed schools that were failing to meet national standards. This consulting work was paid for with five million dollars in private funds (Herszenhorn 2005).

In 2011, former mayor Michael Bloomberg appointed Cathie Black[3] to replace Joel Klein as the chancellor of education. Black, who lacked a graduate degree and had no experience in education or government, is the chairwoman of Hearst magazines. She attended parochial school and sent her children to private schools. Black was the third White chancellor in a row in an educational system where, according to 2009 data, 30.8 percent of students identify as Black, 39.9 percent identify as Hispanic, 14.6 percent identify as Asian, and 14.3 percent identify as White (schools. nyc.gov 2011). Ms. Black met widespread critique, and then resigned ninety-five days after her appointment. Former schools chancellor Rudy Crew (2010) warned that "we're in danger of making New York City schools a plaything for the rich and famous," but Bloomberg's logic seemed to be that in order to demonstrate capability for being in charge of the city's schools, one need only be a good manager. This illustrates further the increasing overlap of competitive market logic with public welfare and advances the pervasive underlying assumption—also found in the logic of philanthropy in relation to public schools (Domanico, Innerst, and Russo 2000)—that public schools and educators lack expertise, and that the outsiders working with the system can provide this expertise with their talent and motivation.[4]

Conclusion

In New York City, on-time graduation rates are slowly increasing, rising to 59 percent for the class of 2009 from 46.5 percent for the class of 2005 and 56.4 percent for the class of 2008 (Medina 2010a); although this is an improvement, David Steiner, the former state education commissioner, called "unacceptable" the fact that almost a third of the city's students do not graduate on time. Just over 50 percent of Hispanic students and 54 percent of Black students graduate on time, compared to 74 percent of White students and 77 percent of Asian students (ibid.). At federal, city, and school level, a widespread political spectacle that equates school choice, competition, and accountability with justice, whether in the context of traditional public or charter schools, does not inspire equity or structural change. Through empowering the elite, and advancing corporate agendas, mainstream educational reform seems to heighten the inequities that it purports to eradicate.

In this chapter, I have argued that the political spectacle of crisis that is often portrayed as educational is actually structural. Beyond the spectacle, arguments about social equity or social justice would be more convincing if they were arguments for redistribution of income (Macedo 2003) or for racial and educational equity, as opposed to arguments for school choice. I have laid out how the political spectacle functions on a macro level in terms of race, private sector involvement, and the political economy of New York City's schools. In the subsequent chapter, and through the remainder of this book, we go inside of College Prep to explore how the spectacle functions on a local level through strategic kinds of image management and agency.

2

The College Prep Look

Managing Image, Marketing Students

Through dramaturgical discourses of college readiness, social justice, student enrichment, and professionalism, College Prep community members sometimes construct a stylized performance that ensures that they will continue to be financially supported by the private sector. While Murray Edelman's theories have been applied to education as a framework for critique of bilingual education policy (Koyama and Bartlett 2011), as well as a critique of the influence of the business world on defining education policy (Smith et al. 2004), I push the conversation further by showing how image management and performance apply to the inextricably intertwined and politicized relationship between public schools and the private sector. Just as politicians and policymakers frame education reforms as beneficial to children, the nation, and the economy, the College Prep community frames itself as deserving of private monies in the context of the marketization of urban schools and students (Cucchiara 2013). Staged productions always necessitate a division between what happens in front of an audience and what is hidden behind the curtain. Thus, College Prep stages an image of an urban school that it believes appeals to funders, such as the one that is portrayed in the College Prep movie. What happens "behind the curtain" is a different story.

The College Prep Movie

It is the first Wednesday of the month at College Prep,[1] which means the bell chimes for student dismissal at 1:48 p.m., and staff stay in the building for a series of meetings. In addition to a weekly tenth-grade team meeting that will last until 3:30, we have a full staff meeting that begins at 3:45 and will end around 5:00. First Wednesdays are long for teachers, and so on meeting days lunch is catered, compliments of the Manhattan firm that is a primary funding agent and founder of our school (hereafter, "the Firm"). Platters of wraps and sandwiches, snack bags of chips and pretzels, cookies, water, and soft drinks are a familiar sight in the guidance suite during fourth and fifth periods—a preemptive reward for the hours we will spend collaborating later. This Wednesday is especially remarkable because we are told that we will be viewing the "College Prep movie," a promotional film created by two filmmakers who, as a way to promote their production company, worked pro bono with the nonprofit organization that the school created (hereafter, "the Foundation") in order to funnel in private donations.

As teachers enter, we notice that there are two celebratory sheet cakes on a table at the side of the room, and that wooden chairs are set up facing a screen and a podium. We take our seats and listen as Sebastian Thomas, the head of the Foundation, wearing a tie and blazer, shares how thrilled he is about the outcome of the movie we are about to watch. He congratulates the filmmakers, two young White women who are sitting in the back. They smile and wave.

Sarah Maxwell and Michelle McLeod, two of College Prep's enrichment coordinators, and Angela Moore, a ninth-grade special education teacher, have been asked by Mr. Thomas to give us a short introduction to the movie, and they approach the podium. Staff members become quiet, waiting to see what is in store, our clipboards on our laps.

Ms. Maxwell, the young, White ninth-grade enrichment coordinator, fills us in on how the movie is going to be used as a tool for eighth-grade recruitment. "Students are the best ones to sell the school," she emphasizes. Ms. McLeod, the tenth-grade enrichment coordinator, tells us that "the film captures the community around each child," and that "it shows what enrichment at College Prep really is." New York City native Ms. Moore, the only teacher and the only African American at the podium, says that the movie "captures the passion, energy, and relentless work ethic that make College Prep set the standard for excellence." She emphasizes that "the film captures the most important parts of the school, including professionalism." We recruit, she says, the best and brightest of New York City teachers, the strongest teachers, those who know what it takes to move students from the bottom to the top. This all comes through, she says, in this short movie.

Mr. Thomas steps back up to the podium. He adds that the movie will also, of course, be shown to prospective funders, such as Time Warner or other corporate philanthropists. "Without further ado," he announces, "we give you the first College Prep movie!" Someone in the back of the room dims the lights and the movie begins. We see Principal McCarren and Mr. Thomas on the screen first. They paint a portrait of the school as an unscreened public school, one that is academically rigorous as well as focused on critical thinking. The face of a young, Black male student flashes onto the screen. "Without education," the student says, "you don't have anything." Other student perspectives are highlighted. One student says, "If things start getting shaky at home, someone at school will get me back on track." Another student warns, "Be prepared to have faculty on your back." Another says, "Especially coming from the environment that I grew up in, it helps me to know that I don't have to go down the wrong path."

The camera cuts to an interview with La'Trice Williams, one of my closest personal friends at College Prep with whom I shared a classroom the previous school year. In the movie, she says that she is from south central Los Angeles, and that "if it weren't for the educators in my life, I wouldn't be here. Working at College Prep gives me the opportunity to give back to my community." I sneak a look at her, seated down the aisle from me next to dean of discipline Jack Sandler. Her face is expressionless as she stares straight ahead at the screen. Months before, she reluctantly agreed to be interviewed for the movie. After the interview took place, I remember that she returned to the classroom we shared, pulled me aside, and told me that the experience had been somewhat discomfiting.

We had already talked at great length about her feeling frequently tokenized by White staff and administrators as one of only a few African American teachers at the school,[2] and as one of the only teachers at the school who grew up in circumstances that were similar to those of many students. Of the interview, she said that "it was obvious why they wanted me to be there, and it was obvious what they wanted me to say. I had to play my role in order to sell College Prep to the White liberals who throw money at us to save these 'poor Black and Brown kids.'" She shook the experience off, but her resentment was obvious, and through the two years that we worked at the school (we left at the same time, me for Austin, Texas, to finish graduate school, her for another job at a charter school advocacy organization in New York), her patience and tolerance for how she was treated by some White staff members wore thin.

I look back at the screen. As the movie continues, during a narrative about higher education, I see a still shot of Keisha Anderson's face flash across the screen. I find this ironic; Keisha's name was one that I learned from her ninth-grade teachers before she set foot into my classroom, as the ringleader of a clique of about twenty African American girls at College Prep who called themselves "BOB," or the "Bang Out Bitches." BOB were notorious for verbal and physical altercations with other students (both boys and girls) outside of and sometimes inside of classrooms, as well as for having a propensity to disrespect teachers and act "unprofessional" (see chapter 3). BOB were also, by and large, intelligent young women who were high academic achievers despite their "unprofessional" demeanor.

Keisha's name would come up during a meeting the following school year, her junior year, as a possible student representative at the annual spring benefit, which I discussed briefly in the introduction. The benefit, which was attended by corporate funders who would donate to our school at the end of an evening of schmoozing with a select group of College Prep students and teachers, took place at the Firm to raise money for the Foundation. Barbara Meehan, a college advisor, suggested to Mr. Thomas that we ask Keisha to represent the school, because she had made great improvements in her behavior and grades since her ninth-grade year. Mr. Thomas immediately refused the idea, saying that the benefit "was not a time to take a chance on a student." Clearly, Keisha could represent our school in a still image on film, but still could not be trusted to manage her behavior among important adults in real time.

The narrator continues: "We offer students as many opportunities as possible to interact with the adult professional world." The movie then cuts to Howard Jackson, an African American twelfth-grade English teacher. "Here," he says, "students can reimagine their possibility." We see Mr. Thomas again, who states, "This school is transformative and life-changing for its students." This is juxtaposed with a statement by an African American male student: "This school set the foundation for helping me to be what I want to be when I want to be it, whether it's president, senator, or lawyer." On this meritocratic note, the movie ends. The lights come up in the library to a chorus of applause. Mr. Thomas tells us to help ourselves to cake, and says that the filmmakers will walk around, ready to answer any questions, and to get our reactions to the movie. Most staff leave the library at that point, eager to either go home or to continue their work in the third- or fourth-floor teachers' offices. In the movie, the school was portrayed so favorably that the gravest threat to students' education and college matriculation seemed to be their own challenging backgrounds and circumstances.[3] Parents and older community members were absent, serving to reinforce the College Prep narrative of urban teachers and students working together, against all odds, to pull students up by their bootstraps, help them to graduate, and securely set them on the road to achievement in the real world—in this case, synonymous with college readiness and a secure place in the middle class.

Ms. Moore, Ms. McLeod, and Ms. Maxwell were right: this movie presents an image of College Prep that showcases the professionalism and hard work of both teachers and students. It demonstrates how well resourced the school is, and how many enrichment opportunities exist for those students who are deemed, in philanthropist Andrew Carnegie's terms, worthy of a hand-up, not a handout (Nasaw 2006).[4] It is expertly produced, and will certainly aid in bringing in more donations to the Foundation, which will translate into more enrichment opportunities for students and more resources for students and teachers. So what does it mean that Ms. Williams feels tokenized, or that Keisha is not invited to represent the school at the benefit, even though her face is used in the video? The portrayal of both women demonstrates a gender and race problem that education scholar Signithia Fordham (1993) has addressed. She discusses the ways in which normalized definitions of femaleness and White middle-class womanhood uphold a two-tiered patriarchy. Because womanhood or femaleness is a norm referenced to one group (White, middle-class Americans), women who do not fall into this group are compelled to silence or gender "passing" (8), either becoming or remaining voiceless or silent, or, alternatively, symbolically impersonating a male image. Keisha was silenced both through the use of her image in the movie and through Mr. Thomas's refusal to invite her to the benefit. Ms. Williams was silenced differently: her voice was mediated and filtered through the production of the movie in order to create an acceptable image for potential funders. In Edelman's terms, both Ms. Williams and Keisha served as props in the spectacle. While College Prep's spectacle, upheld through its graduation and college matriculation rates, as well as through its marketing techniques, shows that the school is an urban success story, I contend that the discrepancy between the spectacle and the reality matters in the pursuit of equity and justice.

College Prep in the Media

An article published in the *New York Times* during College Prep's first year of existence[5] portrays it as a small school that owes its success to its private and nonprofit sponsors, including but not limited to the Firm and the Gates Foundation. The article quotes a student who says that she became interested in law because so many of her relatives have spent time in jail. The article lionizes Claire Cohen, the (then) not yet thirty-year-old principal, as both an older sister figure and a disciplinarian in the eyes of students.[6] In 2006, College Prep was featured on a *Today Show* special that donated thousands of dollars' worth of supplies and equipment to the school. The Firm was featured in a 2005 magazine article that describes its relationship to College Prep as both partner and patron. In addition to these articles, the school's website lists over twenty-five links to newspaper and magazine articles that praise the school for its ambitious mission, its talented teachers, its innovative theme, and its ability to receive generous grants and donations.

The Ideal: Image Management and Climate Control

From the outside, the school building seems like a well-built, friendly, welcoming place. It is located between a corporate hotel and a City University campus, and the school's "college or career-ready" focus seems to be symbolized by the urban academic atmosphere of the campus and the convention / corporate-friendly atmosphere of the hotel. In the two years that I was at the school, I noticed that this school did not escape the gap between the real and the ideal so apparent at many public schools. Climate control (regulating the temperature) of classrooms was a continual battle, and by my second Christmas in the school, most of the clocks in the building had stopped working, and were never repaired.

Twice during my first year at the school the ceiling in the classroom next to mine caved in due to water damage from heavy snow. While college readiness, the student dress code, and student "professionalism" (which I discuss at length in the following chapter) were frequent topics at staff meetings, another frequent topic was building maintenance, which never quite seemed to run smoothly, despite the fact that the school was located in a newly renovated space. At two points in the time that I worked for the school building issues were highlighted in a city newspaper.[7]

The stories pointed out that the school seemed almost booby trapped when students arrived: an unlocked door led to a ten-foot drop onto the roof, and the malfunctioning heat and air-conditioning meant some rooms were hot while others were freezing. There were exposed electrical wires at various locations in the building, and one ceiling leaked for two weeks. Unexplained fire alarms were, at one point when we first moved into the building, going off continuously during the day.

Staff and parents from the school alerted the newspaper to the issues in the building in order to use publicity to get attention and get them fixed. The climate control problems were a big deal because normally (as I emphasize above) it was good publicity, not bad, that surrounded us. Principal McCarren frequently reminded us that we were a high-profile school, and we were advised not to "air our dirty laundry" in official yearly New York City Department of Education surveys, or when teams came to give us our School Quality Review. This was important because we wanted to maintain the "A" we had on our school progress report, as well as our high status in the *New York Post*'s ranking of the top fifty public schools in the city.[8] The school's deliberate spectacle served as what Douglas Foley, drawing on sociologist Erving Goffman, terms a "making out game" (2010) in order to uphold the school's image to outsiders. Foley defines "making out games" in a South Texas high school as humorous classroom speech events where students "con" teachers into breaking from the planned lesson, in order to do the least amount of real work possible while faking their investment or involvement in school to teachers. At College Prep, administrators of the school purposefully create another kind of event through deliberate performance. Both Foley's and College Prep's making out games index racial/ethnic and class hierarchies, but at College Prep, the making out games that administrators perform for outsiders draw on discourses of neoliberal success and marketability to uphold a specific image of the school. Both a lack of attention to building infrastructure in U.S. urban schools (Kozol 1992) and schools' maintenance of race and class hierarchies (Bourdieu 1977; Bowles and Gintis 1976; Ferguson 2001; Kenny 2000; Kozol 1992; A. Lewis 2003) have been documented in earlier studies. College Prep markets itself to its elite funders as being set apart from stereotypical urban high schools in low-income communities (and in many ways it is). But at the same time, it continues to grapple with many of the same issues of building infrastructure and student motivation (which develop largely as a result of structural inequalities beyond the school) while hiding them from funders who want to invest their capital in a successful enterprise.

The mission statement of the school places emphasis on extracurricular activities, rigorous instruction within a themed curriculum, and, most important, college readiness. Just as the façade of the building masked faulty wiring and safety hazards inside, the way College Prep is marketed and the making out games that school administrators play are part of a political spectacle that glazes over other, hidden dynamics of this particular learning environment.

The "College Prep Look" as Spectacle

When asked on a school-wide student questionnaire disseminated in the spring of 2010 (see appendix B) as part of the data collection for this study (but also for the benefit of staff and students, who wanted to get a sense of students' perceptions of the school) what advice she would give to a new student who was just starting at College Prep, a twelfth grader wrote: "College Prep is not what it seems. College Prep is a very slick mixed-up school. A lot of lies are put into promoting this school." This student's perception of the school is telling, in that she seems quite aware of the presence of a "College Prep look" or ideal that is used promotionally. Beneath the ideal, however, there is a reality that is very different. While the ideal is a façade of uniformed professionalism and neediness for staff and students, both parties bend the norms in instrumental ways. Examining both the spectacle of the institution, and how the norms are resisted, serves to expose the ways in which power works in this space, as well as to critique larger social structures.

In an interview, Principal McCarren unknowingly echoed what the student said on the survey:

> To me it seems like there are a couple levels of culture here—there is one level of culture, which is the external public persona, and then there is the internal level, the reality. Listening to all the conversations that we have about this, it seems like that's where our struggle is. We have this reputation that has been branded, that now the expectations are "I'm gonna go to Harvard or Yale 'cause that's what this school does," and then we have the internal culture of what happens in the day to day—and I wonder how do

we get those two things to match or be the same? I can give you one concrete example from today—we had all these district people visit Karla Gomez's class this morning and the kids were amazing. It was first period, and they knew what to do. In this setting, they know what they are doing—they were on their game, it was a great class. But then at the end of the day, we had Nakisha go absolutely insane, and Karla turned to me and said "I'm glad this didn't happen first period!" The feedback from the visitors was "this school is amazing! How do we get our kids to do that?" First period wasn't a show, because they know how to do that stuff, and they practice all the time, but it's amazing how you can have the exact opposite thing happen with the same lesson. Those visitors walked away and said "College Prep has got it and they know how to do it!" And I am thinking "no, we don't," actually.

Principal McCarren highlights the idea here that while students choose to perform school norms and do so under certain circumstances, there are other circumstances where they resist. The choice of students like Nakisha to, as Ms. Williams later put it, "turn it off or turn it on" based on whether funders are in the room, speaks to their level of awareness of the importance of resources and opportunities to their schooling experience. It also speaks to students' critical race and class consciousness because they are very much aware that they are expected to enact an "acceptable" kind of (racialized and classed) performance for an audience. Regardless of how they perform, they are aware that the school has a vested interest in the external public persona that must be upheld. At certain times (like when there is a classroom visitor), students help to do this, and at other times, they choose not to.

Several students picked up on this double standard in responses that they wrote in on the school-wide survey. Knowing that the "College Prep look" does not have room for student failure, in response to a question that read: "How does your experience at College Prep compare with the experiences of your friends/siblings who don't go to College Prep?" three seniors wrote the following:

Academic wise it's great, the teachers teach you in a way that you can't fail. But the kids take advantage of that.

College Prep is a good place, but sometimes babies the students
too much, and doesn't know exactly how or when to let us
fly away.

College Prep is more academic but the students are babied.

While these students show an awareness that the school might be more
academic than schools their friends attend, they also show awareness
that staff hold students up in order to prevent them from failing, sometimes too much. Ralph Fulton, a ninth-grade math teacher, and Assistant
Principal Humphries echoed this sentiment in a conversation at a meeting about school culture:

> MR. FULTON: I wanted to respond about being non-democratic,
> and I think that idea speaks to one of the issues that plagues
> us. We mold situations here in an inauthentic way because we
> so badly want a final product. People that come to work here,
> including myself, have this insane sense of pride. We never let
> kids fail, and they are not accountable. If you don't have a pen,
> I give you one, and if you don't have a printer, I print it out for
> you. We don't allow students to fail. But that triggered in my
> mind, that that's what we do, that we scaffold things so
> much . . .
>
> MS. HUMPHRIES: But that speaks to staff values.
>
> MR. FULTON: And our personalities. Like I wanted my advisory[9]
> to go on a trip, and finally because I am exhausted, I said "you
> guys plan it. Give me three options with budgets," and I've got
> nothing. They just told me paintball and Six Flags prices, but
> we've got nothing written up, and that's what I said they had to
> do. So we are not going on a trip. And there is a part of me that
> might do it for them—part of me wants to do it for them—on
> another day.

These comments demonstrate that staff will go to great lengths to preserve the College Prep look, whether it is based on teachers' pride, on
larger, deeply rooted internalization of neoliberal "savior" discourses in
urban schools (see more on this in chapter 4), or on realizing that the resources that we get depend on a well-managed image of student success,

not failure. Teachers and some students, in a sense, are adept at managing the image of the entire student body to the outside as well, and will go out of their way to cover for students who do not conform or further the school's reputation.

The "College Prep Look": Staff

In addition to teachers managing the image of students in terms of the College Prep look, the external College Prep spectacle is upheld through hiring practices at the school, which seem to favor a particular type. Although there have been explicit attempts to break the mold, especially in terms of hiring more racially diverse staff members, those who fit the mold—young, White, middle-class, mostly but not always female—tend to be the ones who stay. This type (which I discuss further in chapter 4) exemplifies the College Prep look for staff. This is a bit different from the New York City public schools where I worked in the past, where staff seemed of relatively diverse races and ages.

At College Prep, most of the teachers were young (in their twenties or thirties), creative, single, stylish, energetic, and graduates of elite colleges and universities. Many were recruited from programs like the New York City Teaching Fellows and Teach for America (TFA). Fellows and TFA candidates agree to work for a certain amount of time, usually two years, at a "high-need" urban school and to take night courses toward a subsidized master's degree in education. Ms. McGoldrick, a White female teacher, told me that the College Prep type that the school hires are, most important, people who are young, unattached, and idealistic—so that the school can "take advantage of them and their time." As I participated in the hiring process for the fall of 2009, I had to agree.

Although there were always conversations about seeking to hire staff members who were more diverse in color, age, and gender, College Prep's hiring committees had reservations about hiring people who would not have sufficient time to devote to the school's high demands. In addition to creating a more diverse pool of staff members, many of the post-interview conversations about potential hires involved explicitly seeking people who had time to devote to early mornings and late evenings at the school, especially if they were older, or had children or a spouse. Whether candidates would "fit in" with the high demands of the "overachieving," "type A" College Prep staff was frequently a point of contention among an interview panel. I conformed, during the two years that I worked at the school, often working side by side with colleagues until past 7:00 p.m., only to show up the next morning at 8:00 and do the whole thing over. I had, often, up to four regularly scheduled meetings a week, sometimes during and sometimes after the school day. Often, leaving the building late and thinking I was alone, I would run into colleagues who were either still working or on their way out. During the winter, I arrived at school once a week at 6:45 a.m. to coach cheerleading practice. Then too it was a common occurrence to run into a teacher getting an early start on the day. Looking like a hard worker and spending long hours in the building were part of the "College Prep look" for teachers.

What makes us—young, predominantly White, mostly from places other than the city—qualified or motivated to teach students who come from very different backgrounds? There is a problematic duality created here about access to power and knowledge that rests on a banking model of education (Freire 1970), as well as on pathologizing students' families and communities. Power and knowledge rest uniquely in the hands of teachers, who distribute these into the minds and hands of students, seen as empty vessels waiting to be filled. In a neoliberal context, this logic also aligns with the Carnegie-based logic of *philanthrocapitalism* (Bishop and Green 2009), which implies that the privileged know what is best for the oppressed.

I returned to College Prep in the fall of 2010 to present some of the data I gathered from the student questionnaire. Staff learned the following:

- 60 percent of students reported that they gain academic confidence from their families.
- 42 percent of students reported that teachers make "somewhat of an effort" to connect with their neighborhoods or communities.
- 26 percent of students reported that their teachers "do not make an effort" to connect with their neighborhoods or communities.
- 35 percent of students reported that they disapproved of professionalism / professionalism points at College Prep (see chapter 3).

Concerned with these data, one group of staff members asked, "How can we better connect with our students' communities, and how can we connect with the professional people and places in those communities?" Staff members ask the important questions about connecting with students on a broader level, but making these connections everyday is rare.

Race and the "College Prep Look": Staff

In February 2010, Francis Mitchell, the only male and the only non-White person working in College Prep's college office, quit. Mr. Mitchell, who identifies as African American, grew up in public housing projects on the Lower East Side of Manhattan and attended New York City public schools until he was fourteen, when he decided to apply to an elite, mostly White boarding school in Massachusetts. After some convincing, his parents supported him in this decision. After multiple tests and interviews, he was accepted to the boarding school on a full scholarship. He elaborated in our interview on the challenges of this transition. He described feelings of alienation, being caught between two worlds, and sensing that he belonged neither in his home community nor in his boarding school environment. Yet, because of emotional support from an African American teacher in Massachusetts with whom he connected, and from a close-knit group of friends who also came from New York City, he learned how to negotiate both environments: the elite, overwhelmingly White world of high school and college, as well as the poor, working-class, Black and Brown world of his home community.

Following boarding school, he attended a small liberal arts college in the northeast, where he later became an admissions counselor. College Prep then actively recruited him to work in its college office. Because of his background, both personal and professional, he was in many ways a perfect fit for College Prep—a young, educated Black man from the city (sharing a background in a community similar to many of our students) who had succeeded in graduating from high school and college and in pursuing the neoliberal, meritocratic dream of college and middle-class success. He was whom College Prep teachers and administrators hoped our students might someday become.

Despite the fact that he was, on paper, the perfect fit, Mr. Mitchell's tenure in College Prep's college office did not work out as anyone had planned. He had difficulty with Ashley Barnes, a middle-aged White woman originally from a rural area of the United States and the head of the college office (which was funded by the Foundation). According to Mr. Mitchell, he and Ms. Barnes had disagreements in front of students about college office decisions. Tension between the two mounted, and Mr. Mitchell, as he put it, "went above Ms. Barnes" and complained to Sebastian Thomas, the head of the Foundation. Mr. Mitchell thought Mr. Thomas also had difficulty working closely with Ms. Barnes. Mr. Mitchell also went to Principal McCarren about the issues he was having.

In early February 2010, just before winter recess, Principal McCarren called Mr. Mitchell into her office, where Mr. Thomas and Ms. Barnes were waiting. There, Mr. Thomas told Mr. Mitchell that he was "hostile" and "bristled at authority." According to Mr. Mitchell, Ms. Barnes then left the office, and Mr. Mitchell told Mr. Thomas and Principal McCarren that he would quit. He proposed that he stay on and finish through the next five weeks, but Mr. Thomas informed Mr. Mitchell that that following Friday would be his last day at the school and that he would be paid for the next month. Mr. Thomas thought that this would make things less "uncomfortable" in the college office. There was no official announcement made to staff until the day preceding Mr. Mitchell's last. Staff received an e-mail from Mr. Thomas publicly thanking Mr. Mitchell for his hard work and wishing him well.

I became aware of this incident one evening shortly after Mr. Mitchell's last day while socializing with two teachers, Ms. Williams and Mr. Matthews, and support staff member Mr. Davis—all African American staff at the school who were close with Mr. Mitchell. When they shared how Mr. Mitchell had been let go, they were indignant and sad, but not at all surprised. "Put this in your book," they implored, "this" being a hidden story that needed to be told.

Mr. Mitchell's story was similar, they said, to the way another African American staff member, James Howard, a former dean of discipline, had been let go a year earlier. According to the story, College Prep's principal explained to him that he was not "the right fit." Mr. Davis, the parent coordinator who was born in Brooklyn, said that he would not be returning the following school year because he too had a conversation with the principal where she voiced frustration with his alleged lack of competence. According to Ms. Williams, Mr. Matthews, and Mr. Davis, there was an established pattern in place—College Prep was, in Mr. Davis's words, a "racist institution" that often held its own image management above students' best interests. It was a place that aggressively pushed out Black staff who did not conform to the predominantly White power structure.

Mr. Davis said that he was still in close touch with many Black staff who had either been asked to leave by an administrator because they were not "the right fit" or had left of their own volition. He named three, but implied that there were more. According to the group, College Prep is a place that all too clearly mirrors the racist world beyond its walls, as opposed to an ideal, more equitable place of learning. Despite the ostensible fight against "educational inequity," the school does not seem to be a place where hiring practices fight social inequity.[10]

Despite an undertow of racism, the school manages its public image to emphasize the presence of Black staff members. For example, in early publicity about the school, it seems as if every newspaper photo of a classroom teacher with students is of Mr. Battle, the physical education teacher, who is Black. At the school's annual spring benefit, when Mr. Jackson could not attend, Ms. Williams was asked to attend in his place. Both are Black. Ms. Williams and Mr. Jackson are two of four Black teachers at the school who were asked to interview for the College Prep promotional movie; this is a misrepresentation of the racial demographic of the predominantly White College Prep staff, but is part of a system of elaborate image management and political spectacle in promotional material.

As a school, College Prep excels at celebrating its high college acceptance rate, wealth of extracurricular and college preparatory programs for students, and hardworking staff. Yet conversations about students who don't buy in, about how to wrestle with difficult race, class, and gender issues, and what Assistant Principal Humphries calls a "me culture" (as opposed to a "we culture"), were explicitly avoided, or occurred "under the radar." These conversations happened in the stairwells, at teachers' happy hour, or in hushed tones during prep periods in teachers' offices; in other words, forthright discussion was sacrificed to uphold the College Prep look. I knew, based on personal and professional relationships with Mr. Davis, Mr. Howard, and Mr. Mitchell, that all were quite interested in working for racial and educational equity. It just seemed as if the power structure at the school was not friendly to these particular people doing this particular kind of work. Perhaps their very presence challenged the ideals or norms set in place by the institution.

The "College Prep Look": Students

The syllabus for Mr. Randall's tenth-grade Social Studies class stated the following:

Classroom Procedures

1. Upon entering the class on-time and quietly, you must sit in your assigned seat, take off your jacket and your bag and put it on the back of the chair, take out your class binder, a usable writing implement, the assignment that is due that day, and start the do-now which will be on the board. The do-now must be done silently and will affect your classwork/participation grade.
2. Homework and projects/papers that are due must be taken out, have your name on it, and put visibly on top of the desk in order to be checked or collected. This must be done within the first three minutes of class or it will be considered late.
3. After the first three minutes, Mr. Randall will walk around the class, making sure you have done the do-now and will check or collect the homework/project/paper. He will also make sure you have your binder.
4. Bathroom passes will be signed after classroom instruction is finished but not the first or last 10 minutes of class. Do not get out of your seat or ask to get out of your seat for any reason (including to throw away trash or to sharpen a pencil) during classroom instruction time—save it for an appropriate time. When in this class, you must maintain your professionalism. This includes being alert, being organized, being respectful, being responsible, and being appropriate. (Reminders are on the wall.)

Students who are constantly forgetting homework / pens / pencils / paper / handouts / binders / "my jacket in the other room" are not being professional students. Students that swear or yell, are late to class or constantly absent, engage in side conversations or get out of their seat during instruction, have their head down or are asleep, call out without raising their hand or ask to go to the bathroom during instruction, eat food, drink soda, or chew seeds during class, have their binder in a hot mess or can't find their notes are not being professional students. Remember: classwork/ participation is a big part of your grade that includes being professional. Boost your grade! Do not lose out on these points!

Yet, despite his strict regulations, Mr. Randall sent an e-mail out to the tenth-grade teachers during September of 2009 that read:

Teachers–
Things have been a little out of control in our grade this week (especially in my class). Dean Howard is going to come to our grade team tomorrow to discuss a plan. Brainstorm some ideas about what should be done and we'll discuss it tomorrow.

Mr. Randall sent the above e-mail to the tenth-grade teachers the same afternoon that he expressed his frustration to Ms. Williams and me that there were constant "blow-ups" or verbal altercations in his class between tenth-grade girls. Thirty-two years old, White, and adventurous, Mr. Randall was in his fifth year at College Prep. He had a good reputation with students; many spoke to me about how much they enjoyed his class. He came into the classroom that Ms. Williams and I shared with a rare display of intense frustration on his face, and asked whether his class was the only one where the "blow-ups" were happening. Although Ms. Williams and I tried to assure him that he was not the only one, he continued to believe that the issue was the worst in his class. "It has to be something I am doing," he said, shaking his head. "I mean, I am not letting them out of their seats, and I am not letting them talk across the room. I don't know what it is that I am doing wrong!" His rules are clearly delineated on the course syllabus (quoted above), but his e-mail and questions to Ms. Williams and me reveal that although he lays out an ideal for student behavior, and some of his students conform to the ideal, other students resist creating the kind of learning environment that he hopes his rules and routines will inspire.

These routines are part of what I argue is the "College Prep look" for students. Both students and staff expressed that the mainstream classroom College Prep look is a bit different from the hallway College Prep look, and that the ideal College Prep look can be different from the real

College Prep look. Mr. Randall's e-mail about things being "out of control" demonstrates that people sometimes, but not always, enact ideals in the building.

College Prep students, as stated above, are predominantly Black or Latino, and socioeconomically poor, working, or middle class. The College Prep look for students also has to do in some respects with being racially marked (I once witnessed a young, Black, male paraprofessional in teaching clothes be mistaken for a student who was out of uniform by Ms. Brandon, an English teacher who was new to the building). In addition, students are expected to wear uniforms, which also serve as a marker of the College Prep look (although I was once mistaken for a student and asked to sign the attendance sheet by a substitute teacher while I was wearing the school uniform and shadowing a freshman for the day; in this case, the uniform trumped my Whiteness).

Uniformed Bodies / Disciplined Bodies?

The uniform consists of black, khaki, or navy blue pants (or below-the-knee–length skirt for girls), a light blue collared shirt (or blouse for girls), a tie (for boys), and a blue or black V-neck sweater, cardigan, or sweater vest. From September through October 15, and from May 15 until the end of the school year, students have a light blue polo shirt option, but from October 16 through May 14, they can wear button-down long-sleeve dress shirts or blouses only. Hoodies, symbols, patterns, writing, or other colors on clothing are prohibited. Jeans, denim, sweats, stretchy materials, or corduroy are also prohibited. For young men, the uniform policy states, "pants must be pulled up and shirts tucked in. Sandals or flip flops are forbidden, as are hoods, Do Rags or scarves, hats, and belt buckles that depict bad language, violence or sexual content of any kind."

From ninth grade, students are taught to SLANT in class, an acronym that stands for "Sit up straight, Listen, Ask questions, Nod, and Track the speaker with your eyes" (Lemov 2010). In 2009–10, when I assisted Mr. Rodino in his ninth-grade classes, I witnessed many practice SLANTing sessions during the first weeks of school. Mr. Rodino would give students a countdown, after which they were supposed to SLANT. This was often comical, because he would count down from five to one, and the class, on cue, would straighten, stare at him, and begin nodding theatrically, even when he wasn't saying anything. That year, Mr. Rodino often complimented students on how well they were SLANTing toward him during his lessons. SLANTing is part of the ideal College Prep look in classrooms.

In addition to SLANTing, there are norms of behavior that are set in place by the institution. These include being punctual and speaking Standard English, which includes knowing how to speak Standard English at a "reasonable" volume (this is a point of contention, as Ms. Franklin, a Black support staff member of Caribbean heritage, informed me. She shared an incident where a White, middle-class, female teacher repeatedly told a student to "stop yelling," but from Ms. Franklin's perspective the student was speaking at a reasonable volume). Other institutional norms require that students do the "do-now" exercise, a three- to five-minute assignment, when they arrive to class, and that they remain calm while SLANTing through the class period, whether engaged in group work or activities or direct instruction from the teacher.

Students are expected to remain in class; after staff struggled with students "abusing their bathroom privileges" (e.g., using the restroom too much, or for too long, or wandering through the halls of the building when they were supposed to be using the bathroom), the school implemented a pass system. In 2009–10, students were issued a piece of paper with six bathroom passes per six-week marking period on it. Each time they needed to use the restroom, a teacher was supposed to sign and date one of the passes. Staff members were instructed to refuse to let students leave the classroom after they exhausted their six passes.

During the 2008–9 school year, the institution had a merit/demerit point system in place. This meant that for certain activities, students could earn (or lose) points that would place them on a certain level (gold, silver, bronze, caution, or penalty). Students who were on penalty level were prohibited from participating in field trips, dances, after-school, or extracurricular activities. To gain merit points that year, students could tutor peers, assist teachers, return lost items, excel academically, demonstrate school spirit or citizenship, provide staff with information that could prevent or help resolve violent or threatening situations, lead clubs or social service events or activities, or otherwise serve the College Prep community at large. If students enhanced their "College Prep look" by earning merit points, teachers filled out and signed a piece of paper that students would take to the dean's office. The secretary would enter the points earned into the system, raising the student's merit level.[11]

Certain students, like Steven Davis, Cassandra Goodridge, and Sydney Falkland (all of whom I taught during the 2008–09 school year), were named by staff and students as some of the "most professional" in their class. They often told me that year that they wished that there were a "platinum" merit level—they had already reached "gold," and continued to gain merit points from teachers for exemplifying the College Prep look. They were straight-A students, and were always prepared. They followed teachers' rules in class, and always wore their uniforms. They switched to Standard English while in class, but spoke African American Vernacular English (Rickford 1999)[12] with friends on their own time. They were calm in class, organized, and used their planners. They were unfailingly polite to adults in the building. They played on the school's basketball teams, and participated in other extracurricular activities, including summer internships. They arrived to school early and stayed late. These students unfailingly and consistently were professionals at demonstrating the ideal College Prep look and working to uphold the school's spectacle, and they were rewarded by the institution for doing so. They were not, however, representative of the majority of students at the school.

Discipline and Incentives

Students would also accrue demerits, which were subtracted from a student's merit points for any violation of the school's discipline code—from coming to school out of uniform, to having/using electronics in class, to engaging in activities that were "disruptive" or physically harmful to other students or teachers. In addition to demerits, there was a detention and suspension system in place based on the gravity of the violations.

For example, level-one behavior, worth between five and twenty demerits, included an unexcused absence from school, a dress code infraction, cutting class, being late to class or school, not being in the assigned place on school premises, disrupting the educational process or engaging in verbally rude or "disruptive" behavior, wearing "disruptive" headgear or clothing, bringing prohibited electronics, posting or distributing inappropriate material on school premises, or using school electronics without permission. Level-two behavior, worth between fifteen and twenty demerits, involved smoking, gambling, using profane, vulgar, lewd, or abusive language or gestures, lying to school staff, destroying or misusing property belonging to the school or others, or persistent level-

one behavior. Level-three behavior involved leaving class or school premises without permission, defying or disobeying the instructions of school
staff, trying to enter the building without permission, engaging in gang-
related behavior, tampering with school records, stealing, cheating, or
vandalizing property. Level-four behavior, which resulted in "immediate
penalty level," was making inappropriate sexual comments or engaging
in sexually inappropriate behaviors, posting or distributing threatening
material, physical fighting, possessing drugs, making a bomb threat, setting
off a false fire alarm, inciting or causing a riot, or possessing a weapon.
When I taught at College Prep, most of the infractions that I witnessed or
noticed other teachers writing up were level one.

Students were classified based on their merit/demerit levels into five
categories: gold, silver, bronze, caution, or penalty. Students who were on
penalty level were not permitted to attend dances, field trips, or participate in extracurricular activities, while students on caution level were not
allowed to attend social events but were able to attend extracurricular
activities.

During the 2009–10 school year, the merit/demerit system was sim-
plified from five levels to two levels: students were either "eligible" or
"ineligible." If students accrued detentions for infractions listed on the
discipline code, they had to serve these detentions or they would be put
on the ineligible list, also known as the "I-List." E-mailed to teachers
weekly and posted on each floor of the school, the I-List functioned the
same way the penalty level did during the system the previous year: students who were on the I-List were barred from dances, field trips, talent
shows, and extracurricular activities. In order to enforce this rule, deans
of discipline attended dances, field trips, and basketball games, to bar
ineligible students from entry. Students who were eligible, on the other
hand, were permitted to engage in these activities. If a student missed
three detentions, they were automatically put on the I-List, and any student who returned from a suspension and was on disciplinary probation
remained on the I-List until the probation period was over.

Whether the system manifested itself in the form of a "penalty level"
or an "I-List," however, students seemed relatively apathetic to both rewards
and punishments. Because of its complexity, the merit system allowed for
fewer students to be on punishment: on October 15, 2009, for example, I
counted thirty-four students on penalty level; during the week of October 9, 2010, there were 184 students (40 percent of the student body) who

were ineligible. During the week of February 23, there were 158 students who were ineligible (35 percent of the student body). The list was cleared each semester; if students ended the fall semester ineligible, they were eligible at the start of the spring semester. Numbers rose later in the year: the I-List during the week of May 17, 2010, had 342 students on it. There are 450 students on the school's register, so this meant that 76 percent of the students in school were not eligible to participate in any extracurricular activities. Students on this list had between three and fifty unserved detentions. These data expose part of what happens "behind the curtain" of the political spectacle of College Prep. Students, staff, and administrators are aware that resources depend on constructing an image of a school where extracurricular opportunities are available to every student. However, even if extracurricular activities exist, what good do they do if students are not permitted to participate in them?

Behind the "curtain," some staff members demonstrated various forms of resistant agency in the face of the I-List. In a follow-up interview in 2014, Ms. McLeod told me that those who worked for the Foundation's student enrichment office agreed that when it came to extracurricular opportunities where deans or administrators would be present (like dances or basketball games), they had to enforce the I-List, but when it came to off-site extracurricular opportunities that did not involve deans or administrators, "we're not doing that"; in other words, they would ignore the I-List and continue to do their best to ensure that the most students got the most opportunities possible.

One snafu in the eligible/ineligible system was that there were no repercussions for not serving detentions and for letting them build up. The situation prompted Nakisha, an African American student whom I taught as a sophomore in English during the 2008–9 school year and whom I shadowed during the 2009–10 school year, to comment: "We don't have to serve detention . . . like we're just going to be ineligible, but we are not forced to serve detention." Students like Nakisha, who had a reputation at the school for being troublemakers (or according to her, having "fun" or "acting goofy" in class), didn't necessarily have an incentive to get off the I-List once they were on it. Especially when detentions built up for level-one infractions, serving all of one's detentions seemed a tall mountain to climb. Instead, students became apathetic.

This tone was evident in the announcement of a "dress down challenge" in November 2009, when students were promised a school-wide "dress down" where they could come to school out of uniform if they could all come to school in uniform for two weeks straight. In the advisory class that I co-taught with Mr. Horowitz, I noticed that no one reacted the morning the dress-down announcement was made (I counted five students out of fifteen in the room who were in dress-code violation). Students were not able to successfully meet the dress down challenge, and they were expected to arrive at school in uniform, as usual. While most staff and administrators at the school seemed to try their best to get students to buy into school rules and regulations, the ways in which this was communicated to students seemed to be top down—done to, as opposed to done with, students.

Concluding Thoughts

Prevailing attitudes at College Prep supported a political spectacle that aggressively upheld the school's image in the interest of media recognition and financial support. This spectacle attempts to hide the gap between the ideal and the real. Oftentimes, critique of the spectacle is sacrificed in the name of the ideal, in order to make funders comfortable. While staff members at College Prep engage reasons for the absence (or presence) of student motivation to succeed in school (in several faculty meetings, as well as the meeting where I presented questionnaire data to staff, students, and parents), these conversations do not reach a social or structural level. They exist to satisfy the story that is sold to funders about the school. They are not (and perhaps at the institutional level, cannot be) located at the level of structural critique that interrogates continuing social and economic inequities and asks why students and some staff members choose not to buy into the spectacle that the school is selling. Politicians and policymakers do not engage these questions in the discourse around school choice either; conversations that equate a "good education" in the United States with competition or choice masquerade as being about social justice and enhanced opportunity, but in reality can depend on an inequitable balance of resources, opportunities, power, and privilege.

College Prep and its staff are marketed as students' "neoliberal saviors" (see chapter 4 for more on this). In other words, College Prep constructs itself as "rescuing" students from their home communities, and deems them worthy of salvation as they are given the "bundles of skill sets" necessary to graduate from high school and matriculate into college

(Spears-Bunton and Powell 2008). While a small number of Black teachers represent the staff in the school's promotional materials, feeding into a politically liberal dream of ethnic diversity (without a real shift in hierarchies of power or privilege), those same teachers are often told by White administration that they are "not the right fit," and asked to leave. Although they are the "faces" of the school, their perspectives are often pushed out of the school in real time. Students, meanwhile, are expected to wear uniforms and to behave according to the school's codes as one way to cultivate their marketability for college. Obscuring both the neoliberal marketing of students and the school's racist policies is a kind of color-blind or meritocratic logic that provides a convenient escape from critiquing the fact that the school's model depends on class and race inequity to exist.

Like many of New York City's SSCs, College Prep is not a neighborhood school. Students commute from each borough of the city, in some cases from as far as Staten Island. This model is inherently discouraging of community or family involvement in school, and provides another challenge to creating alternatives to a market-based model. Forms of knowledge and epistemologies that are rooted in students' home lives, but are alternative to those of the school, are not encouraged (Moll et al. 1992; Valenzuela 1999). This may be one explanation for students' resistance to the school's ostensibly stringent uniform policy and apathy about the school's discipline code. Seen as "bundles of skill sets," students opt out in their own ironic system of "school choice" in an effort to maintain a sense of self-determination and agency (Spears-Bunton and Powell 2008).

Students' (and some staff members') decisions to opt out of becoming props in the spectacle, although not necessarily transformative, represent a kind of political agency. So does teachers' rethinking of student privileges, rights, and responsibilities in the wake of a negative school climate, Foundation employees' overt resistance to the I-List, or teachers wondering how to involve students' parents or communities in school. So do some Black teachers' critiques of College Prep's racist policies. These actions and conversations represent the idea that other options exist. In the case of mainstream discourses about school choice, in the rush to achieve in standards-based or federally sanctioned ways, it is easier to praise or blame schools and teachers for their failures or successes in the game of test-taking and college or career readiness than to critique (or change) the game itself. As we shall see in subsequent chapters, the image

of College Prep as an urban miracle further entrenches deep-seated inequities that are increasingly more pronounced given the current of educational reform in New York City, and in many cities across the United
States. These inequities are hidden in a political spectacle of choice and
market-based competition as educational justice.

3

Walk the Walk, Talk the Talk

Professionalism at College Prep

I took my place at an empty desk in Ms. Brandon's tenth-grade English classroom, and watched as she struggled to quiet her class. Despite the fact that the bell rang, and the "do-now" was on the board, students continued to chat with one another. Ms. Brandon was new to College Prep, but had been a teacher in another public school in the city for several years before. She shushed the students a couple of times to no avail. She reminded students that they only had five minutes to complete the "do-now," their introductory assignment, but this still seemed not to make much of a difference. The chatter continued, and I recorded in my field notes:

> A female student is laughing at a table just in front of us and to our right, and Ms. Brandon says, "Listening to me, please, listening to me, please." Students are still talking. She says, "I hear all this chatter and people are still not doing the right thing." When students still don't quiet down, one or two minutes later, she says, "what happened to us over the weekend? It looks like we are going to eat up this five minutes today." She looks frustrated. She shushes again twice, trying to settle the class down. A girl sitting in front of me tosses a black plastic bag on the floor. Ms. Brandon says, "I am seeing only about four people around the room who are getting their professionalism points." She complains: "My God, you guys are so noisy today!"

The above anecdote highlights an important aspect of teaching and learning at College Prep. Teachers were encouraged to give students a daily grade based on their display of "professionalism" (or lack thereof) in classes. Professionalism points most often functioned as a metric to evaluate students on their speech, dress, or conduct in the classroom.

Students' professionalism grades were factored into their marking period grades, and usually counted for about 10 percent.

Corporate values like professionalism in schools are emblematic of a newer version of classic liberal economic ideology that is based on tenets of individualism, meritocracy, and the freedom of the market. I contend that the school's focus on credentialing and students' performance of professionalism are another part of a problematic political spectacle in education that places the responsibility for upward mobility (or the failure to be upwardly mobile) solely on individuals, and justifies existent social inequalities that are ostensibly color-blind, yet in actuality are fundamental to racial capitalism (Robinson 1983). In addition to high graduation and college matriculation rates, the practice and assessment of student professionalism are another way in which the school is able to demonstrate its deservedness to funders; that is, despite being constructed as needy, College Prep students are also trained in professionalism, and thus demonstrate the potential for upward mobility if given the right kind of help.

I find it useful to conceptualize the racial project of this school predominantly through the lens of radical Black scholars. While this choice may prevent me from effectively theorizing the nuanced racial subjectivities and experiences of Latino or Asian participants, and I run the risk of being accused of furthering a false Black/White binary of racial experience in the United States, I find these scholars' particular views on the ways in which White hegemony attempts to circumscribe non-White identity through creating an "other" to be extremely useful. While much qualitative research in education focuses either on the maintenance of racial hierarchy (Ferguson 2001; A. Lewis 2003; Marx 2006; P. Perry 2002; Pollock 2004) or on the insidiousness of neoliberalism in school settings (Apple 2001; Davies and Bansel 2007; Giroux 2004), my analysis of professionalism in this chapter synthesizes the two, demonstrating the relationship between neoliberalism and racism in the context of a political spectacle that acknowledges neither.

On some level, the very existence of a system that evaluates students on their professionalism makes the assumption that they come into the school as "unprofessionals" who must reshape their political identities and transcend their racial positionalities in order to be valued in a neoliberal world. It is up to students to behave as "professionals" and thus demonstrate the potential to transcend their racialized and classed positionalities and become players on the free market. This ties into College Prep's participation in a political spectacle that upholds a neoliberal system of expertise that furthers social inequity; criteria for professionalism function as "props" in the spectacle that constructs students and their communities as problems, and teachers and funders as saviors in a neoliberal world.

A surface reading of College Prep professionalism might lead one to believe that it functions only as a top-down instrument of oppression. Rather than simply argue that the discourse and use of College Prep professionalism should be abolished, I profile the multiple and nuanced ways that some students and teachers take up the practice of professionalism in agentic ways. In some sense, this is emblematic of Frantz Fanon's analysis of the stages of resistance by the colonized in *A Dying Colonialism* (1965). This resistance is characterized first, he argues, by their refusal to embrace elements of local life that are the targets of imperial attention. Then, he argues, it is characterized by a reappropriation and remaking of these tools to forge a postcolonial future. I argue that the ambivalence around the practice of professionalism at College Prep, despite depending on ostensibly oppressive neoliberal systems of expertise, may also demonstrate potential for a postneoliberal future. I'll return to this idea in this chapter's conclusion.

College Prep Professionalism

I was first introduced to the concept of *professionalism* at College Prep in August 2008, during a tenth-grade team meeting before the first day of school. During this meeting, Mr. Randall, a White history teacher and head of the tenth-grade team, told faculty that we all needed to "be on the same page" in terms of how much professionalism counted for students' grades. "Professionalism is great," Mr. Randall told Ms. Williams and me, just after we were hired. "Students really care about their professionalism points, and it's a great management tool. Like if you see them doing something bad, just start docking their professionalism points, and they'll stop," he said.

When the bell was heard, teachers were encouraged to begin circling the room and using an ink stamp to give do-now credit on students' papers when complete and collecting any homework. If a student disrupted the silence during the do-now, teachers were encouraged to take off professionalism points from that student on their clipboard, which would impact that student's marking period grade. The do-now would move into the daily routines of the class, which in most subject areas was a mini-lesson, ideally between five and fifteen minutes of direct instruction. If any student disrupted the mini-lesson, teachers were encouraged to deduct professionalism points. From the mini-lesson, teachers were encouraged to give students guided practice, in which the class practiced together the skills demonstrated by the teacher during the mini-lesson. Guided practice was to move into independent practice, when students, individually or in groups, continued to practice the mini-lesson skill themselves. Class was to close with a summary, an assessment, or an exit slip, which would demonstrate what students learned that day. Again, during any given moment of class, if a student was not following what a teacher deemed to be "professional behavior," points could be taken off on the clipboard, impacting that student's grade for the marking period. Students were often told to see teachers after class or during their office hours for questions about their professionalism points. This was supposed to minimize conflict about point deduction in the classroom, if students saw teachers making marks on their clipboards.

A flyer that hung on the wall of the school during the spring of 2010 is reproduced in Figure 1. This was just one of many pro-professionalism flyers that hung throughout the building. Note the gendered nature of this flyer, as well as the equation of professionalism with one's school uniform, and note that the very existence of the flyer belies the amount of resistance that teachers and administrators experienced to school-sanctioned norms of professionalism.

Professionalism points were most commonly taken from students when they were out of uniform, when they came into class late, when they fell asleep in class, when they cut class, or when they exhibited any other behavior that was not deemed "professional" by the teacher in charge. Although do-nows, mini-lessons, and exit slips were common elements in the two New York City schools where I taught before College Prep, this was the first school where I encountered "professionalism." Ms. Stein, a twenty-nine-year-old, White, New York City–born English teacher, expressed to me in an interview that "professional culture" was not unique to our school. In fact, professionalism is a common term at many small, themed, New York City schools that are structured to make students "college or career ready" (Dillon 2010) by the time they graduate.

Students and Teachers Define Professionalism

Smith et al. (2004) define professionalism as having the existence of a specialized knowledge base as well as authority, autonomy, and control over one's practice and over how aspirants may join one's group. However, College Prep students seemed to define professionalism differently. For example, when I asked Michael, an African American, tenth-grade student whom I shadowed during the school day and interviewed, how he would define professionalism, he said:

Professionalism is when you don't interrupt teachers and students in the classroom, and you are respectful . . . you are not sitting there, like you are not sitting there when the teacher is talking, like you are not interfering with what she is saying, like a teacher will be talking and you are not like, oh, I'm going to talk to my friend.

Destiny, an African American eleventh grader, defines professionalism as "dress code, like especially for Ms. Elliott. Principal McCarren, for her, it's get to class on time . . . or not talking [in class]." Students' equation of professionalism with silence was also affirmed during a December 2009 academic intervention with Martine, an African American ninth-grade student who didn't have grades good enough to cheer on the squad during games (an average of seventy or above in all major subjects). In front of her mother, me (the cheerleading coach that season), and three of her teachers, when asked what she was going to do to be better in her classes, she stated, "I am just going to come in and be quiet, be professional, just not say anything." As I mentioned in chapter 2 in relation to Keisha, Martine's position here is a direct reiteration of Fordham's argument (1993) about Black female students' silence or gender "passing" (8), either becoming or remaining voiceless or silent in the context of White supremacist patriarchy. Although some teachers, including me, said that being professional didn't just mean being silent, I find this definition of professionalism—as silence, deference, and an attempt at invisibility—to be particularly troubling, especially because of the degree to which College Prep constructs itself as a social justice school. This definition lends itself to an exceptionally problematic construction not only of students, their needs, their perspectives, and their experience, but also of education itself.

When I spoke with Assistant Principal Paula Humphries, an African American, about professionalism, she called it "nebulous" and "hard to define." Despite a lack of a solid definition, College Prep normalizes the discourse of professionalism in order to make college-bound students more "marketable" by mainstream neoliberal standards. When Ms. Carr, a White teacher, and I spoke about professionalism in 2009, she said:

> I think that [professionalism] is about . . . giving students an opportunity to practice the social skills required for middle-class success, upper-middle or upper-class success. I think that it's about equipping them for what's expected or required in a university setting and in a professional job setting. I mean, I think that some kids learn that at home; I mean, I think a lot of kids learn that at home, but I think that having a place to practice that where that expectation is constant, I think that's what we provide. Because when they are hanging out with their friends, and say, for instance, when they live in the projects, and they are surrounded by people that are . . . not necessarily following those values, it's easy to fall into the trap of, well I don't have to excuse myself, because nobody else does, or I don't have to expect this of myself because nobody else does.

At first glance, this quote might seem to demonstrate that Ms. Carr feels that while some students learn "professional" (which she calls "middle-class" or "upper-middle-class") codes of culture in their homes (Fine et al. 1997; Heath 1983), she ascribes a deficit discourse to those for whom she assumes this is not the case, conflating race, class, and place as she uses students who live in public housing as an example of students who lack the social skills required for upward mobility and personhood in a neoliberal context. Yet in a follow-up interview in 2013, Ms. Carr elaborated on her sentiments above: "There are so many roles one can play in educating a child. I have to think of myself in terms of the change I can effect," she said. She continued:

> Am I cognizant of the fact that poverty is a sinkhole? Absolutely! I mean how do you pull yourself up when you have no opportunity to save money, expensive day cares for your kids, you're working two jobs, you're dealing with food insecurity? . . . I don't think

students are unaware of the fact that life isn't fair. If I can help students find their voice, access the halls of power, then they can write new rules.

Ms. Carr's statements show how professionalism, central to discourse about college and career readiness at College Prep, represents an area of great tension for teachers and for students, who are aware of the realities of a neoliberal and quite nonmeritocratic world beyond College Prep. Ms. Carr mused over what professionalism at College Prep would look like if we lived in a society that was actually democratic, and for the time being, it was clear that she saw professionalism as evidence that we do not. In other words, despite internal conflict, she is cognizant of what she feels is the necessity of adhering to the spectacle in order to someday move beyond it. Her statements represent a fundamental question for educators: how can teachers teach students to survive and thrive in a fundamentally inequitable and undemocratic world without reinscribing these same inequities, especially when teachers also represent groups who have historically oppressed others? While teachers who implemented professionalism points in their classrooms had the best of intentions, students often interpreted the professionalism point system (as we shall see below) as both oppressive and grounded in deficit discourse.

At College Prep, to demonstrate professionalism is to demonstrate potential in the market. Rather than a critical consideration of the inequities that are fundamental to racial capitalism, corporate paradigms in education encourage local actors to uphold the spectacle by supporting, rather than critiquing, a flawed system. This performance shapes the political identities of teachers and students in both raced and classed ways. Students and teachers simultaneously give into and critique College Prep professionalism, demonstrating their discomfort, ambivalence, and critical race and class consciousness.

Performing Unprofessionalism in the Classroom

Much like the asylum patients in sociologist Erving Goffman's analysis (1961), College Prep students seem to define themselves both within and against the norms of the institution. As I demonstrate below, some students seem to recognize and enact a critique of the school's participation in a political spectacle (Edelman 1988; Smith et al. 2004). On a school-wide student questionnaire that I distributed to students in 2010 (appendix B), students voiced a fair amount of resistance to professionalism. A ninth grade student reported that "[professionalism / professionalism points are] bull, I'm already professional." In accordance, another student wrote, "it's ridiculous, we're not little kids. It's important, but repeating it every day is not necessary." Another wrote, "it's stupid. It absolutely positively makes no sense." Another demonstrated the discrepancy between the school's desire for students' performance of professionalism and the reality: "College Prep instills a professional environment but us as students don't uphold it, i.e. dress code, respect for ourselves and others." An eleventh-grade student demonstrated a sense of the deficit-grounded logic of professionalism, stating, "I don't think professionalism points should make up a majority of our grades because it pulls down our GPA significantly. Plus, schools aren't supposed to do that." A twelfth-grade student seemed to agree, stating, "nobody is good in being professional"; and another twelfth-grade student spoke about his negative experience with professionalism points, saying, "they hurt me a lot." Students also seemed to be aware of the arbitrariness of professionalism points; one twelfth grader wrote, "sometimes points are taken away because of extremely frivolous things like not directly looking at a teacher during a lesson."

These students' perspectives illustrate the negative or critical opinions of professionalism that students hold. These comments represent 35 percent of the students who took the survey. Based on the above quotes, we see that some students align professionalism (and the point system that often comes along with it) with being both infantilized and academically penalized for their behavior. Students voiced their frustration with professionalism, and one student, quoted above, critiques the idea of teenagers having to perform it. According to this student, College Prep students are "just teens," and shouldn't have to conform to such a strict behavior standard. Some students critique professionalism through performing "unprofessionalism" in the classroom.

Ninth-grade teachers documented demonstrations of unprofessionalism in their classes through e-mails, listing behaviors that were characteristic of students' resistance. Teachers' critiques of students' unprofessionalism were gendered: girls were more likely to be policed for sexually provocative dress (as we see in Figure 1), behavior, or language, while boys were much more likely to be chastised for unprofessionalism due to wearing hoodies, baggy pants, a fitted baseball cap, a do-rag, or any other items of clothing that could be construed as "hood," (from a stereotypically Black urban neighborhood, or ghetto). As I observed in classrooms, some female students would wear low-cut tank tops or T-shirts underneath their uniforms, and would unbutton their uniforms to reveal the shirts underneath. I noticed several teachers in all grades, usually female, telling female students that they needed to button up their uniform blouses in order to appear more professional. Male staff members were reluctant to address this "sexually provocative" improvisation on the uniform. Behaviors such as cursing, fighting, or speaking in Black vernacular were construed as unprofessional for male and female students, as was interrupting teachers, grooming or eating in class, wandering the halls, or using the bathroom during class too much.

Senator Daniel Patrick Moynihan (1965) is notorious for misusing anthropologist Oscar Lewis's culture of poverty theory (1959) to describe family life in U.S. Black communities as constituting a "tangle of pathology" that continues to "perpetuate the cycle of poverty and deprivation." This problematic ideology continues through the present: some U.S. social scientists and educational researchers who focus on social class denigrate the "culture" of the poor and seem to blame them for their economic situation (Harrington 1997; Payne 1996; Riessman 1962). While scholars made (and continue to make) critiques of the concept of the culture of poverty (Akom 2008; Goode and Eames 1996; M. Katz 2013; Pierre 2004; Valencia 1997), social science has not been successful at replacing the culture concept as a heuristic for understanding poverty. This explains why, Michael Katz (2013) asserts, economists took the lead in poverty research, also influencing educational policy. The school's conflation of some students' behaviors with unprofessionalism is a direct reflection of many of the popularized images of the Black teenage mothers and Black jobless youths reflected in the Moynihan report (1965), as well as other stereotypical images of Black urban poverty (Collins 1990, 2004; M. Katz 2013), and, again, supports College Prep's role in a political spectacle that constructs students and their communities as the problem, and the school, its staff, and its funders as saviors.

Some teachers often got quite upset when students showed that they had not internalized the logic of professionalism and did not self-regulate their behavior—in other words, participation in the spectacle was only a stylized (and temporary) performance. This frustration was demonstrated in a series of faculty meetings where the agenda included how to "change

Figure 1. A 2010 flyer advocating for College Prep student professionalism.

school culture" and "get students to buy in." When I interviewed Mr. Fulton, a White ninth-grade teacher, he said:

> Kids will do fine in the classroom, but . . . the way kids behave in
> the hallways is evident of the culture you have built in the school.
> Like you can walk into the worst school, with a particular teacher
> and a group of kids, and you can see great things happening. But
> when you let kids just walk around, without an authority figure
> hovering over them, that then you see how this school is. And
> it makes me really sad because I almost don't think there is an
> adult that can walk into a hallway here and kids will listen to
> them—principal, dean, nothing. And it's almost like they step out
> there, and it's just like, "Fuck you" to everyone—we're cursing,
> we're play fighting, we're throwing garbage on the floor, we throw
> food, we're going late to class, the bathrooms . . . I feel like you can
> walk into a school bathroom and you can see evidence of how
> happy kids are. Every day, written in the bathroom here: "College
> Prep sucks, Fuck this." The paper towels are in the urinal toilet by
> 10:00. Where is this coming from? 'Cause I know they are not
> doing this in their homes. And it's like wow, this is the place
> where they spend the majority of their teenage years and they
> hate it. And I don't know how to change it.

Mr. Fulton takes issue here with the fact that while some students at College Prep might work well in supervised classrooms, students demonstrate that they have not internalized school-sanctioned professional values or culture where there is no visible controlling power. Perhaps this is not due to defiance on the students' part; rather, it is due to agency in the face of the school's deficit discourse and participation in a problematic political spectacle (Smith et al. 2004; Spears-Bunton and Powell 2008).

During the spring of 2010 students took their hallway unprofessionalism to the next level; many chose to ignore the late bell to talk and laugh with friends. To ameliorate this, teachers tried locking their doors after the bell rang, so that students would have to knock before they came in. This proved ineffective, especially because students would knock on the door after class had started to be let in. The deans of discipline tried hallway sweeps, where any student caught after the bell was marched to the guidance suite, and issued a detention. But not only did these students come even later to class, they cut their detentions. When they did this, they were barred from privileges like school dances, basketball games, or extra-curricular activities. But this did not seem to be enough of a disincentive.

In May 2010, Ms. McGoldrick, a White ninth-grade teacher, said during what the ninth-grade team named an "emergency meltdown" meeting about student discipline:

> They say to themselves: why do I care if I have twenty-seven
> detentions? They feel that we (adults) are fighting the fight and
> that they don't have to—they know that we have to make our
> school look good. Students know that our results are published,
> and that it makes the school look better if our numbers look good.

Despite the fact that some students don't demonstrate that they have internalized the class culture that teachers deem necessary for their college and career readiness, for some teachers, the school's image and competitiveness for funding take precedence over finding other creative ways to get all students to invest. Students, meanwhile, achieve the right to opt out of professionalism while teachers feel ignored and overpowered. At the same time, teachers are aware of students' metacognitive and evaluative power based on their recognition of student agency.

Principal McCarren tried to ameliorate the issues of student unprofessionalism and noncompliance in the ninth grade by attending a ninth-grade team meeting in 2010. At this meeting, although short-term fixes were one of the topics, the larger conversation was about how to convince students to take more ownership over their learning and the school. This fell under the topic of what Principal McCarren called "long-term culture shifts." Mr. Fulton and Mr. Matthews, an African American teacher, suggested hallway monitors, peer counselors and tutors, and an active student council as ideas about how to get students to invest in their schooling. Because it was May, and the year was close to over, it was agreed that none of these suggestions would be implemented right away, although they would be considered for the following school year.

As they performed unprofessionalism through behavior, dress, and language, some students seemed to be sending an important message to staff about the deficit view that the professionalism point system, and the political spectacle that it was a part of, conveyed about students' ability to be professional from the beginning. If the institution did not demonstrate that it valued elements of students' experience and realities that they brought from outside of school, students refused to valorize the code of ethics and behaviors endorsed by the institution. This code of ethics contributed to the school's essentialization of students as "needy," "college-fragile," or "at-risk" urban youth who needed College Prep to "save" them.

Students Advocate Professionalism

While some students and teachers seemed to demonstrate a critique of professionalism points at College Prep, others seemed to show that they advocated for it. On the school-wide questionnaire (appendix B), one ninth grader put professionalism points into the context of college-readiness, stating, "I think professionalism points are needed. Because children will carry the same attitude on to college," while an eleventh grader put it into the context of success beyond college, stating, "I think being professional is an important thing to do if you want to be successful." Another ninth-grade student saw professionalism points as an asset to her transcript, writing, "I think College Prep's professionalism points is a great idea. It gives us another grade so that if we screw up academically, behavior can help." A twelfth grader echoed this sentiment, saying, "I think it is good because it helps increase my grade in class for something that comes natural." The above quotes illustrate a few of the positive opinions of professionalism that students held, and represent 45 percent of the students who took the survey. These students seem to align professionalism (and the point system that often comes along with it) with getting better grades, as well as setting one up for success. Often, students who have the reputation for being the most professional are the ones who are selected first for extracurricular opportunities, especially those that explicitly represent the school.

Students like Elise, an African American student whom I shadowed during spring 2010, shared with me how excited she was to go on an upcoming overnight college trip with the school. Not every student had been accepted to go, and so she was thrilled that she had been chosen. When I interviewed her, she named this as one of the reasons why she was glad that she had not transferred out of College Prep, which she had wanted earlier in the year. She said:

I did want to transfer, but I decided not to, and from the result of me saying that I want to get out of the school, like I kept hearing so much about colleges, like the college trip was good, like I was hearing that from seniors, this college, and that college, and like we spent the night, and it made me like want to stay 'cause I didn't have that experience, and once I found that I was accepted on this college trip, that made me so happy, like I bought like a whole new professional outfit so I could see like what colleges I want and how they like see me as a person, cause they will see that I am very professional and very determined and I want to get that note across to them.

Here, her language is interesting. Elise aligns professional dress with being successful, and with putting forth a determined image, showing that she is confident in her skills. This is evident in terms of how she defines professionalism:

How you represent yourself, how you dress, how you act with others, students, adults . . . I could say sometimes, like I am not the most professional 'cause of how students want to make a joke to me or come at me in classrooms, and I take it seriously.

When visiting a college, she is aware that the impression that she makes will be determined by her "professional" look. Elise demonstrates another important aspect of the practice of professionalism. While professionalism as it is enacted and critiqued at College Prep may embody a problematic reification of race and class hierarchies, Elise shows an awareness of the importance of what Goffman would call the "presentation of self" (1959) in the reality of a neoliberal, corporate world, and a neoliberal political spectacle. In the context of neoliberalism, the ostensibly individualized subject imagines him- or herself to be free; yet, a discourse of consumption strongly governs desires and agency; the "responsible citizen" must become the "economic entrepreneur" of his or her own life (Davies and Bansel 2007); Elise demonstrates this logic here.

Sometimes, students adopt this idea of professionalism and use it to critique teachers in the same way that they are critiqued. As I sat in the teachers' office working one afternoon, I overheard an eleventh grader speaking loudly to Ms. Elliott, a White teacher, in the hallway after she was pulled out of class for disrespecting Ms. Connell, a Black teacher-in-training:

> STUDENT: She gave me attitude and she rolled her neck and she acted unprofessional and she is in an environment where teachers are acting professional so she needs to tame herself!
> MS. ELLIOTT: You said it in a voice that was loud enough for the entire class to hear.
> STUDENT: So what?!
> MS. ELLIOTT: She is a teacher and the appropriate thing to do is to ask her to step outside and have the conversation with her.

Here, we see a student adopting the language of professionalism to criticize an adult. This, especially late in the school year, was also a common occurrence. Students called each other "unprofessional" at times, and they called adults (whether teachers-in-training or teachers), "unprofessional" at times when they were upset, as in the above example. In some sense, some students use the discourse and practice of professionalism to demonstrate their potential and power to read and navigate the political spectacle that operates in tandem with a neoliberal and racist world. In this sense, students construct themselves as authorities on professionalism, as opposed to their teachers. Perhaps this represents potential in the practice of professionalism, if it is framed more as a critical asset, rather than in a deficit-based way. Can the master's tools dismantle the master's house?

Some students' rejection of professional performance at College Prep may be what James Scott would call a "weapon of the weak," yet will this form of resistance to the norms of the institution actually have an impact on mitigating social hierarchies over time (D. Foley 2010; Scott 1985; Willis 1977)? Is College Prep professionalism what Du Preez (1980) calls an "identity trap," an identity frame that allows little room for maneuver, that denies other possibilities, and allows too little freedom? Or might some students and teachers embrace a more critical model of professionalism that does not rest on pathologizing them in the interest of garnering funding, but rather on emphasizing simultaneous awareness and critique of race and class hierarchies within the political spectacle of color-blind meritocracy in the interest of educational and social equity? Does the regulation of conduct through professionalism lead to students' potential to "work from within" (Urrieta 2009)?

Discussion: Is Reframing Professionalism Possible?

On the questionnaire, when asked to define professionalism, one twelfth-grade student wrote: "Professionalism: Being dressed and well behaviored and manored [sic] for the real world here in 'White America.'" This student expresses an awareness of "playing the game" as a Black agent in a market that is grounded in a dominant White racial order. She clearly positions herself in the context of the racial state (Fine et al. 1997; Omi and Winant 1994), and demonstrates awareness of the pervasive discourses of neoliberal capitalism and marketability (Hursh 2007, 2009) in a political spectacle that ostensibly values justice, fairness, and professionalism. Are there possibilities for professionalism at College Prep that both critique White hegemony and neoliberalism and set students up for success (Delpit 1998; Giroux 2004; Spears-Bunton and Powell 2008)?

In this chapter, I have argued that students' resistance (and sometimes their strategic rearticulation of) College Prep professionalism demonstrates an agentic critique of socially situated systems of expertise, work, and labor (D. Foley 2010; Giddens 1991; Willis 1977). This exposes a rift in certain aspects that are endemic to a popularized political spectacle of education reform in the United States. The reinscription of and resistance to social hierarchies at the school level have implications for political economy and the construction of political identities in broader society. Perhaps professional identity, in the context of College Prep and beyond, does not have to demean the political identities of many of its students, demonstrated by those who agentically adhere to and adopt the discourse and practice of professionalism. In a more radical sense, according to Howard Winant, movements and articulations of the possible influence the creation of political identity (2004). Some of the students who creatively rearticulate the discourse of professionalism demonstrate that there may be potential in the practice of school professionalism if it is redefined, and if the spectacle is named and critiqued.

Principal McCarren expressed a desire for a "long-term culture shift"; this desire is based on astute observations. Some students and teachers are aware that in many ways, the practice of professionalism is based on problematic assumptions about students, their families, and their communities. These assumptions are grounded in sociohistorically constructed and racist controlling images of a Black and Brown urban underclass (Collins 1990), as well as in a neoliberal ideology that does not address the need for social change. These controlling images and neoliberal ideologies support a political spectacle of marketability and opportunity that seems, at first glance, to be just.

Perhaps in some sense, evaluating students on their professionalism allows teachers to construct themselves as authorities on professionalism, and thus as professionals despite their deprofessionalization in the context of an industrialist model of schooling, marked by an emphasis on efficiency, accountability, and high-stakes tests (Kumashiro 2012). While empowering teachers' racial and class positionalities in some ways, this masks the oppressive conditions that affect both teachers' and students' potential for power and agency. Teachers who act as the evaluators of professionalism also serve to solidify a political spectacle that reinforces dominant models of cultural capital, in addition to need and deservedness. This tension, in front of and behind the curtain, represents potential for a more empowering approach to professionalism practices at College Prep that might denaturalize the deficit model of teaching professionalism by exposing the arbitrary, racially normative, and culturally constructed nature of unquestioned professionalism. The realization of the oppressiveness of unquestioned professionalism for teachers and students might represent the possibility for a kind of collusion amongst both parties that would lead to a pedagogy that explicitly values students' ability to deftly navigate between different kinds of cultural spaces. This collusion might represent the possibility to move toward a postneoliberal future, one that acknowledges and critiques the oppressiveness of a political spectacle that supports neoliberalization, and works toward something else.

College Prep's dependence on corporate philanthropy, as well as its commitment to evaluating students based on their professionalism, is concomitant with a political spectacle that defines social justice in a neoliberal sense. In other words, College Prep provides an example of how social justice in education is defined as creating the condition for students to become marketable, without a critique of the race, class, and gender inequities that capitalism produces. This furthers what Cindi Katz (2001) calls the "necessity of social reproduction" of global capitalism and runs directly counter to a model of social justice that is based on a critique of domination and oppression (Young 1990).

As it stands now, much of the practice of professionalism at College Prep seems to function as another part of the psychic violence and systematic pedagogy of self-hatred that Cornel West argues have been a part of the White exploitation of Black labor in the United States for nearly four hundred years (2001). Predominantly White teachers define and evaluate Black and Latino students on their potential to perform professionalism in the context of White capitalist hegemony without ever naming it as such. At the same time, many of these teachers and students form critiques of this deficit-based and undemocratic system. The political spectacle that College Prep's unquestioned version of professionalism supports is emblematic of the "new racism"—White hegemony maintains itself under the guise of color blindness or a "post-race" world (Balibar and Wallerstein 1991; Bonilla-Silva 2014; Winant 2004). Thus, the practice of professionalism furthers an identity system of not only class hierarchy but also race hierarchy in and beyond College Prep. Indeed (as students and teachers are aware), College Prep needs a cultural shift: a shift away from a view of students that rests on a culture of poverty, and toward one that is grounded in what Black scholars (Baldwin 1993; hooks 2001; Rose 2008) have called both affirmational and transformational love: one that is grounded in the richness of students' lives, agency, and experience but also sees the potential for growth. The students who rearticulate and resist College Prep professionalism demonstrate the potential for a more critical and intellectual practice that might empower them to become experts not only in professionalism, but also in a self- and community-affirming critique of a color-blind and meritocratic political spectacle that actually rests upon existent social hierarchies.

4

Waiting for Superwoman

White Female Teachers as "Neoliberal Saviors"

I ran into Ms. Barnes, the head of the college office, leaving the building on a spring day in 2009, just before some alumni elected to return for homecoming. In her excitement about the upcoming event, Ms. Barnes, who is White, told me how proud she felt about the fact that College Prep plays the role of "family around the dinner table" for its urban, college-bound students. A fabulously dedicated college advisor, Ms. Barnes was widely known at College Prep for working tirelessly to be sure that every student matriculated to college. She cared deeply for students and wanted to ensure their stable futures. Yet her statement raised some provocative questions about the role of schools, families, and communities in terms of students' educational success. Was College Prep solely responsible for its students' success? Ms. Barnes's good intentions and hard work manifested, in the context of the racialized and neoliberal spectacle of the institution, into a statement that represented an important narrative for funders. This narrative problematically constructed students and their families through a deficit lens; they could only be "saved" with the school's help—and, of course, with funders' support.

As Ms. Barnes shared her thoughts, I thought back to the interview I had conducted with Howard Jackson just one week previously. Mr. Jackson, one of the few African American male teachers at College Prep, was planning on leaving this institution for a PhD program the following year. In the interview, I asked him why he was leaving. He spoke about the fact that he felt he had "hit the glass ceiling" at College Prep. He stated,

> There is this belief by some of my White colleagues in this idea of "White savior." And I think this is true of Hollywood, of all the many movies we see. I may need to get better skills so that I may not run up against this . . . but I may always run up against this, I

don't know. I have felt great difficulty in my work here because I have had to deal with this and navigate this.

Using the image of the dinner table to signify middle-class security and the image of the family to signify care, support, and love, Ms. Barnes seems to demonstrate the savior ideology that Mr. Jackson critiques. This ideology, critical to maintaining support from funders, is built upon a deficit discourse about students' families, who are not expected or invited by the school to be involved in students' college application process nearly to the degree that the school's college office is. It is important to emphasize that I do not believe that this set of beliefs is uniquely attributable to Ms. Barnes, nor to any other individual at the school. In reality, Ms. Barnes as well as many White staff members who could easily be construed as "savior figures" are participants in social structures and ideologies that permeate all of us. I write this chapter not to critique any individual or individuals, but rather to name the potentially problematic ways in which ideologies can inform our actions, and sometimes inflict forms of symbolic violence despite our best intentions. In this case, I argue that the ways in which White female bodies are commodified and consumed through the spectacle of mainstream popular media, and media about College Prep and other U.S. urban schools, strongly governs people's agency, and exploits *both* the students whom the media profiles as needy as well as the teachers profiled as saviors. As Edelman puts it, "The language of affection, pity, compassion and helping masks from the self and from others the importance of exploiting these groups for the maintenance of the social order" (1988, 72). It is my hope that by using the tools of qualitative research to name the ways in which these potentially violent or oppressive ideologies manifest, we can become more vigilant in critiquing a political spectacle of secular saviorism, and in creating, as I shall discuss later, a social justice practice that is grounded in affirmational, transformational love (Baldwin 1993; hooks 2001; Rose 2008) and "agonistic solidarity" (Chouliaraki 2011).

The school's college office, partly funded by the Foundation, plays a key role in the institution. Students begin to work with the college office from their freshman year, and are mandated to apply to at least seven CUNY (City University of New York) campuses during their junior year. As a result (and as I noted in the introduction), almost the entire senior class matriculates into college (although, according to NYC.gov's 2014 school progress report, only 69.3 percent of the students from the 2011 cohort persisted in college past the third semester). "College readiness" takes up a great deal of the conversation in classrooms and at faculty meetings. I contend that the school's model, which is dependent on corporate charity to create a "college-going culture," demonstrates a problematic kind of savior mentality. I begin with a critique of popular images of White female teachers, and then contrast these images with ethnographic portrayals of White female teachers at College Prep. I conclude with an analysis of how my data articulates with ideologies of Whiteness, and a spectacle of neoliberalism and secular saviorism at College Prep and beyond. I then share advice on possible alternatives to the troubling trope of the White neoliberal savior.

College Prep must maintain a relationship with its funders. Therefore, the school manages its image by constructing urban teachers and students as both needy and deserving of corporate charity. This particular definition of social justice, which is dependent upon a savior mentality both on an institutional and an individual level, ironically reifies the hierarchies of race and class that it purports to alleviate.

Nice White Ladies

I mentioned the popular documentary *Waiting for "Superman"* (Guggenheim 2010) in chapter 1. The film profiles five students in five different cities in the United States, each of whom attempts to get accepted to a charter school (as opposed to their neighborhood public school) through a lottery system. The beginning of the film is an interview with Geoffrey Canada, the president and CEO of Harlem Children's Zone, a charter school in New York City. Canada explains his reaction, as a young boy growing up in Harlem, when his mother told him that Superman didn't exist: "he always shows up and he saves all the good people . . . I was crying because there was no one coming with enough power to save us." Not without its critics (R. Ayers 2010; Ravitch 2011b), the film vilifies teachers' unions, valorizes privately supported charter schools as the antidote to failing traditional public schools in the United States, and supports the claim that individuals such as Bill Gates, Michelle Rhee (former chancellor of Washington, D.C., public schools), and Canada can act as saviors within the context of a failing public school system. The film focuses heavily on school reformers and on students and their families, but, for the most part, does not focus on teachers. Racialized and classed discourses of saviorism operate not just in terms of school reform in a broad sense, but rather in classrooms, in regard to the construction of the White female savior teacher.

Movies like *Dangerous Minds* (J. Smith 1995) and *Freedom Writers* (LaGravenese 2007) feature a young, straight, attractive White female protagonist who goes to an inner-city school to "save" Black and Brown students from their communities and themselves. *Nice White Lady* (Leddy, Grossman, and Bearse 2007), a popular MadTV skit, is a spoof of these films. This narrative of the gendered White savior in urban classrooms, or the "great White hope," is ubiquitous not only in film (Craven 1999; LaGravenese 2007; Mandel 1996; Mulligan 1967; Ritchie 1986; J. Smith 1995), but also in popular and academic literature. The film versions of *Dangerous Minds* and *Freedom Writers* are both based on "true stories"—the autobiographical writing of LouAnne Johnson (1992) and Erin Gruwell (1999), respectively. Besides Johnson's book, several other books tell, from various White female perspectives, stories of time spent as educators in segregated Black and Brown urban classrooms (Baldacci 2004; Codell 1999; Landsman 2001; Paley 1979).

While in the past dominant images of urban teachers in film were male (Ayers 1996), women increasingly seem to dominate the image of the "urban teacher." The popular trope of the White female teacher reflects a trend in K–12 U.S. classrooms: a 2005 article in the *New York Times* entitled "Teaching the Teachers: Those Who Can, and Can't" reveals that since the year 2000, 500,000 more teachers have taken jobs in U.S. elementary and secondary school classrooms (Simon 2005). These teachers are primarily women (75 percent) and primarily White (84 percent).[1]

Ferguson (2001), Hyland (2005), and King (1991) have noted the ways in which racist ideologies can masquerade under White teachers' good intentions, even in the cases of White women who mark themselves as "good teachers of Black students," but there are other, broader implications to the ideology of the savior teacher. This ideology exists within a spectacle of teacher blaming and vilification that constructs the "ideal" teacher as one who sacrifices her personal life as well as a demand for fair compensation for the good of her students. In a *Huffington Post* editorial, public education advocate Sabrina Stevens writes:

> Just as with the "ideal" woman in a broader sense, there is much praise lavished on the "ideal" teacher who quietly, unobtrusively and selflessly does her work. But when teachers try to have a voice in the decisions that affect them, or advocate for better pay and working conditions, they're derided as being selfish. (2012)

Stevens goes on to remind readers that despite the fact that teachers' working conditions are also students' learning conditions, all too often female teachers enforce the role of the savior, buying into the rhetoric of self-sacrifice, "to their own—and their colleagues—detriment."

It is important to note that this trope is reproduced in teachers' minds through mass media, through teacher training and professional development programs, and through national policy debates in education. This enduring production is illustrated by ongoing critiques of deficit discourse in schools (Valencia 2010), as well as critiques of pseudoscientific recycled "culture of poverty" discourse in teacher training (Bomer 2008; D. Foley 1997, 2008; Valencia 2010). Mainstream, racialized "ideal types" (Weber 1999) of teachers and students are often overly dramatized, but teachers at College Prep often cited mainstream literature and film in their critiques of the "savior teacher." They believe many new and underprepared teachers who enter New York City's classrooms employ these tropes when structuring classroom practices and structuring relationships with students and their families.

Freedom Writers (LaGravenese 2007), the story of White teacher Erin Gruwell, differs from other films of its kind in an important way; I argue that this is a direct reflection of neoliberal capitalism. Gruwell's narrative, although still that of the savior, embodies another trope that I call the "White neoliberal savior." While Gruwell still has a social or moral agenda, she also courts the favoritism of private donors who help to fund her mission of not only saving students from their backgrounds, families, and communities, but also helping them access material gain and social mobility through college. The neoliberal savior's social justice agenda includes a moneyed logic intertwined with the liberal agenda of tokenistic diversity and equality that is suspiciously absent of a critique of social privilege and oppression, while being supportive of color-blind meritocracy (Akom 2008; Apple 2001). There seems to be a similar ideology permeating College Prep.

Not unlike the antebellum White proselytizers who expanded the influence of the church by teaching Black slaves, whom they called the "heathen of the new world," to read so that they could read the Bible and one day find salvation (Woodson 1919), or the officials who started the U.S. federal government and Bureau of Indian Affairs' nineteenth- and twentieth-century projects of Native American assimilation through schooling (Farb 1991; Hunt 2012; Lomawaima 1995), young teachers in urban classrooms have ideals characterized by missionary zeal. The same zeal lies behind much of the discourse of urban alternative certification programs. These programs, through "populational reasoning," can serve to normalize young, predominantly White middle-class teachers while constructing "urban" or "at-risk" students as an "other" who needs to be saved (Popkewitz 1998). Yet, salvation does not come through helping the oppressed to assimilate and find God in the neoliberal era; rather, it comes through helping the oppressed to pursue dreams of social mobility and material success and to market oneself even, ironically, in a world with fewer and fewer economic or social opportunities. Becoming "marketable" for college or a career becomes synonymous with salvation in a neoliberal political spectacle. Besides *The Freedom Writers Diary* book, and subsequent *Freedom Writers* film (Gruwell and the Freedom Writers 1999; LaGravenese 2007), this recent turn is not encapsulated in many of the ideal type of White teachers who are so common in popular film and literature. Much of the academic literature that critiques White racism in urban classrooms discusses unintentional, passive, color-blind, or dysconscious racism (Hyland 2005; King 1991; A. Lewis 2003; Marx 2006; Solomon et al. 2005). I am naming another way in which racism and misogyny operate in tandem with classism in a specifically neoliberal sense: in order to remain competitive, schools use the discourse of meritocracy and college readiness to market urban students and predominantly White, female teachers in an explicitly racialized, gendered, and classed sense, furthering rather than alleviating social hierarchies.

Systems of higher education in the United States tend to reproduce structures of privilege and social status, and for a few, it is the key to upward social mobility (Weber 1999). Access to higher education is still strongly correlated to a privileged family background, and U.S. higher education is still highly stratified (Roska et al. 2007).

In the narrative of College Prep that is disseminated in the media and sold to funders, College Prep staff members are profiled—and sometimes act—as "saviors," deeming some students deserving of the opportunities and extracurricular activities that will give them the "measurable virtues" (M. Stevens 2007) that make them more attractive to colleges. The presumed cultural superiority of College Prep norms ascribes deficits to students and their communities. It also perpetuates an uncritical myth of meritocracy, because students are ostensibly taught to believe that if they behave "professionally enough" in the context of neoliberalism, they will be afforded all the opportunities of their White and/or middle-class counterparts. At College Prep, while students and teachers are supposed to work together to be the "economic entrepreneurs of [students'] lives" (Davies and Bansel 2007), families are expected to take a back seat. The school has what Assistant Principal Paula Humphries calls a "me" culture, as opposed to a "we" culture. In other words, rather than a nonindividualistic school culture that advocates a strong, common culture of achievement for all students to buffer them from the experience of racism (T. Perry 2003), this ideology is part of a spectacle that valorizes individualism and competition in the context of the myth of a color- and class-blind meritocracy.

Methods: Research and Writing

Thirteen of the teachers whom I interviewed at College Prep were White women. I observed each of their classes at least once. Out of those thirteen, for the purposes of this chapter, I focus closely on three. I conducted weekly classroom (or extracurricular) observations of each for an entire semester. Parents, students, and colleagues see each of these three as effective pedagogues; students demonstrate evidence of learning in their classes; and each sees herself as a social justice educator. I recorded and transcribed one formal interview with each teacher, which lasted between one and two hours. In addition to observing these teachers' classes or extracurricular activities, I also observed the teachers at faculty meetings and professional development events and listened closely to what parents/guardians, colleagues, and students said *about* these women relative to their teaching and interpersonal relationships with students, staff, and families.

In an attempt to preserve the anonymity of my participants, I altered small details about the their lives or backgrounds. In order to synthesize the data for this project, I read transcripts from interviews with teachers and coded for emergent themes of race, class, gender, college readiness, social justice, teaching practice, views on philanthropy and education, views on the savior mentality, and views of students and parents.

Dangerous Minds or Dangerous Myths? LouAnne Johnson, Erin Gruwell, and the "White Savior" Model

In her book, originally titled *My Posse Don't Do Homework* but renamed *Dangerous Minds* (1992) after its film version, LouAnne Johnson, a White marine turned teacher, tells the story of her first years in the high school classroom. Thirty-five years old, from a working-class background in Pennsylvania, she is hired to teach English to a class of intelligent but at-risk students at a high school in Palo Alto, California. She uses a combination of intimidation techniques (she compares her first days in the class to a war [ibid. 26], threatens to punch a student in the "weenie" [79], threatens to kill a student [88]), and demonstrates "caring" to manage the class (she drives students home from school to meet their families and loans one student, Raul, one hundred dollars to pay for a stolen coat that he bought on the street [6]). Most of the problems that she has in the classroom have to do with male students, and involve students fighting and acting as discipline problems. Throughout the book, she mentions her father's strict standards of discipline for her and her four siblings, but never mentions having any friends or partners, and never discusses her own positionality as a White woman (Frankenberg 1993).

Johnson (1992) highlights the poverty and low social class status of her students, who go to a special luncheon donated by a hotel, which partnered with the school to reward students who are meeting academic standards. She buys one student a suit for the occasion (teaching them to "consider their appearance") and highlights students' impoverished circumstances and social class status as she discusses a student who did not know what filet mignon was and his amazement at their water glasses getting continually refilled (12). She attempts to teach students literacy and empathy and prepares them for "office jobs" (232) and, in a few cases, community college (277). She portrays herself as the teacher who uniquely sees potential in each of her students, an unconditionally loving savior figure.

Gruwell's story (1999) is somewhat similar to Johnson's in that she is a high school English teacher of predominantly minority urban youth who are profiled as "at risk" or as "underachievers." Pearl-clad and naïve, but ever more enthusiastic, Gruwell is shocked during the first weeks of school when one student draws a caricature of another one with big lips. She yells "this was the type of propaganda used by the Nazis during the Holocaust!" (2). She then realizes that her students don't know what the Holocaust is, and she decides to teach them about it, especially because when she asks students how many of them had been shot at, every hand goes up (6). Paralleling Johnson's narrative, Gruwell writes about how other teachers, and the administration, try to discourage her unorthodox teaching habits, but she perseveres. The majority of the book is filled with diary entries from her at-risk students (part of her unorthodox pedagogical methods include journaling), who at first write that she is "too young and too White to be working here" (6).

The student journals often focus on themes of neighborhood and community violence, including absent fathers, sexual violence and molestation, homelessness, abusive and neglectful parents, and hunger. Ms. Gruwell, or "Ms. G." as her students call her, writes in her own journal about being "in the trenches" with kids (32).

She teaches color blindness to her students, and they internalize this, as seen through their journal writing (38, 93). As she teaches students about the Holocaust and invites several guests to the class to talk about their experience (including Holocaust survivors and survivors of the war in Bosnia), she inspires wealthy people to invest in her curriculum, such as millionaire John Tu, who donates computers to the class. Like Johnson, Gruwell is portrayed as the only person who believes in her "unteachable" students, a "guardian angel" (160) who stays with her students in the building sometimes until 11:00 p.m. (158).

In a scene similar to the hotel dinner in *Dangerous Minds,* Gruwell's book also profiles her students' lack of class privilege by bringing them to a formal dinner, sponsored by the Marriott, with a survivor of the war in Bosnia. Of the dinner, one student wrote: "waiters in tuxedos and white gloves served us appetizers off silver trays . . . there must have been at least five courses. There were so many knives and forks at our table. I'm glad Ms. Gruwell went over which ones we're supposed to use first" (91). Unlike Johnson, Gruwell sees herself as a "mom to 150 college-bound kids" (193), and creates a graduate student mentor program for her students, as well as a nonprofit organization to help fund her students' tuition.

Especially in the cases of Gruwell's and Johnson's narratives, which are so successful in the mainstream culture that, worldwide, the *Freedom Writers* film grossed $43,090,741 (IMDb 2011b) and the *Dangerous Minds* film $177,900,000 (IMDb 2011a), problematic ideas about what makes a "good teacher" of minority urban youth are popularized. While the ideas of good teachers, dedicated students, and social justice are important to explore and interrogate, both the published and film versions of Johnson's and Gruwell's stories uphold a spectacle about "successful" urban high school teachers, the ideal types of whom are White, straight, pretty, and female. This spectacle panders to raced and classed inequities and further supports rhetoric made popular in education by figures like Michelle Rhee. The spectacle encourages the idea that teachers are the sole providers of opportunity, love, safety, acceptance, and caring for students, while deficits are ascribed to their families and communities. Meritocracy and color blindness are the underlying values.

Teachers in these idealized versions of urban schools are also, bafflingly, most successful with the least amount of experience and professional development, and the least amount of input from colleagues. In fact, they are competitive with colleagues, and do not collaborate. They find individual success in the classroom by inspiring students mostly through "caring" and intimidation techniques.

The White female teacher is often portrayed as a feminized version of the "rugged individual": she singlehandedly takes on school administration's bureaucratic structures, and is the sole believer in her students, who ultimately succeed. Her narrative becomes one not only of White exceptionality and risk-taking in the face of a group of non-White students who are labeled "at-risk" (Hartigan 2009), but also one of White missionary-like sacrifice and color-blind, heartwarming success: we are all people, the films seem to say, and given help from the right (White) missionary, even those who have all their cards stacked against them can get on the right path. Typically, the goals for the ideal type of White teacher's students are literacy, empathy, and nonviolent conflict resolution, as opposed to college readiness.[2]

In its idealized model of U.S. classrooms, Johnson's narrative embodies what I call the trope of the "White liberal savior." In this model, the White teacher saves her Black and Brown students from their "violent," "immoral," "uncivilized," and "illiterate" backgrounds and communities. She sacrifices herself, her time, and often her personal relationships for the "good" of her students, who see her as a surrogate mother who uniquely recognizes their potential. The end of the narrative of the White liberal savior is that students emerge as better, less violent, or more moral people.

At College Prep, Mr. Jackson (quoted at the beginning of this chapter) and the teachers I profile below recognize that, though popular movies portray the missionary-like "great White hope" in urban schools and the at-risk, ignorant, troubled, or violent Black or Brown student, the reality is far from these images both in regard to the work of the activist, anti-racist pedagogue and the curious, critical student. Teachers who come into classrooms expecting to embody the plotlines of mainstream films and literature about urban teachers and their students cannot be effective agents of social change, because the spectacle that includes the "great White hope" perpetuates racist, deficit discourse about students and their communities while problematically and uncritically elevating the teacher and her community to the paragon of goodness and perfection.

The White Neoliberal Savior Model at College Prep

Although the spectacle that College Prep encourages as it markets itself to its funders depends on the narrative of the White neoliberal savior, the politics and pedagogies of these three teachers in some ways complicate the ideal type of White female teacher. Many dominant popular-culture film and text narratives about White teachers maintain White privilege through aligning White femaleness with "goodness," "patience," "peace," "sacrifice," "individualism," and "taking risks." In contrast, White privilege is maintained differently in the College Prep narrative, where it is aligned with middle-classness and the proper performance of a corporate, market-consumer identity.

The White female teachers whom I examine here fall on a spectrum of politics in regard to race. All are considered to be effective teachers by students and parents. Their classes (or in one case, extracurricular activities) are well organized, and students show evidence of learning. Yet, two of the teachers valorize students' experiences and communities and demonstrate a more overt critique of the neoliberal mission of the institution itself (and are more encouraging of critiques by colleagues and students), while one does not. All care deeply for students, and are invested in improving as self-reflexive and humanizing educators.

Because the themes that emerged from two of the teachers closely resembled one another, while one stood apart, it is important to emphasize that all three of these teachers were seen as excellent and hardworking educators. While all were open about being at different points in terms of racial politics, each one admitted her struggle to be an effective, self-reflexive, and critical pedagogue who teaches toward a more socially just world.

Kevin Kumashiro (2012) critiques the ways in which teacher blaming obscures social or systemic issues that are endemic to the "achievement gap" that is, in reality, an "education debt" (Ladson-Billings 2006). In addition to our nation's historical legacy of chattel slavery, segregation, and racial capitalism, these issues include health care, affordable housing and food, environmental justice, and widely accessible early childhood education. The "bad teacher" stereotype scapegoats teachers while obscuring the real issues, and Kumashiro writes against the ideology embodied by former Washington, D.C., school chancellor Michelle Rhee, who discouraged teachers' unions and resorted to dismissing teachers based on performance, as opposed to making larger, systemic changes (Lewin 2010). Kumashiro urges us not to ask who is winning or losing, but rather, to ask who made the rules and who benefits from them. A "witch hunt" for "bad teachers" (or, for that matter, "neoliberal saviors") obscures much more important conversations that serve to name widely pervasive and oftentimes common-sensical ideologies that construct, marginalize, and oppress an "other." This argument undergirds my analysis in this chapter.

Case Study: Ms. Elliott

Thirty years old, Ms. Elliott was in her fifth year teaching at College Prep when I interviewed her. She graduated from a small liberal arts college in the northeastern United States, and is originally from a city in the southern United States.

She said that she attended a "very selective private school." Because the school had extremely small classes, she said, there were "zero classroom management problems anywhere." Ms. Elliott told me that the school was predominantly White, with the exception of two African American students, and that most students came from very privileged backgrounds. There were many international students at the school who spoke languages other than English.

During our interview, I asked her what kept her teaching at College Prep. She had been on a recent visit to her old school, and remarked to me how awestruck she was at how students respected and internalized the "culture" of the school:

> It was like a half an hour before class started, the kids were just milling about, sitting in front of their lockers, talking to their friends. All the classrooms were open whether there was a teacher in there or not. Students were, like, helping out in classrooms. They were helping teachers get ready. They were just like reading a book, or they were just sitting talking to their friends. It was like the whole place had this aura of just like, it was like a college campus in that sense. It was just like, "oh yeah, we're all here to learn and we're all happy to be here" . . . I was just like, "oh my gosh! If our students would just like mill about the hallways like this, we would have no problem." But they don't . . . we've had so much trouble in the mornings, and students who like sneak up the back staircase, and they like literally run and scream and curse and chase and hit each other in the hallway.

She seemed so nostalgic for the self-motivation and class culture of the students at her old high school, and given her portrayal in the above comments of her own high school versus ours, I wondered what moved her to stay at College Prep, especially since the reason for her visit to her high school was that she was considering moving back there to work. I also wondered what motivated her to teach. When I asked her this, she responded that she saw teaching as a career and as a profession. She continued:

> I did not come into teaching because I wanted to save kids. I think that the relationships with students, and seeing the success of students, that is the reward of a job well done. And definitely kind of the intrinsic motivation that goes with it. But I came into teaching because I thought I would like teaching. I thought I would like the material and the discussions about texts and you know, and that somewhat academic aspect to it.

Ms. Elliott's statement here was provocative in that she explicitly negated the idea of the teacher-as-savior. She came into teaching because she thought that she would enjoy a career of talking about texts, and she liked to be pushed as a professional. While not completely satisfied at College Prep (she said that had the economy not been so bad, she might have found another job for this year), and aware that she did not see herself in "this kind of environment" for life, she said College Prep was "the devil I know, versus the devil I don't."

Ms. Elliott and Her Students

Students said that "Ms. Elliott doesn't play," and when I sat in her fast-paced Research Writing class, I saw what they meant. Ms. Elliott's "teacher moves" were calculated. She used an egg timer to keep herself on track, and after students had completed the do-now in their notebooks, she asked them to spontaneously share examples. She wasn't shy about correcting students if their sentences did not align with her definition. For example, when one student volunteered the sentence "Ms. Carr is not always conscientious about grading papers," Ms. Elliott corrected the student, saying that the word has more to do with keeping one's mind on something than on doing something fast. I thought this example was particularly interesting, because rather than engage the fact that a student was making a critique of her colleague, Ms. Elliott kept the focus on the matter at hand: the do-now. Her whole class worked like this; it felt businesslike, and moved quickly. There was the sense that everyone was getting something done.

When Ms. Elliott joked with students, it was often about her own intellectualism, by being comically formal, or through showcasing her difference from her students. The day when she tried to teach satire, for example, she projected an image from a political cartoon in front of the class. The class discussed the meaning of the cartoon, and Ms. Elliott tied in the ways it was a satire. Then, taking the cartoon down, she said, "that guy was such an exaggeration, he was such a hyperbole!" Hearing this, one student smiled and imitated her: "such a hyperbole!" She smiled too, and asked the student, "Mr. Sanford, would you like to teach this class?" On another occasion, Ms. Elliott put up an example of an essay that she was assigning the class. She had written the essay, and the first paragraph that she projected was somewhat lengthy. A few students began to complain and suck their teeth. She began to jokingly imitate them, but in trying to suck her teeth started to giggle, and said, "I can't even do it!"

Students did not seem to find this funny, but that didn't matter; it didn't change the pace of the class, and students were still responsible for the assignment, regardless of their laughter or complaints.

Ms. Elliott and Parents

When I spoke with Ms. Smith, whose daughter, Princess, was in eleventh grade (see chapter 5 for a case study of Princess), Ms. Smith told me that Ms. Elliott kept Princess "in check." She elaborated:

> Princess's grandfather died and we had to go to his wake. And Princess's report was due the next day and she is in the funeral hall typing her report! And I said, "why don't you tell Ms. Elliott that you were at a funeral?" And she told me that there was a boy who told her that his grandmother was sick, and Ms. Elliott said, "your grandma would want you to do your work!" No excuses.

Ms. Smith liked what she heard about Ms. Elliott's class, because she set high standards. According to Ms. Elliott, however, not every parent was equally supportive of her work with students. Going into greater detail about why she continued to work at College Prep, she said:

> I know that the principal respects me as a professional and I know that I am safe as a teacher. Like I know that when a parent screams at me and curses at me and hangs up on me, which has happened to me a couple times now, that when I send that e-mail to the principal that if the parent's next phone call is to the principal that she has my back.

Princess is a high-achieving student who does not challenge her teachers, yet she may not be representative of the majority of College Prep students, according to Ms. Elliott.

I wondered what caused such conflict between Ms. Elliott and the parents who had cursed and hung up on her. Evidently, she had not made the kind of impression on every parent that she had on Ms. Smith. I formed a hypothesis later in the interview, when Ms. Elliott and I talked about student behavior. I asked her why our students don't just calmly "mill about the hallways" as did the students at the high school she attended. She responded:

> I mean I really don't know. I really—I mean, to sound terribly classist and terribly racist, I mean like they're just predominantly White kids from two-parent families that are raised in homes that it's not appropriate to run around and scream and curse and hit people—like they don't do it. That is not okay.

Ms. Elliott revealed here a great disconnect between her expectations and educational autobiography and students who did not obey the school's norms. She marked this disconnect by race and family structure, which were the most visible ways it manifested for her. The assumption that she seemed to make here (with the caveat that it "sounds incredibly classist and racist") was that in the homes of non-White students who come from single-parent families, it was okay to "run around and scream and curse and hit people." I wondered how this rift manifested when Ms. Elliott called the parents of students who were not behaving in her class according to her expectations. Perhaps this was one reason for parents' defensiveness during her phone calls. Her statement raises questions about how teachers who may have very different histories and experiences from students can be pushed to question the assumptions that may come from that. It is important to stress here that students reported that they enjoyed learning from Ms. Elliott. Might students' learning experiences (and Ms. Elliott's) have been even more powerful and meaningful if Ms. Elliott had found ways to appreciate and validate students' out-of-school identities to a greater extent?

Ms. Elliott, Social Structure, and Social Justice

Ms. Elliott described her classroom persona to me as "prim and proper." She said, in relation to her students:

> I am not going to try to be your friend, I am not going to try to be your buddy. I am not going to get down and boogie with you. I am not going to speak your language. And, so, in a way, it's like I

showcase the difference, rather than trying to conceal it . . . and it's a personality thing as well . . . like I am the "please and thank you," I am the "sir and ma'am."

Her belief in "proper" behavior and language manifested one day when I observed a grammar lesson in her class. Students were supposed to be labeling subject, verb, and object in the following sentences:

1. My brother go to school in Flatbush.
2. When you cut it, it send a bitter, sharp, unpleasant smell to your nose.

When the class came back together after students had labeled subjects and objects, Ms. Elliott stood at the front of the room and helped students to make the corrections. She asked students what the "correct" version of the sentences would be in "grammatical language." When students said that it should be "goes" to school as opposed to "go," and "sends" instead of "send" she said, "most of you know the correction because it sounds bad [in Standard American English]."

While the overt curriculum here was about grammar, I found the hidden curriculum to be particularly provocative as a racial project (Omi and Winant 1994). Alim (2006), Delpit (1998), Gee (1996), and Smitherman (2001), among many others, have argued the importance of an explicit curriculum of linguistic and discursive code switching for students, especially in predominantly African American classrooms. While it is important, these scholars concede, to teach Standard American English (SAE) or the Language of Wider Communication (LWC) to prepare students for socioeconomic success, it is just as important not to demean students' home discourses by marking them as "improper," "wrong," or "incorrect." The scholars listed above argue for conveying to students that African American Vernacular English (AAVE) (or any other language or discourse) is just as "correct" as SAE, but is just used in different scenarios. They show that AAVE is just as complex and nuanced as SAE, but is not recognized as such due to hierarchies of racial and linguistic supremacy. To name SAE as the only correct way of expressing oneself is a covert project of White supremacy, since SAE is most commonly conflated with White middle-classness in the United States, and AAVE most commonly associated with Blackness.

Ms. Elliott's use of "Flatbush" in the first sentence also becomes part of the same racial project. College Prep is not a neighborhood school, and many of our students come from communities all over New York City. Some live in Flatbush, which is a predominantly African American and Caribbean community. Not only is the sentence written in AAVE, it also refers to a geographic area that is racially marked. This further patholo-gizes the grammar of the "incorrect" sentence by associating it with a geographic area of Brooklyn that is marked as "Black." Ms. Elliott seems to elevate her own raced and classed discourse above that of her Black and Brown students, without explicit social critique or self-reflexivity.

On the other hand, some might argue that Ms. Elliott is giving stu-dents the tools they need to succeed in an unforgiving, fundamentally neoliberal and racist world. Here, it seems as if Ms. Elliott's actions raise similar questions to those brought up by Ms. Carr in relation to profes-sionalism in her follow-up interview (see chapter 3): that is, how does one teach students the skills necessary to survive in a fundamentally undemo-cratic and inequitable world without reinscribing those same inequities? This moment represents a fundamental struggle for teachers, including me. Ms. Elliott's ideology here, in some sense, embodies that of the neo-liberal savior, yet in another demonstrates an awareness of the urgency of teaching students to navigate the political spectacle of a White suprema-cist world outside of College Prep.

I asked Ms. Elliott to describe to me when she was most aware of her Whiteness as she moved through College Prep. Part of the reason why Ms. Elliott may be quite reluctant to address issues of race and language in the classroom came out in her response:

MS. ELLIOTT: Race questions are very difficult for me because I've got a supreme amount of racial guilt in my background, um, and like why all these conversations we have had at school have been really really hard for me because like [the German] side of my family killed all the Jews and the [southern U.S. side] of my family enslaved all the Blacks, so I mean, I am kind of screwed both ways . . . I've kind of been very much raised with kind of like a racial, ethnic, cultural guilt. But the problem is that if I am asked about it, I get all tongue tied, and I get all nervous, and when people talk to me, what I hear, even if it's not what they are saying is that: because you are White you can't teach our Black students. That's what I hear, like I hear it over and over again.

AB: From the other people on staff? Or from . . .

MS. ELLIOTT: Yeah, well, when we had these conversations.

AB: Oh, the "Courageous Conversations about Race."

MS. ELLIOTT: That we had in PD (professional development), well that's very much what I hear, but then on the other hand, I want to say, well obviously I can teach these students, you know, because I have taught every single grade that's in this school right now, and they did learn, and I think that the way that I do that is by saying "I am about learning . . . and the way that I am going to connect to you is by giving you an opportunity to succeed by giving you high standards," and I kind of bridge that difference by being like "oh, I am super formal, and I am stuffy," and all that kind of stuff. And then it becomes funny because we have these moments where students say to me "oh, Miss, you know, that's mad wack" and I say [inflecting a very clipped tone] "yes, Stephen, it is, indeed, mad . . . wack." And that gets a good laugh out of the students because you know, I am then able to make fun of myself, and I am then able to make fun of them.

Ms. Elliott grapples here with an incredibly difficult question. How can White teachers of Black and Brown students come to terms with historical and present racial terror, genocide, and oppression, especially when those White teachers are explicitly in institutional positions of power that normalize their own epistemologies (Spears-Bunton and Powell 2008)? She expresses here that she resolves this in two ways, (1) through initiating a relatively formal teacher/student relationship with members of her class, and (2) through performing humorous caricatures that showcase the differences between her home discourse and students' own. These are the ways Ms. Elliott protects herself, and resists coming to painful terms with the White guilt that she harbors, and with her status as an oppressor who is also in a position of institutional power. Her statement above represents her deep desire to work through this guilt, and to have opportunities to process it in an affirming way.

She also referred to the difficulty she encountered during two consecutive professional development sessions called "Courageous Conversations about Race." These conversations came from a recommendation from Mr. Jackson of Mica Pollock's edited volume, *Everyday Antiracism* (2008a), to Ms. Sands.

Ms. Sands then recommended the book to Principal McCarren, who, inspired by an essay in the book entitled "Beginning Courageous Conversations about Race" (Singleton and Hays 2008), during the fall of 2008 sent an e-mail to the staff saying that it was time to begin "our own courageous conversations." She asked for teacher volunteers to help her plan the first meeting, which would take place during our full staff development meeting in October. I could not attend the first planning meeting, but did attend the second planning meeting, as well as both full staff "courageous conversation" meetings (Ms. McGoldrick, who is profiled later in this chapter, attended all planning meetings).

At the start of the first staff meeting, we formed groups of four to establish norms for productive discussion. Ms. Elliott was in this small group with me, but waited until the full staff reconvened to volunteer her opinion that "there should be no attacking . . . I think we can hold ourselves to that standard . . . there will be ideas that upset us and anger us, but I am saying that we should question the idea instead of attack the idea." Her explicit caution even before the conversations began reveals the anxiety and fear that she holds in terms of talking about race. This, in tandem with her self-professed racial guilt, shows that she protects herself from self-reflexivity because it has the potential to cause great pain and suffering that she is not sure how to handle.

Although Ms. Elliott explicitly avoids talking about race with other staff or with her students because she does not see it as part of her own mission, or the mission of the school, I pushed her during our interview, asking whether the school maintains or contests racial disparities. She responded:

> I think the thing that we are doing in order to challenge ideas about race is not so much in our discussion of like, "what does it mean to be Black?" but that we as teachers are trying to confer as much of our privilege that we were lucky enough or coincidentally fortunate enough to grow up with on our students. We are trying to send students out into the world more likely to go to college, more likely to be academically successful, you know, with a kind of . . . give them the opportunity to have them enter whatever social sphere they would like to . . . we give them the opportunities that their racial group traditionally or stereotypically doesn't have.

Ms. Elliott's case study both embodies and complicates the trope of the neoliberal savior in some important ways. She could easily be read as embodying the characteristics of the neoliberal savior because of her beliefs in College Prep's "professionalizing" discourse, because of her somewhat deficit-grounded beliefs of students, and because of her confidence in a political spectacle that valorizes neoliberal systems and standards for measuring one's worth. However, we might also read Ms. Elliott as demonstrating her wish to find better ways of dealing with her fear and guilt around her students (racialized "others"), and as someone who works hard to ensure that students learn important skills. In a sense, she represents possibility because she is aware of her need for growth. She is dedicated to students and to being a good teacher, and communicates that she wishes she had the tools and a safe space to work through her problematic racial politics.

Conclusions: Ms. Elliott

When I spoke with Mr. Jackson about how he experienced race and gender at College Prep as the only Black male teacher in the English department, he said that he was "incredibly aware [of Blackness]; at English department meetings, for example, I am incredibly aware of both my gender and my race—there is a hyperawareness there, first I am Black, then I am a male, and then I am a teacher, in that order; that's how I experience it." What made him even more aware was that while most of his White colleagues, he thought, would say that we fight race and gender disparities at College Prep, he sees things very differently. These opinions, he said, were a "manifestation or a reproduction of things that already exist." His first example was that College Prep's leadership was predominantly White (he used Ms. Barnes and Mr. Thomas here as examples; Ms. Humphries had not yet been hired). In other words, Whiteness is visibly synonymous with power at College Prep. Then, he added:

> And then, I think I told you before about my interactions with Lisa Elliott, for the first year, year and a half that I knew her, she refused to acknowledge my presence, until I confirmed in her eyes that I had the potential to be on par with her intellectually. For me, this is the difficulty of working with individuals who believe deep down in their hearts in their own progressive and liberal nature.

No matter how we teach, it is impossible to transfer our own race and class privilege or oppression onto others. No matter who we are, we are products of our environments and experiences. It is possible, however, to cultivate tools of empathy, critique, openness, and self-reflexivity. Mr. Jackson revealed the ways Ms. Elliott's deep-seated racial guilt, and conflation of Blackness with deficit, manifested through her interactions with him, a Black colleague. Even she remarked that she has work to do when it comes to race. Thus, she maintains a tenuous relation with her position, and with her positionality at College Prep. Her White liberalism leads her to work hard and to set high standards for her students, but also leads her to have difficulty confronting the reality of her students' experiences. Students learn from her, and have fun in her class, even as she demonstrates a deep desire to confront her guilt and fear.

In the next case study, I focus on another White teacher who complicates the trope of the feminized, White neoliberal savior.

Case Study: Ms. McGoldrick

Brooklyn-born and -raised, Ms. McGoldrick, who identifies as White, reported to me that many students ask her if she is Puerto Rican, because of the way she talks. Indeed, her accent marks her immediately as a local. This is rare among teachers at College Prep; most are not originally from New York City. When we taught at College Prep, Ms. McGoldrick and I were neighbors in Bedford-Stuyvesant, a predominantly African American neighborhood in Brooklyn, but we met in 2005, when we were colleagues at another school in New York City. At that time, she was teaching middle school, but at College Prep, she taught ninth-grade science, served as the chair of the Science department, and facilitated the Young Women's Association (YWA). Additionally, she was pursuing her doctorate during the evenings.

I knew that she had been raised in Brooklyn, but she filled in some of the gaps in my knowledge. Born in Park Slope in the late 1970s, she witnessed the gentrification of her community firsthand. Until fifth grade, she attended one public school, which she describes demographically as 60 percent White and 40 percent Puerto Rican. For sixth grade, she attended a different public school where, she tells me, she was one of the few White students. She describes the school as "kinda rough," and says that her parents pulled her out of the public school system after the sixth grade and put her in Catholic school. She began at the all-girls school where her mother teaches. The tuition was exceptionally high for its students, and so she said that many wealthy Italian families sent their daughters there; Ms. McGoldrick describes this school as "super snobby." She marks the experience as a sort of "racial awakening": out of a class of five hundred girls, only five were African American. She witnessed a teacher who frequently mixed up the Black girls' names, and she was shocked that these girls seemed to be "all the same" in the teacher's eyes. Ms. McGoldrick marks this as the first time she became aware of her Whiteness. She subsequently transferred to another private Catholic school where the tuition was much lower and the students were more diverse, both racially and socioeconomically. She said that this was a more comfortable environment for her, since, growing up in Brooklyn, "[you] went on the block and you played with whoever was there," White, Black, or otherwise. She told me that several of College Prep's students also attended her elementary school, and that this helped her relate to students. She knew what was available to her students because their backgrounds were part of her own childhood. She added:

> I don't know what it's like to come to New York and be in this brand-new place and try and situate yourself, and try and deal with kids, but I can imagine it would be a lot more difficult, not understanding where they are coming from and where they are growing up. And there's a lot of people that do make the effort to get in and understand and talk to people that live in this neighborhood [Bedford-Stuyvesant, where we conducted our interview], for example, but then you also have the people that have like seen some movie about teaching in New York City and base their knowledge off of that.

Her critical awareness of media-based ideas that inspire some people to go into teaching is one of many factors that motivate her to stay in the classroom. When I interviewed Ms. McGoldrick, she was in her ninth year of teaching, between working at a Catholic school and working in Brooklyn public schools. Even though she was busy teaching full-time, chairing the department, running the YWA, and pursuing a PhD, she saw it as her responsibility not to leave the classroom: "I think I have a responsibility to the kids, and I don't know how to say this without sounding conceited, but I just feel like I've seen a lot of really bad teaching, and I've seen a lot of people in teaching for the wrong reasons." She continued, telling me that while there were many people in teaching, not all of them were good at relating to the students. Ms. McGoldrick is not in the classroom to confer her own privilege on her students, and she has a clear critique of the popular mainstream narrative of teacher-as-missionary or savior. Rather, she stays in the classroom because she relates well to her students and she is good at teaching. In looking at many of the adults around her, she does not see these qualities reflected. She loves the students, and sees it as her responsibility to continue to teach them, although she expresses her doubt during our interview that she will be able to sustain working at College Prep for a long period of time, because of the job's high demands on her time and energy. In her words, College Prep is not a place that can be "sustainable for teachers."

Ms. McGoldrick and Students

Ms. McGoldrick makes up for her petite size in the way that she commands authority in the classroom. Throughout my observations, I never heard her raise her voice above a conversational tone with students. In fact, the quieter she got, the more attention students paid. She emphatically does not use professionalism points in her room,[3] but students are invested in her class and care about pleasing her.

The few times when I saw her lecture in class, students listened attentively, but most of the times when I observed her classes, students were working in pairs to co-edit their written work or they were working in small groups on a lab. I witnessed Ms. McGoldrick trying different strategies to motivate students to complete their homework, including posting the class's daily homework average at the end of class, and setting goals for the following week. In addition to trying to boost homework completion, she is invested in her class working as a team: rather than making homework a competition, she turns it into a community effort. This is one way in which Ms. McGoldrick incorporates a critique of the model of individual competitiveness, or what Assistant Principal Humphries calls the "me" culture that seems so prevalent at College Prep.

An important part of getting to know her students and exploring how to best engage them, Ms. McGoldrick tells me, is through her work at the school with the Young Women's Association. The YWA meets twice a week and is open to girls in all grades. At the beginning of each school year, YWA goes on an October camping trip in upstate New York. I volunteered to help Ms. McGoldrick chaperone. On a Friday afternoon, we took the train from Grand Central Station with twenty YWA girls, in addition to the twenty Young Men's Association (YMA) boys and their facilitators, Mr. Fulton and Mr. Matthews. Even on the two-hour train ride to the campsite, I found it telling that while I sat and shared snacks with Mr. Fulton and Mr. Matthews in the front of the car, Ms. McGoldrick sat with the YWA girls in the back. Although Mr. Fulton, Mr. Matthews, Ms. McGoldrick, and I frequently socialized outside of work, her priorities on this trip were clearly to enjoy time with students.

We split from the boys, and with our guides, hiked our way into the woods to the campsite. After taking hours to build a campfire in the rain, cooking dinner, and cleaning up, we spent the cold night in sleeping bags on a covered wooden platform, and spent the day together on Saturday. Both days were packed with trust games, teambuilding, and bonding activities in the woods. On Friday night, after the other girls went to bed, I stayed up late into the night with Ms. McGoldrick and with two of the eleventh-grade girls, who were in my class as tenth-graders, and who Ms. McGoldrick taught as ninth-graders. Over the dying fire, the girls asked us about college, about love, about our backgrounds and families, and they told us about their own.

On Saturday, we hiked through the woods to a rock-climbing wall, and I watched the girls cheer Ms. McGoldrick on as she scaled the most challenging portion of the wall. She cheered them on too, no matter which portion of the wall they tried. It was on this trip that I really got a sense of why it is so important for Ms. McGoldrick to balance teaching with YWA while pursuing her doctorate. While intellectual engagement outside of College Prep is important to her, she is an effective and experienced teacher whose pedagogy is made more effective by the deep understanding and sense of community she cultivates with her students.

She views her job as giving students both a science and a character education. For her, this practice is explicitly gendered.

MS. McGOLDRICK: YWA has affected my teaching, like I feel the need to say something to a girl if they are doing something that doesn't show that they respect themselves, like even if it's in the middle of class, like I'll feel the need to go and talk to them about it if I feel like it's something that they need to hear.

AB: And is that what YWA does, teaches young women self-respect?

MS. MCGOLDRICK: That's part of it—part of it is how do you respect yourself, and then another part is how do you have a healthy relationship with others after you do that?

Part of the character education that Ms. McGoldrick feels is so critical for girls is to develop a reputation of self-respect, to cultivate healthy friendships with other young women, and to be involved in a community that supports that. YWA provides both the opportunity for her to model this for young women and opportunities for leadership for older students in the program. The effort and time that Ms. McGoldrick puts into YWA, as well as into creating an intellectually engaging and supportive class, pays off in the close and fulfilling relationships that she is able to have with her students.

She is concerned about the college-only option that College Prep perpetuates for its students. She sees this, in a way, as perpetuating an unrealistic meritocratic narrative of achievement for students who are set up to fail:

I think our whole like college push actually like not focuses on the middle, but kind of like creates this one only path that people can take—is the system created so that we know only a certain percentage of kids can get accepted anyway, so are we creating a certain percentage that has to fail?

Ms. McGoldrick's goal goes beyond simple college preparation; it is to provide students with a character education and with work habits that will contribute to them being competent, critical, and empathetic adults.

Ms. McGoldrick and Parents

When I asked Ms. McGoldrick whether she had a strong partnership with parents now, she said,

Not necessarily this year, 'cause I have so many just absent parents, and that's probably why so many kids in my advisory are failing. My first year of advisory was awesome. I had really good relationships with those kids, and I had pretty close relationships with some of those parents like Alan Chaplin's mother and Barrett Sanford's parents; I talked to them a lot. We definitely need more parent involvement at the school. That's one important link. And I think that could be a bias that people in public education have. At many Catholic schools, so you pay like $200 in dues at the beginning, or you do so many hours of community service. And I feel like if I were to bring that up at College Prep, they would be like, "well you can't expect our kids' parents to do that, you know like they have to work or they come from poor communities," and I am like: "what do you mean, they are poor, so they can't come to the school? They can't be involved?" I feel like we just make their decision for them; we use that as an excuse.

Ms. McGoldrick believes that teachers and students are more successful when schools work in partnership with families.

Ms. McGoldrick, Social Structure, and Social Justice

As a child in Brooklyn, Ms. McGoldrick was accustomed to being in diverse settings, and says that she feels uncomfortable in settings that are too homogenous. When I asked her about racial politics and segregation among the adults at College Prep, she spoke about how teachers' backgrounds influence the ways they were able to get along with students, as well as their initial reasons for teaching:

MS. MCGOLDRICK: There was someone who was touted as this amazing teacher here, but this was someone who I knew would never be able to relate to kids because of like, because they couldn't get past that, like they couldn't be in their world, like, ever. And I think a lot of it had to do with, like not just race, but also with like socioeconomic status and education.

AB: So you are talking about someone with a White, elite background.

MS. MCGOLDRICK: I am talking about like, "Oh I am gonna come in and like save these kids."

AB: Yeah, the White missionary complex?

MS. MCGOLDRICK: Right, but without the idea of who you are even giving to, you know? Like if I come in and tell you that everything that I know is going to make your life better because my life is good.

While Ms. Elliott and Ms. McGoldrick both voice a critique of White missionary discourse in urban schools, they do so for different reasons.

Unlike Ms. Elliott, Ms. McGoldrick sees part of her job as a teacher as being able to know and deeply connect with where students are coming from. She knows that there are important skills, content, and knowledge (including class discourses) that teachers need to incorporate into students' learning experience, but that this cannot happen until teachers cultivate a deep respect for and understanding of their students. While she acknowledges that race might be a part of this, she also cites the importance of class background as it intersects with race in terms of teachers' alienation from students, and from one another. Not only are White teachers from elite backgrounds at higher risk of being alienated from their students, they seem more likely to be alienated from colleagues who don't share their background.

MS. MCGOLDRICK: Although I saw this more last year than the first year at College Prep, there is a very clear divide amongst the staff. Like I am not sure about this year, because there's like a lot of new people, but last year, there was a definite, like quite a few of those people left, but there was definitely like one side, and another side.

AB: Black/White?

MS. MCGOLDRICK: White, and "other."

In other words, according to Ms. McGoldrick, there are staff members who segregate themselves, and there are staff members who don't. There are White staff members, as well as non-White staff in the second group, who make it a point to embody a version of what Prudence Carter calls multicultural navigators (2005). As adults, these teachers enact connecting with people of diverse backgrounds and positionalities, and are able to strategically negotiate different kinds of interactions, perhaps because, as in Ms. McGoldrick's case, they come from backgrounds where this kind of interaction was normalized. This changes the ways they engage with students in the classroom, because the classroom becomes another setting to enact the same politics, which come from a foundation of genuine courage, curiosity, respect, and critique of power hierarchies, as opposed to a foundation of White guilt and fear of difference.

As she discusses whether College Prep perpetuates or contests social disparities in race and gender, Ms. McGoldrick expresses recognition that this is part of a larger issue and disappointment that these larger social/structural issues are not part of a regular conversation or critique at College Prep. She recalls a YWA conversation where students voiced a critique of present-day segregation in U.S. public schools, and expresses frustration that staff and administration gave up so quickly on the "Courageous Conversations about Race" that she had volunteered to help plan.

While critical conversations about social structures and inequities should be a regular part of schooling, she recognizes that this is not sufficient to combat the inequities perpetuated by segregation by race and class. Regardless of what kind of education College Prep students get, unless larger patterns of social structures change, talk about fighting race, class, and gender disparities can only go so far. Ms. McGoldrick sees the necessity of fighting for social equity both in and outside of schools. Educating students in a segregated environment, no matter how well, is not going to effect change. This mentality forms her critique of the school's ongoing participation in a problematic spectacle.

Conclusions: Ms. McGoldrick

In participating in the planning committee for the "Courageous Conversations about Race," as well as in trying to have critical conversations with YWA about race, gender, self-esteem, and continuing inequity, Ms. McGoldrick attempts to work toward what she sees as a more integrated and just world; however, she sees the limits of this when she looks at dominant patterns of school experiences in the United States. She feels a responsibility to stay at the school because she can connect deeply with students, and she finds the work to be fulfilling, despite being somewhat taxing. She seems unsure, though, that there is any way that we could inspire change on a micro level if social structure remains the same.

In the next case study, I focus on another White woman, an employee of the Foundation, who complicates and critiques the White neoliberal savior mentality.

Case Study: Ms. Meehan

Before Ms. Meehan was hired at College Prep as a teaching artist, then a health teacher, then a college advisor, she taught a social studies class called "Social Justice" at another school that she describes as "a very chaotic place that resembles many of the portraits you hear of NYC public high schools. There was a lack of strong leadership and lots of academic issues with students, and no buy-in from anyone. It was a really depressing place." Initially, she was excited about it because it was created in a partnership between the community and the Department of Education, but her hopes were quickly dashed, she said, when the community partnership eventually became meaningless. She elaborated:

> All these things that the community wanted, like for example, there was a room that said "Darkroom" on a little sign. And it was not a darkroom. And there was a room that said "TV / Radio Station" and that was an empty room. So there were clearly all of these things that were supposed to happen in the planning stage and in the dreaming stage that maybe could have made it to reality 'cause they had signs on the doors indicating these things that should be there and they just weren't there.

Overall, she appreciates College Prep's dual missions of college matriculation and extracurricular opportunities for its students, especially in comparison to the school where she was before. She says: "College Prep is a very high-functioning institution. I feel like it's full of people who are very dedicated, very hardworking, very creative, and I like that there's so much collaborative work and planning among colleagues here." Ms. Meehan is a strong believer in change through critical community input. In October 2010 at a professional development meeting for staff, I saw this ethic come to fruition when I presented data from the school-wide student questionnaire (appendix B). In response to a question that compared College Prep to a prison, a typical NYC school, a private school, a second home or family, a university, a corporation or business, a party, or "other," 37 percent of students responded that College Prep was like a prison. Mr. Thomas, the director of the Foundation and Ms. Meehan's boss, shared that he did not agree with the wording of the question, and thought that the results were skewed by the extreme nature of the choices. Ms. Meehan quickly shot back: "Why is it that we always try to make excuses to get out of looking at what we don't want to see? Students are telling us something important here; we can't ignore it!" She believes in making her point regardless of whether it will be popular or accepted, and frequently does so. She listens, weighing others' opinions, but is not afraid to make her opinions known.

Ms. Meehan and Students

Ms. Meehan's interactions with students are often through extracurricular activities or through the college office, where she spends much of her time at the school. Early in the 2008–9 school year, when I told her that I was interested in exploring contested definitions of *social justice* at College Prep for my research, she asked me if I was interested in helping her facilitate an exchange program between our students and a group of predominantly White, working-class students in rural Maine. Several after-school meetings with our students would lead to a December trip to Maine, where we would stay for four days. Our students would stay in the homes of their Maine counterparts, and teacher chaperones would stay in the homes of Maine teachers. Later in the spring, the Maine students would come to New York City to stay in the homes of their counterparts, and Maine teachers would stay with New York City teachers.

As we planned the after-school sessions that we would conduct with students, I got a better sense of Ms. Meehan's politics regarding students and the trip itself. She told me that while, traditionally, the trip has been focused on furthering a color-blind multiculturalism between predominantly Black New York City students and predominantly White Maine students, she wanted this time to be different. She hoped that we could bring in activities that would help all students to notice and be critical of differences, as opposed to ignoring them. In a flyer for tenth- and eleventh-grade students who were going on the trip (they had all been to Maine in their previous years at College Prep), she wrote:

You should consider your Maine partner your investigative counterpart this year. The two of you will bring together your different identities, different experiences, and different perspectives to an investigation of how stereotypes and discrimination function in our society. As allies, you will have to think about how you can promote understanding and connection across differences.

We decided that, in order to do this, we would experiment with some of Augusto Boal's "Theatre of the Oppressed" methods and activities (1979) as a creative and engaging way to inspire critical conversations about privilege and oppression. One week in November, we got off track from our planned activity, and just sat around talking. Tenth- and eleventh-grade College Prep students who had been on the Maine trip in previous years started discussing how much their counterparts in Maine are "allowed to get away with." I wrote in my field notes:

> Students expressed that they [Maine kids] don't do any work in school, that they can leave school to smoke cigarettes (sometimes, said one student, her host family's grandma would even give her Maine partner cigarettes), they drink (sometimes in school), smoke a lot of weed, and drive. They do all this stuff, and get away with it, and no one seems to notice. Barbara [Meehan] used this organic opportunity to say: "it's called privilege, that's what that is—when you are born with all these opportunities that you didn't earn. And that's the thing—you guys have to work twice as hard to get the same things." Here, Tina [an eleventh-grade student] made an observation: that if you think about the stereotypes that prevail about us [Black and Brown urban kids], the Maine kids are [ironically] the ones who actually embody these behaviors—and it's the New York City kids that are the most surveilled, the most watched.

Ms. Meehan makes it a point to create opportunities to make structures of privilege obvious to students through conversation, in the same ways that she does with her colleagues. In another activity we did where students were asked to contrast stereotypes about New York City and Maine families, Ms. Meehan debriefed the activity in the following way: "Everyone comes back and says 'Oh, in so many ways we are the same'—but this trip might actually be about being honest about our differences."

Part of the work that Ms. Meehan does with students is in getting them to feel comfortable engaging race with her, even though she is White and they are not. When I asked her about the times when she was aware of her Whiteness at College Prep, she said:

> I think I am always aware; I think the racial difference can be transcended when you have close long-term relationships with students. When you have a relationship of trust it doesn't mean that those differences go away, or that the power dynamics go away, but bridges can be built. You know, I've been working with teenagers since I was a teenager, so I have had students in the past say: "you are White but you help us to understand each other," and I think, I have learned that being able to connect with people is possible across lots of difference and lots of hurt, and lots of fears. But it takes time and I feel like you have to prove yourself to people. I find myself more aware of racial differences when I am dealing with kids that I don't know that well. Or when I have to take on a role of authority with a kid I don't have a relationship with, and it becomes this scene of caricatures. If I have to tell a young man to take off his hat, and like stop acting crazy and like go to class, and I am just some White lady, and he doesn't know my name and I don't know his . . . it's harder to have those conversations with no relationship, and all that can really be seen is the obvious, the surface stuff.

She understands that cultivating a relationship of trust with students and engaging, rather than ignoring, difference is an important point of human connection. Ms. Meehan foregrounds the ways she is an oppressor by cultivating self-awareness as she moves through the space of the building and in her interactions with students. Unlike other White teachers that I interviewed, Ms. Meehan said that she had explicit conversations with students about race "often." When I asked her how they normally went, she elaborated:

> I find kids to be a little wary, like they don't know that it's okay to talk about race, or they call White people "Caucasian" or some-

thing like that. They are trying to respect me, but I don't need that level of not talking about the issue. So I think you have to give them the clues that you are cool to talk about stuff, and that you don't have any interest in defending White people. So, yeah, I find them to be cautious, and maybe waiting to see that it's okay to speak their minds. I think that everybody is more comfortable talking about race with their own groups. And I know when I am around White people, I wish I didn't hear the things that I hear, but I do, and I am offended that you think that I am a part of this group and that I would be okay with that. White people are really not used to having discussions about race. I think my kids are [used to having these discussions], but I just don't think that they think they can have it around me.

Ms. Meehan engages with students and critiques her status as an oppressor (along with critiquing social structures of privilege and oppression), as opposed to ignoring it. In fact, she sees this engagement as an essential way to combat the caricature that she feels she embodies as a White person in a position of power who must act as a disciplinarian to non-White students.

Ms. Meehan and Parents

I interviewed Ms. Meehan in June 2009. Earlier in the day, a meeting was scheduled at the school with parents, because of a fight between two cliques of girls that morning just outside of the school. Principal McCarren and the deans of discipline called the parents in for a conference. Yet, when the parents arrived, a physical altercation arose between them just outside the school's main office. School safety agents broke up the fight. The College Office, where Ms. Meehan works, is just down the hallway from the main office, and she witnessed the altercation. Rather than blaming the parents for what occurred, Ms. Meehan interpreted the situation as parents advocating for their children when the school would not. She recognized that the altercation demonstrated a kind of cultural conflict between what she calls "school and street culture." She wondered aloud to me whether "there is a way to be more accepting but still give students skills to transcend, being more than just in street culture, but keeping their alliance to the streets if they want it." This is one area, she said, where staff fall short.

She added that after the fight, she saw an angry parent talking to Principal McCarren. Ms. Meehan believes from what she overheard that the parent was implicating the school in the fight, because the school was aware of the conflict as it was developing and did nothing to stop it. Ideally, Ms. Meehan said, schools should be in partnership with families, but at College Prep they seem set in opposition to one another. Ms. Meehan recognizes that while College Prep may have good intentions, the school needs to get better both at being in partnership with parents and at giving students a viable option to pursue a successful academic identity at school while maintaining allegiance to their home communities. Rather than blaming parents or students for incidents of violence, Ms. Meehan wants to explore the possibilities for students to embrace school norms of behavior, especially in relation to resolving conflicts peacefully or through talk, without ascribing a deficit to the realities of students' lives outside of the building.

Ms. Meehan, Social Structure, and Social Justice

When I asked Ms. Meehan whether the school, in her opinion, furthered or combated race and gender inequities, she broke the question down herself. She began with gender, because she said that she had a lot of passion for and commitment to working with young women and used gender as a platform to connect with them and inspire them to have positive relationships with other young women. Teenagers, she says, are hyper-aware of "gender stuff," because they are coming into their own sexuality. She told me that girls who form tight cliques with one another (like BOB [see chapter 2] or another clique of junior and senior girls who called themselves the "Poppin' Seven") are the ones who often have the most social issues with other girls and who act in opposition to the norms of the school. Yet, these are also the girls who align themselves more deeply along gender lines and care more deeply about what other girls think. She elaborated:

> The things that make us fight as young women are the things that we really need to come together on; the way that we feel about ourselves, our self-esteem, the challenges that we face are the things that we get at each others' throats about. These are the reasons why we need to support each other.

Like Ms. McGoldrick, Ms. Meehan strives to teach young women how to cultivate self-respect and engage in respectful relationships with others.

When she finished discussing gender, Ms. Meehan asked me: "And then what was the other part of the question? What are we doing to combat White supremacy?" I answered affirmatively, thinking that it was interesting that she chose to employ the vocabulary of "White supremacy" when I had not. She answered:

> I think we are providing our Students of Color with one of the better, more stable, learning environments than they would be offered anywhere else, and I think that anywhere they look, they will find people who believe in them, and I think that people who don't ignore their race, but understand how racism works in the world or how it works in education, are doing things to combat that. I don't think people are ignorant about race or racism. I think we've gathered a lot of resources.

While she acknowledges that College Prep is far from perfect, Ms. Meehan sees the school as farther along in terms of combating White supremacy than other New York City schools.

Conclusions: Ms. Meehan

Like Ms. McGoldrick, Ms. Meehan sees the "Courageous Conversations about Race" as a good start in the right direction. However, she believes the conversations did not have the intended outcome. While she says that Pollock's book (2008) was great because it had "tangible concrete action steps" to take, it's hard to have a discussion about something and then translate that discussion into action steps. Ms. Meehan sees part of her job as a teacher as being able to deeply connect with students and families. This is directly counter to the school's participation in a political spectacle of secular saviorism. Like Ms. McGoldrick, Ms. Meehan recognizes the importance of teachers incorporating students' learning experience into the classroom. She recognizes that gender, social class, and race intersect and that differences, if not addressed critically, compassionately, and courageously, can function to alienate teachers and students. And like Ms. McGoldrick, Ms. Meehan knows that critical conversations about social structures and inequities are not sufficient to combat the inequities perpetuated by gender inequality and class segregation. Ms. Meehan sees the necessity of fighting for social equity both in and outside of schools.

Brayboy, Castagno, and Maughan remind us that equity (a system where unequal goods are redistributed to move toward a society where there is a greater likelihood of equality) is not the same thing as equality (sameness) (2007). The future of race scholarship in education, these scholars write, should be based on a goal of equity and justice, as opposed to one of equality. It seems that while Ms. Elliott demonstrates a somewhat reluctant acceptance of the "real world" beyond College Prep (and a political spectacle that supports it), Ms. Meehan's ideology is equity-based—teaching and learning have to start from critiquing and engaging differences in privilege, power, and positionality, and moving beyond the spectacle, both in and beyond the classroom.

Concluding Thoughts

None of the case studies that I document above align with the "ideal type" of White teacher as "Christian" or "liberal" savior that is so common in many movies and literature, and all critique the idea of the White savior in different ways. Each teacher complicates this trope through her words and actions. The school's spectacle, as well as funders' uncritical support of the school's mission, represents, to some extent, buy-in to the school's neoliberal and market-based ideology. The school markets itself as doing the impossible: saving students from a socioeconomic crisis that already exists, as opposed to religious or moral crisis. Ms. Elliott demonstrates ambivalence about the school's mission, while Ms. McGoldrick and Ms. Meehan demonstrate an overarching critique that takes place "behind the curtain." They refuse to be props in the spectacle. Perhaps embodying the trope of the White savior or missionary, in some sense, provides a way for some White teachers to cope with the discomfort of a White ambivalence that is also the product of economic privilege, while not yet confronting their own privilege, (nor White supremacist social and economic structures) head-on (Fine et al. 1997). In other ways, embodying the trope feeds into a mainstream political spectacle that rationalizes social inequities through ideologies of pity and saviorism.

How, in a corporatized and increasingly privatized school system where the concept of social justice is often ironically equated with schools' and students' marketability, as well as teachers' saviorism, might we forge toward a system of equity? How might we move past what Lilie Chouliaraki (2011), drawing on Richard Rorty, calls the "banal morality of ironic solidarity," in other words, a form of solidarity that relies on the difference between "us" and "them," that is based on self-distance and self-empowerment, and on realizing our own humanity while excluding the humanity of the sufferer outside of our own empathetic imagination? Each teacher profiled here demonstrates a desire to get to a point of what Chouliaraki calls "agonistic solidarity," that is, a radical way of cultivating solidarity as if the world were common and shared among all, with an awareness of different standpoints and a problematizing of human vulnerability as a question of global injustice, collective responsibility, and social change.

These case studies help to nuance the "ideal types" of urban teachers so popularized in political spectacles, literature, media, and film. While students, parents, and colleagues see each teacher as an effective pedagogue and classroom manager, there are marked differences between their views of their work and the socially charged, raced, classed, and gendered issues they are willing to discuss with their students, and marked differences in the roles they play in the school's spectacle. Ms. Meehan and Ms. McGoldrick are practiced at voicing and embodying a move toward a more agonistic solidarity with students through an awareness of students and communities as complex, diverse, and possessing value. These teachers critique the irony inherent in the model of the school, and critique the politics of their colleagues when they see it as necessary. Their pedagogy is emblematic of self-reflective and critical race, gender, and class politics, and they recognize their activist work as serving their own interests as well, because it demonstrates a critique of intersectional oppression (Collins 1990; Crenshaw 1995). Ms. Elliott voices a desire to arrive at this point, and expresses a politics of self-awareness and critique, even as she is less critical of the school's mission. All of these case studies represent excellent, committed, and engaged teachers who are to some degree unsatisfied with the conditions in which they work, and who are effective, despite the circumstances.

Each of these teachers, in her own way, talks back to popularized ideal types of White teachers, yet Ms. Meehan and Ms. McGoldrick more explicitly critique the neoliberal White savior model that Mr. Jackson marks as the problematic prototype of social justice at College Prep. Ms. Meehan understands that to challenge the social positions of her students, she must challenge her own social position and think critically about how the institution maintains differentiated social positions for predominantly White teachers and predominantly non-White students. While she believes that some aspects of the institution's mission (a college-preparatory curriculum, encouragement of critical thought, social justice) are noble, she continues to be critical of those aspects of the institution that further the hegemony of racial and class dominance and that purport an uncritical narrative of meritocracy. She does not see her work as conferring privilege upon her students, but rather sees relationships with students, colleagues, and parents as mutually beneficial in effecting change. She challenges racial ideology by "not only reconceptualizing [her] own racial identity, but [reformulating] the meaning of race in general" (Omi and Winant 1994, 91). Ms. McGoldrick succeeds in relating to colleagues, students, and parents in a self-critical and humanizing way while engaging in important conversations about difference, privilege, oppression, and power. She is open to what students teach her about their families and communities, as well as about how to be an effective and respected teacher in a power-laden and complex educational space.

It is not my intention here to vilify the pedagogy or politics of Ms. Elliott while idealizing those of Ms. McGoldrick and Ms. Meehan. I find it more useful to conceptualize these case studies as representative of the ways in which individuals enact ideologies through agency. I am building here upon Ullman and Hecsh's assertion that teachers' sociocultural consciousness is a continuum (2011), and that it is essential for administrators and teaching practitioners as well as teacher educators to conceptualize it as such in order to design teacher training that inspires critical reflexivity, informed agency, and cultural competence. Neoliberal social practices exacerbate inequalities (Apple 2001; Giroux 2004; Hursh 2009; Lipman 2004), and democratic practices in classrooms become a necessary but not sufficient condition for social justice pedagogy, human agency, and participatory democracy (Young 1990). In a moment of increasing privatization in public education, educators are encouraged to participate in a spectacle that equates social justice with the classic liberal ideals of individual freedom and equality of opportunity in the free market (Friedman 1962; A. Smith [1776] 2010). I argue that action must be continually coupled with skepticism about the goals of social justice teaching, as well as a spectacle of beneficence and saviorism as it relates to the hegemony of the free market.

Although I am not prepared to quantify the ways in which White female teachers critical of social inequity might impact students' learning, mental or emotional well-being, or success, it does seem that teachers can make choices about their level of affiliation with or critique of the racial and class projects of their institutions. My observations reiterate Ladson-Billings's "culturally relevant pedagogy" (1995) to some degree, yet demonstrate that we cannot conceive of "culture" outside of a critical awareness of the salience of how race, class, and neoliberalism intersect. My findings speak to the importance of recruiting and maintaining teachers who have thought deeply about the fact that race, gender, and economic inequities continue to increase and who therefore are willing to engage in a structural and intersectional critique of these disparities, as well as teachers who are prepared to authentically connect with students and their families. While the teaching profession needs to be diversified, many of the predominantly White women who are already in classrooms must demonstrate willingness to critique the trope of the "great White hope" in its neoliberal form, and deepen their investment in fighting inequity through a critical and embodied discomfort with intersectional oppressions. These case studies demonstrate the ways the trope of the White neoliberal savior embodied in the spectacle in which College Prep participates emphasizes performance and image management while unfortunately downplaying teacher–student relationships and the possibility of agonistic solidarity.

In the following chapter, in contrast to the trope of White, female liberal and neoliberal saviors in urban classrooms, I discuss another aspect of the spectacle: the trope of the urban, Black, adolescent girl, as portrayed both in teacher narratives and films and in mainstream College Prep discourse.

5
_____

Girl Drama

Black Female Students and the Spectacle of Risk

This chapter advances my critique of College Prep's support of a problematic political spectacle. Instead of focusing on the role teachers are expected to play in the context of the spectacle, and how they sometimes resist, in this chapter I focus on students. I profile College Prep students whose circumstances, histories, personalities, aspirations, and perspectives complicate mainstream ideas of the "at-risk" urban adolescent. Just as with its teachers, the school's heavy-handed image management and marketing of its students to funders depends on many of the stereotypes found in mainstream films and teacher narratives, promising social change with the help of a sufficient amount of private funding. Media and school discourse that constructs these students as "problems" plays another part in the political spectacle that reinforces the racialized and classed hierarchy of funder/teacher/student, masking the ways in which philanthropy in public schools is often in fundamental conflict with the aims of what we know about good teaching.

I begin with the most popularized portrayals of Black, urban female adolescents in Johnson's (1992) and Gruwell's (1999) narratives. Young African American women in Johnson's book are usually portrayed as wanting to do well academically, and as making an effort to help Ms. Johnson manage the difficult boys in her class (1992, 37). They are timid, talking through their fingers (50), and although they sometimes show her "an attitude" (61), they are easily tamed by a little positive reinforcement or a complimentary note home to parents or guardians. In the story, there is one gang-related "girlfight" between two Latinas (70) that starts when one girl bumps into another's purse. There is another fight between a Latino boy and girl. Usually though, the girls in the story provide the background to Ms. Johnson's struggles with the boys, and sometimes the girls are the messengers between Ms. Johnson and the boys among whom conflicts were brewing (220). One young woman, Shamica, gets pregnant, and Ms. Johnson fights for her to remain in her class and not get put into a separate program (245). Johnson's book does little to convince the reader that any of her students (male or female) have any extracurricular interests beyond expensive-looking clothes, fighting, or sex. The reader also has no picture of students' aspirations, or of their peer groups, unless they happen to be involved in a gang or a fight. Overall, Johnson profiles her successes and her failures with her male students, while her female students provide the backdrop to her story of how she thrived in the "trenches" of an urban classroom.

Even though most of Gruwell's book is made up of journal entries written by students, Gruwell (1999), like Johnson, also leaves the reader unconvinced that students have any conventional extracurricular interests at all. This is especially ironic because of Gruwell's portrayal at the conclusion of the book of her students as being all bound for college, thanks to her nonprofit organization. Gruwell demonstrates that as the trope of the White liberal savior may shift to that of the neoliberal savior (see the previous chapter), the trope of the urban adolescent remains static. The journal entries written by Gruwell's anonymous female students detail a catalog of problems, including physically and sexually abusive love and family relationships (35, 72, 75, 126, 129, 131, 150, 200), being bullied (61), testifying against a former boyfriend in court (64), alcoholism (67), shoplifting (69), drug addiction (99), an incarcerated parent (116), misogyny (125), homelessness and an absent father (134), living in violent, drug-ridden housing projects (145, 179, 195, 259), pregnancy and abortion (151), AIDS (164), neglectful parents (189), illegal immigration (200), early death of a parent (219), sexuality (244), rape (248), and drug-addicted parents (261).

Again, although students (and Ms. Gruwell) in their journal entries sometimes compare the class to a "family," there is little expression in their journals of any interests in peer groups, hobbies, or even popular culture. It seems that none of the students in her class actually come from family backgrounds that include any support or love at all. While the problems that students detail through their journal entries are prevalent and all too real in communities across the United States, this conflation of, as Gregory (1998) has argued, race, class, and place helps to further the empty and useless tropes of the "Black ghetto" and "inner city," neglecting the fact that all social groups are diverse, that all poverty is political (251), and here, I argue (as does Henry Giroux [1996] in critiquing the film *Kids*), neglecting the fact that urban teenagers are complex people, with interests and personalities that go beyond the deficits that outsiders often unknowingly apply to their families and communities. Going further, the construction of these students as an objectifiable, entertaining, and commodifiable problem in mainstream media diverts attention from the sociopolitical problems (in which all of us are complicit) that give rise to continuing urban poverty: inequitable funding; lack of access to affordable food, housing, healthcare, or early childhood education; and a legacy of White supremacy that is indelibly woven into our national (and global) past and present.

This raced, classed, and gendered mainstream spectacle as applied to Black and Brown urban youth serves simultaneously to circumscribe and problematize non-White identities while ascribing a limitless kind of invisibility to privileged Whiteness. In other words, the creation and perpetuation of this trope furthers White privilege through essentializing and "othering," in the above examples, a young, Black, poor, urban, female identity (Collins 2004; hooks 1992). In College Prep's marketing to funders and its advertising to outsiders, the trope of the White neoliberal savior is offset by the trope of the at-risk Black urban adolescent. The following discussion of College Prep explores the ways in which, behind the curtain, young, urban, Black women complicate these social constructions. Much of the same literature that portrays the White savior teacher portrays African American adolescent girls as at risk of academic failure or of problems in school (see K. Brown 2010; Valencia 2010). I complicate this portrayal through a more nuanced picture of these students' backgrounds, as well as through highlighting their own versions of how the College Prep model articulates with their lives and experiences. I also examine how and why the political spectacle in which College Prep participates needs the problematic trope of the at-risk adolescent to function, and I argue against its use in any school environment.

"Girl Drama"

At College Prep, the student population is primarily female (72 percent) and African American (81 percent) (nysed.gov 2008–9). Often, school staff and students view young women as more likely than their male counterparts to be troublemakers, or as particularly resistant to school norms and expectations. When I asked a group of four students in my summer book club / cultural circle (see chapter 6) whether College Prep girls behave differently from College Prep boys, all agreed that there is a difference between the way in which the girls and the boys at the school behaved. Destiny Jones (see case study below) said: "Everybody loves the boys, and the girls are out of control!" Elise Miller, an African American student whom I shadowed and interviewed when she was a junior, explained:

> Boys, when they see girls arguing, will either watch, and most that I know are mature; they will just walk away. They don't have time for that . . . and then when they bring it up in class, they will say like "oh, that's crazy" and everything, they won't exactly get themselves involved in it. But girls, they just keep it going constantly throughout the whole day until the day is ended.

Alex Parker, an African American student whom I shadowed when he was a senior, describes College Prep girls as "bipolar." I asked him what kinds of girls go to College Prep.

ALEX: Hmm, I don't know . . . 'cause sometimes, like they'll be cool, and then sometimes, like there's just days where like all hell breaks loose, so it's like bipolar, somewhat?
AB: Smart?
ALEX: Yeah, definitely. For the most part.
AB: Okay, but bipolar meaning that they are kind of moody and dramatic sometimes?
ALEX: Oh, very moody and dramatic.

Staff members too often vent in person or e-mail about incidents and altercations between girls. In addition to having and overhearing several personal conversations with and between staff members about "girl drama" at the school, I searched through e-mails from the 2008 and 2010 school years (I was included in e-mails sent to the ninth- and tenth-grade teams, but not the eleventh and twelfth). I found 110 e-mails that mentioned the word *girls*, of which twenty-seven were about altercations, conflicts, interventions, or mediations. When I looked at the twenty e-mails that mentioned the word *boys* over the two years, there were no altercations, conflicts, interventions, or mediations mentioned. I searched for *young men* in my in-box, and found only two e-mails that mentioned conflicts between male students.[1]

The e-mails about girls' behavior detail students entering class late, being "disruptive," eating or drinking in class, talking over teachers, having screaming matches, getting into physical altercations, or bullying one another. Incidents like these between girls seemed quite common at the school, while those between boys seemed much more rare. Because such a great amount of emphasis and energy is placed on girls' behavior at the school, in this chapter, I focus closely on case studies of three young women at College Prep. All were in tenth grade when I met them and finished eleventh grade the same year I left the school. These young women were my English students as tenth graders, and attended my summer book club / cultural circle during the summer after their sophomore year. I shadowed and interviewed them in eleventh grade, and I interviewed their parents.

Blackness, Privilege, and Performance at College Prep: Need and *Richesse Oblige*

While girls at College Prep are often profiled in everyday conversation among students and staff as particularly volatile in terms of behavior, the school plays down this volatility as it markets itself, while playing up the "at-risk" status of its students. Because students are sold as underprivileged, those who are chosen to publicly represent the school must be able to indulge the *richesse oblige* of the corporate class who donate to the school by playing the part of the at-risk but deserving youth who demonstrate their potential through the ability to perform professionalism.

One example of this deliberate kind of representation is the annual spring benefit, which I described in the introduction to this book. One of the invited juniors was unable to attend, and so there was a debate about whom to invite in his place. The conversation between Mr. Thomas, Ms. Meehan from the college office, and me provides an interesting window into how students were selected to represent the school. Ms. Meehan wanted to ask Keisha Anderson. Keisha was an eleventh-grade student who during ninth and tenth grades had been part of a clique of about twenty girls who called themselves "BOB" (an acronym for "Bang Out Bitches"; see chapter 2). Some staff members saw BOB as a gang, others as a clique. BOB members were popular among their peers and had a tough reputation, but prided themselves on being high academic performers. Before I began teaching tenth grade at the school, I was warned about BOB, given a list of girls who were in the group, and told to alert the deans immediately if I heard any talk about BOB in school. The girls had told deans and teachers at the end of their freshman year that BOB was obsolete, but staff members were doubtful.

During Keisha's tenth-grade year, when I was her English teacher, her name frequently came up in staff meetings for screaming at other students in the hallway, for getting involved in physical fights, and for bullying or threatening other students, sometimes in the middle of class (she once got up in my class and shoved a male student out of his chair because, she said, he had thrown a ball of paper in her face in the class before mine). She was frequently cited for being late to class, for sometimes cutting class altogether to wander the halls or hang out in the gym locker room, and for coming to school out of uniform. In September of her sophomore year, I intercepted a note passed between her and a boy in class where she asked him if he wanted to "eat da box" (perform cunnilingus). At the end of her tenth-grade year, she was arrested during a fight she got into with several other girls outside of the school building. In my class, she maintained a C average; even though there were times when her behavior became an issue in my classroom, she got her assignments in and demonstrated an understanding of the course material.

Through her opposition to school norms and policies, Keisha demonstrated overt defiance not only to rules that were standard within the building, but also to the mainstream College Prep discourse of femininity, which does not sanction fighting, overt displays of sexuality, or disruptive verbal altercations. Keisha's defiance, however, never extended to a rejection of an academic identity; she maintained a B average in her classes. From a list put out by the deans of discipline in 2008 of twenty BOB girls who were pulled from class and scheduled for weekly "gang prevention" workshops by NYPD, I pulled BOB members' transcripts and calculated their average GPA at 76 percent, or a C average. From my observations in class, I noticed that most of the BOB girls, with the exception of those who had extremely low reading and writing skills, excelled academically, while at the same time rejecting "professional" norms of behavior. Since College Prep teachers are encouraged to factor professionalism as a part of a students grade, I hypothesize that BOB's averages were often lower than they may have been had professionalism not been factored into their grades. In short, BOB girls were playing the College Prep game by demonstrating intellectual prowess while rejecting the school's norms of behavior and instead upholding their peer pride and tough reputation. Behind the curtain, they rejected the spectacle.

BOB was a close-knit, all-girl peer group. The girls supported one another in academic achievement and in rejecting the behavioral norms of the school. Their behavior demonstrates an alternative to the hotly contested "burden of acting White" for social and academic success for African American students in academic institutions, as originally argued by Signithia Fordham and John Ogbu (1986) (but also see Fordham 2008). Fordham (2008) writes,

> Today, "acting White" is a scripted, even racialized performance, the goal of which is—perhaps unconsciously—something approximating attempted identity theft, not in the colloquial sense of stealing someone's credit card or bank account information, but, more critically, in exchange for what is conventionally defined as success, racially defined Black bodies are compelled to perform a White identity by mimicking the cultural, linguistic, and economic practices historically affiliated with the hegemonic rule of Euro-Americans. In other words, the wholesale appropriation of a society's hegemonic social and cultural personae—its identity—by another group. (234)

Many scholars have made important critiques of the implications of the "acting White" hypothesis (Ainsworth-Darnell and Downey 1998; Carter 2005; Cook and Ludwig 1998; Diamond 2013; Diamond, Lewis, and Gordon 2007; Harris 2011; Tyson 2011), and in fact have found that even in the face of positive peer pressure to do better in school, Black students are more affected by low expectations from White teachers and peers than they are from a perceived fear of "acting White" (Diamond 2013; Diamond, Lewis, and Gordon 2007). I find, similarly to John Diamond and his colleagues, who conducted a study of race and school achievement in a desegregated suburban high school (2007), that Black students at College Prep affiliated with BOB experience positive peer pressure to succeed academically. Yet they do this while rejecting the school's behavioral norms, creating their own kind of alternative cultural and academic practice. Most of the BOB girls choose which norms they want to embrace; they succeed academically, but do not conform to the structures of behavior that are set into place by predominantly White staff and administrators who put forth ideals of school-sanctioned professionalism, or who are involved in marketing to the school's funders.

Importantly, one cannot equate Keisha or BOB's behavior with poverty, or with a poor or working-class identity. Rather, I argue that their discourse was often in overt competition with that of the school's. I went to Keisha's home to interview her mother, who is a soft-spoken, polite Caribbean woman. She invited me to sit on the couch in her tidy living room while we talked. While I do not discuss the myriad factors that signify one's social class standing in the United States here, Keisha's home life did not strike me as a particularly unstable or "hard living" situation. I went to the homes of students who were visibly in much harder living situations. Students who lived in Section 8 housing or in public housing projects were not always the school's biggest discipline problems.

BOB girls performed according to the school's norms when they chose to, and rejected the school's norms when they wanted to. Much like Bettie documents in her ethnography (2003), there are girls who perform a school-sanctioned version of femininity or class identity, and then there are those who create alternative symbolic economies where they earn and wear different "badges of dignity." They may have been rebelling against the way the school profiled them as not professional enough, not middle class enough, or not marketable enough. The school then chastised them by keeping them behind the curtain, overtly excluding them from public displays that functioned to support its spectacle.

In contrast to her sophomore year, during junior year Keisha's teachers saw a marked change in her behavior. She was quieter, more focused and disciplined, and she participated in class in school-sanctioned ways. School detention records for the spring semester of the 2009–10 school year show that between February and June she was written up once for cutting class, twelve times for violating the dress code, seven times for being late to school, and one time for leaving class or school without an excuse. Despite these write-ups, there was no more talk of her being involved in a gang, and, noticeably, none of her violations were for overt behavior issues like fighting or disrupting the educational process. She was no longer a major in-class discipline problem for her teachers. For this reason, Ms. Meehan wanted to invite her to reward her good behavior, and to give a chance to a student who had been oppositional to school norms and policies, but now seemed to buy into school norms.

As I mentioned in chapter 2, Mr. Thomas refused to invite Keisha to represent the school at the benefit (although an image of her face was used in College Prep's promotional film), saying that this event was too important and not the time to take a chance on a "potentially volatile" student. Despite the fact that Keisha seemed more adept at performing the school-sanctioned norms dictated by the spectacle, she had not successfully transcended her reputation. When I looked at the detention records for the other three junior girls who were chosen to go to the benefit, I noticed that the two who had originally been chosen, Sydney and Cassandra, had never been written up for a discipline violation, and Alita, who was asked to go instead of Keisha, had been written up four times for being late to school. In terms of uniform and punctuality, Mr. Thomas knew that there was no risk of these students putting funds for the school in jeopardy.

According to the New York City Department of Education's profile of College Prep, 62 percent of its students are eligible for free lunches and 16 percent are eligible for reduced-price lunches. More than half of the school's students, based solely on household income, are not middle class. Yet, those who can effectively perform "professionally" as if they are members of a middle-class status group are rewarded and put on display, while those who do not perform are not rewarded.

Ironically, the students chosen to represent the school at the benefit were the ones who could perform the school's version of middle-classness believably, regardless of their actual class status. These were students who could engage middle- or upper-class adults in polite conversation, and who would highlight positive experiences with the school. These students were adept at Standard English (or at code-switching into Standard English if it was not their primary dialect), were punctual, were involved in extracurricular activities, did their homework, did not get involved in physical or verbal altercations in or out of school, conformed to the dress code, and had relatively high GPAs. In other words, to be chosen to represent the school to outsiders, students are expected to blend seamlessly into corporate-class social settings; they are expected to "cover" (Goffman 1963; Yoshino 2006) those aspects of their identities that do not align with corporate-class norms. This is not to say that nonconformity is limited to students who are not middle class. Rather, those students who are picked to represent the school are the ones who choose to show that they can fluidly move between the "cash language" (Little 2003) of corporate-class America and their home discourse, whatever it may be.

Mr. Mitchell, a native New Yorker and the only African American member of the college office staff in 2009–10, shared with me in his interview that an African American female alumna who had been invited to represent students at the benefit when she was a junior told him that she resented the school's tendency to portray all the students as poor and Black or Brown. Although that might be the case for some students, it is certainly not the case for all students. She knew that portraying the students this way benefitted the school financially because of its dependence on private funding, but at the same time, she found it upsetting that she was expected to embody a stereotype that she didn't connect to. Students and staff are caught in a bind in relation to race, class, and political spectacle. In order to get the resources that College Prep depends on, school representatives must accentuate the image of College Prep that image makers think funders want to see—that is, middle-class and predominantly White teachers showing poor, working class, and predominantly Black and Brown urban students how to perform "professionalism" and rise above their economic circumstances and enter the middle class. Some students are instructed that they must cover (Goffman 1963; Yoshino 2006) to appear middle class and disguise their identities, language, and backgrounds, and therefore fit into corporate norms and pursue middle-class success. Other students who actually come from the middle class (although income is not the sole factor that determines one's social class, 22 percent of students do not qualify for free or reduced-price lunch) have to assume the opposite cover when representing the school in order to appear needy to the school's benefactors.

For the remainder of this chapter, I focus on three students who complicate both the mainstream media's and College Prep's discourse about needy, at-risk, urban, Black teenage girls. It is my hope that these case studies reveal the contradiction between the ways these students are constructed and exploited through the political spectacle supported both by College Prep and the mainstream media. Each case study begins with a poem on the theme "Raised By" that students wrote as an English class assignment. The students' words provide context for the discussion that follows.

Case Study: Destiny Jones

Destiny's "Raised By" Poem

I was brought up by
Slick talking
Neat freak
On time every day or you gon' get it
"Get the hell out of my house" kind of mother

Keeps to himself
Bob Marley
Redemption Song listening
Turn that foolishness you listening to off
Type father

The better get good grades
Go to school on time
Listen to your teachers
"Where that 60 come from?"
strict parents

From the "call the cops if you think you bad"
To the "I'm gon' tear your behind up!"
Threatening always, but their
Hearts are in the right place
Parents

Caribbean Proud
Fatty food cooking
Always trying to get me to eat right
And forever taunting
Parents

I am loved by my parents[2]

Destiny Jones is goal oriented and driven. She was my advisory student, as well as my English student as a sophomore. That year, she came on the trip that I chaperoned to Maine, and she also participated in my summer book club / cultural circle. As a junior, she participates in four extracurricular activities, including the school's dance company, which practices three days a week. The other three activities that she participates in are a university-based high school law institute, an internship at the Firm, and SAT prep. She told me that she was often at the school until 7:00 or 8:00 p.m. While she told me that she often stayed at school for activities, she also stayed to do work. She likes to stay at school, she says, because it helps her to get to know her teachers better and to build relationships with them. Destiny lives in Brownsville, Brooklyn, in a modest, immaculate apartment with her younger sister, her older brother, and her parents, Orwell and Maria Jones. Her parents met in New York but are from the Caribbean islands of St. Kitts and St. Lucia, respectively. Like its neighboring East New York, Brownsville is a predominantly African American neighborhood where the median annual household income is $20,839, compared to the national average of $56,604 (NeighborhoodLink 2010). Destiny and her siblings visit the Caribbean with their parents periodically. On an academic level, Destiny is confident, and she told me that she had wanted to be a lawyer since she was eight years old. She described herself as

> ambitious, like I know what I want, and I have known what I want since I was eight years old . . . I want to get my MBA, then go on to law school, and work hard to help my parents retire to the Caribbean 'cause that's what they want to do. They are pushing me. Everything they wanted to do they couldn't 'cause of me and my brother and my sister. I am gonna be the first one to go off to college. So when—my father already said if by the time I am seventeen and I don't know what I want to do—he is not going to support me, 'cause he is not here to waste time and money, especially living in New York and in this economy, he is not here to play games.

She told me that she came to College Prep not only because of its theme, but also because, back in the school's third year, students were required to write an essay about how their career aspirations related to that theme. Over the two years that I maintained a close relationship with Destiny as her teacher, she told me repeatedly that she loves to learn.

Destiny and Her Peers

In my advisory class, Destiny was a member of the clique who bought into school norms and were called "lames" by the clique who did not. When I asked her in an interview what the word *lame* meant, she said, shrugging: "it just means you study a lot—I consider myself a lame." Despite this classification, she has a close-knit group of friends. She likes the classes where she gets to work with her friends and do hands-on projects the best, like her physics class, where that day students had been allowed to go as a group into the hallway to conduct an experiment about waves using a slinky.

When I spoke about Destiny's experience at College Prep with her mother, Mrs. Jones, she called Destiny a "chatterbox," and did not seem to believe me when I said that I loved having Destiny in class. Destiny admits that when she is seated next to a group of her friends, specifically four other girls in her class, she has a hard time refraining from side conversations, and teachers have called home about this. Yet when I shadowed Destiny during her junior year, I sat next to her in most of her classes and at lunch, and I noticed that while she had what teachers would call "side conversations" in classes with her friends, all of these conversations were either about books (her favorites are the *Twilight* saga and the *Harry Potter* series) or about school. Destiny often spoke with her friends about how stressed she was about deadlines for assignments and papers. And although she has side conversations, she often finishes copying notes or doing classwork before most other students.

Even during lunch, the time when most students play games, listen to music on their phones, or socialize, as soon as Destiny sat down with the peanut butter and jelly sandwich she got from the lunch line, she took out her math homework and worked on this through the period. Her friend Tameka did the same thing, working on homework for another class. At one point, I noted that Tameka asked Destiny if she wanted to copy her math homework when they thought I was not listening. Destiny shook her head. "I'm not going to just copy it if I don't understand it," she said. This demonstrates her drive and work ethic (although her decision may have been influenced by my presence). While her core group of friends is important to her and she enjoys them, she told me in our debrief interview that many of her friends are not her greatest social support:

DESTINY: When I tell my friends things I want to do, they look at me like I am crazy.

AB: Really? Carmen and Tameka look at you like you're crazy?

DESTINY: Yeah. 'Cause the years that I want to spend in school, like they just want to do their four years and be done, and I can't do that, 'cause I won't feel that that satisfies me.

I asked her whether she felt that she was the minority in school in terms of her dreams or goals, or whether she saw a lot of students around her who shared her ideals of the future. Her answer is telling: "They share the same vision," she said, "but they want to do all the shortcuts, and to get where you want to go, there is no shortcut the way I see it." Destiny believes working hard will lead her to accomplish her goals. While she has fun with her peers and notices that many of them have the same goals that she does, she prides herself on consistently doing the work that will lead her to accomplish her vision.

Destiny and Her Family

When I was Destiny's advisor, it was my job to call all advisory students' homes every three weeks after they received progress reports or report cards and to report their grades to their parents. Ideally, students were already supposed to have shown their grades to their parents, but this was not always the case. Although Destiny was usually an A student, in February she received a D in biology on her progress report. I called her home in the middle of the day on a Thursday. Mrs. Jones picked up. When I reported the news, her mother lost her initial politeness. Her voice raised, she said, "Destiny does not get Ds on her progress report! Where is she now?" When I said that Destiny was in class, she demanded that I pull Destiny out of class immediately and put her on the phone so that she could speak to her. I looked up Destiny's schedule and found her in American History. I brought her down to the teachers' office, telling her on the way that I had just spoken to her mother regarding her D, and that her mother wanted to speak with her. When Destiny got on the phone, she was mostly quiet. Her mother did the talking. Destiny knew better than to try to make excuses, and as she "uh-huh"-ed, and "okay"-ed her way through her mother's angry words, it was apparent to me that Destiny would be pulling her grade up quickly.

Mr. Jones attended school in St. Kitts and technical college where he studied carpentry until he came to New York in 1987 when he was 19. Mrs. Jones dropped out of school after sixth grade. Destiny's father applied for a visa for Destiny and her sister, who attends a public elementary school, and her brother, who attends another public high school (not College Prep). Mrs. Jones does not work, but takes care of the family's needs at home. Mr. Jones works in construction. He drops off and picks up Destiny at the school, including for field trips and extracurricular activities, and he attends open school nights. Mrs. Jones takes calls from the school, and made it clear to me when I spoke with her throughout Destiny's tenth-grade year that she most appreciated the teachers who called home frequently about Destiny's behavior and progress in their classes.

Although her parents are content that their children were born in the United States and attend U.S. schools, they are concerned about the education that U.S. students get compared to students in the Caribbean. While the opportunities to attend college are greater here, they told me, schools in the Caribbean are stricter and can use corporal punishment and enforce a strict uniform policy. Mr. Jones told me that while he felt that educational standards were higher in the Caribbean, there were more opportunities in the United States.

Destiny speaks often about what she is reading, or what books she buys. This habit is supported by her father, who she says, every week "puts a bunch of books on [her] bed, like 'read this' and 'read that.'" She speaks proudly of the books that her father owns, including those by important Black radicals like Angela Davis, George Jackson, and Eldridge Cleaver. She tells me that he often gives her books that she does not feel she is ready for (such as Nelson Mandela's autobiography), but that she appreciates the challenge. She says that she wants to push herself to keep reading higher-level books, and that even though her parents try to enforce a 9:00 p.m. bedtime and allow no television after school, she often stays up until 1:00, 2:00, or 3:00 a.m. in her room doing homework or reading on her own.

Destiny makes it clear as she talks about her family that their example is what supports her ambition:

> In the Caribbean, they get out of school at sixteen, and some don't go back to school till they are like nineteen, and I don't want that for myself, and I don't want that for my family. My mother, she

lost her mother at nine years old, and so her grandmother raised her and she [my mother] couldn't finish school because she had to help take care of her family. And my father, he went to college in the Caribbean so to come here, he would have to go through the whole process over to get a degree and everything. And plus, he always, every day, he reminds me and my brother that after high school, you have two choices, college or a minimum wage job, and I don't want to work at no fast food restaurant. So my thing is, and I tell everybody, there is a difference between having a job and having a career. A job is only temporary, and a career is something that you can see yourself doing forever. So I want a career.

Destiny's parents are a primary reason for her determination and motivation. Through a combination of discipline and encouragement for career goals and the pursuit of knowledge, they support Destiny's dreams of educational and economic upward mobility.

Destiny and Her Teachers

In addition to drawing motivation from her parents, Destiny draws motivation from her teachers' commitment to her education:

We have tutoring like four days a week and I really need help with my math, and sometimes in physics, like she gives us formulas that I don't understand, I like sit in the back and I don't really pay attention or focus very easily, so I'll go to school like Thursdays or Tuesdays, and like, I'll be there for like an hour or two. I think it was last week, I had dance practice, and that finished at 5:00, and then they still had Global History tutoring, so I went there, and I left at 6:00. That shows that teachers are committed to doing what they are here to do, and that is to help us. And sometimes they will get upset when students don't show up to tutoring—like I would think that they are happy to go home early, but no!

Because her teachers are willing to stay, Destiny stays. Rather than getting frustrated and giving up in classes where she needs more help, she puts extra time into those classes in order to do better. While she expresses that her teachers make their support clear, she is critical of teachers' age. Because most of the teachers are young, she explained to me, many of them act more like students' friends than students' teachers. She elaborated:

> Freshmen and sophomore year, like some teachers try to act like they are best friends to the students and then when they fail the students, the students get upset. And it's so funny 'cause like they start cursing out the teachers, and then the teachers get so upset, like, you shouldn't have befriended the students, like you are here to work, so work! Like the first year, our advisory had a big, huge problem, like worse than this year, because the teacher tried to befriend some of them, and then when half of us would speak out against it, they would get kicked out. It was very divided.

Destiny says she appreciates teachers who do not try to befriend students. She explains:

> Ms. Barton does not play—she really doesn't, especially because every day I come to her class, she reminds us that we are applying for college next year, and that college is really important if we want to make something of our lives. A lot of people don't like her because they think she is really sarcastic, but she pushes you to do what you wanna do. If you go to other schools, you don't have teachers like that—she believes in us, and she doesn't let us take advantage of ourselves. 'Cause she knows—I wrote two papers, and one was based on the Holocaust and I went deep with that paper. And then we did another paper, I forgot what it was, and I was lazy, I did not want to do it, so I just wrote two pages, and the assignment was to write four pages, and then she wrote on my paper, 'don't be lazy,' 'cause she knows about my writing ability.

Destiny appreciates teachers who connect with her academically first, as opposed to personally or socially. Her priority in school is learning and developing a solid foundation for her career. Teachers who show her that they believe in her through expecting disciplined work and pushing her are the teachers she most admires and respects, as opposed to those she gets along with on a personal level.

Destiny is so self-motivated and is so strongly supported by her family that she feeds off teachers who push her to achieve academically. Destiny does not often get into trouble with teachers at school. Although she was written up a total of thirty-six times for disciplinary infractions during the 2009–10 school year, twenty-one of them were for being late to school and fifteen were for violations of the school's dress code. She puts a great deal of effort into her schooling, because she believes that school is a worthwhile investment in her future and assurance of a successful career.

Destiny and Her Aspirations

Destiny has big goals. Becoming a lawyer is the last step in what she envisions as years of school for herself. At the beginning of her junior year, when I spoke with her, she informed me (and her parents when I was at their house for the interview) that she wants to have five majors in college. Her father remained quiet, but her mother's jaw dropped.

> DESTINY: [I want] to go for prelaw, for child development and
> psychology, business administration and management,
> history . . .
> MRS. JONES: How many . . . um . . . how many things you taking
> like that?
> DESTINY: It's like five.
> MR. JONES: I thought you was going for law only?
> DESTINY: No . . .
> AB: You are gonna be busy, Destiny! Five majors!
> MR. JONES: Destiny is taking five majors! I thought it was one she
> was going for, and she is going for five!
> DESTINY: But they all pique my interest, so I want to try all of
> them!
> MR. JONES: But that might be different later.
> AB: It's true, a lot of freshmen come in as one major and then
> totally change.
> MR. JONES: Yeah.
> DESTINY: That's why I have five.
> MR. JONES: Yeah, they change.

Later in her junior year, when I shadowed and interviewed her, she had reduced her goal of five majors to three. She said that she wanted to go to either NYU or Howard. She informed me that she plans on triple-majoring in psychology, child development, and business administration, and still going for her MBA. Although she is nervous about her financial situation, especially if she goes to NYU (which she tells me costs $56,000 per year), she is determined that she will achieve her educational goals somehow. Thus far at College Prep, she has not wavered from her path.

Conclusions: Destiny

Destiny told me that she didn't think that professionalism at College Prep would prepare her for college, although she thought that it might prepare her for job interviews. While she expresses a critique of College Prep professionalism, saying that it's "over the top," she buys into the school's mission of college matriculation for all students. Her daily decisions and demeanor at the school show that she buys into the school's discipline policies as well. She sees herself as someday becoming the sole source of support for her parents, and also of attaining upward class mobility: that is, of being the one who will work her way into achieving the American dream as her parents imagine it. She tells me that she sees freshmen and sophomores who don't take their work seriously, and this concerns her because they don't know how important it is for their future. Because her career goal of being a lawyer seems attainable to her, she sees admission to a good college as a necessary step along the way, one that College Prep promises to help her accomplish if she keeps her part of the bargain, working hard and embracing professionalism. She is adept setting goals that fit in with the meritocratic narrative of the spectacle, but at the same time, her nuanced and complex identity and the strong social support she gets from her parents negate another facet of the spectacle: the idea of her needing to be "saved" by College Prep.

Case Study: Carmen Fletcher

Carmen's "Raised By" Poem

I was raised by a shopper
Always worrying 'bout my grades, loves the computer

"Pour me some ginger ale"
Mother

I was raised by a Black,
Young, sleeps and eats,
College worryin', "your
Report card ain't bad—
Just that grade," lovin'
Mother

I was raised by a listener
True friend, crazy, funny
"Don't make me have to come to your school" "Carmen I love
You, bestie"
Mother

Carmen is a close friend of Destiny's. Like Destiny, Carmen was a student in my English class and was also in my advisory. She came on the trip that I chaperoned to Maine, and participated in my summer book club / cultural circle. During the year that Carmen was in my advisory, I developed a close relationship with her mother, Jessica Fletcher, because I called home frequently to discuss Carmen's progress in her classes. Her mother later told me that she loved having my number on speed dial for the year. She took advantage of being able to contact me, frequently getting in touch with me for Carmen's whereabouts after school, or for whether Carmen had homework in my English class. My close relationship with Carmen's mother paid off, I believe, in my relationship with Carmen, who often confided in me about issues that she was having with other students or teachers.

Carmen is a self-professed "natural-born flirt." Demonstrating this, Carmen told me about the "drama" she was dealing with when she tried to remain "Facebook friends" with her ex-boyfriend, whose new girlfriend did not want Carmen and him to talk. She also shared with me that she was romantically interested in a freshman girl whom her best friend, Tracy, was also interested in. Carmen swore to me (and to Tracy, who was talking with us), that she wasn't trying to flirt with the freshman girl, but that the girl "just started kissing her" in front of Tracy as they walked down the stairs to catch the subway one Wednesday evening.

Hearing this story, Tracy laughed, and said, "It's true, everybody finds a way to kiss her!"

Carmen also has a very serious side. Profoundly affected by pain and suffering, whether other people's or her own, she had many difficult challenges to contend with in her two years at the school, and outwardly expressed this through talk and action. When an old friend from her neighborhood was killed in a shooting, she taped his picture to her binder and carried it for weeks. Her father died suddenly at the beginning of her junior year, and she wore a button with a picture of his face to school for days afterward in his memory. She described to me that one of her most frustrating memories of College Prep was the year before in advisory, when we were planning a trip to volunteer together at a soup kitchen for people who are HIV positive. There were three members of the class who refused to go because they didn't want to catch HIV from touching or feeding people there. Despite my explanations and other students' explanations about the ways you can and cannot catch HIV, these students still refused to attend the trip. Carmen became extremely frustrated at these students' ignorance, especially because, she told the class and emphasized to me later, she and her mother were the primary caretakers of her aunt who had died of AIDS. Not only were those students not in danger of catching the virus from working at the soup kitchen, they were giving up a chance to do important work in the city. Carmen found this inexcusable.

Carmen came to New York City, and to College Prep, from Virginia at the end of her freshman year. Ms. Fletcher's stories about why Carmen ended up at College Prep differed from Carmen's. While Carmen said that when she moved to New York, there were no other schools that would take her, because they were all full, so she had to go to College Prep, her mother told a different story. "I said, 'you are going to be a lawyer, you just don't know it yet'; I did my research," she told me. She wanted Carmen to attend College Prep, because she had read that the school had good graduation and college matriculation rates and a rigorous curriculum. She met with Ms. Franklin, the school social worker, who she said "took pity on her" and admitted Carmen to the school. Ms. Fletcher was even more impressed when the school asked Carmen to come for an interview with the school social worker and with the principal.

Carmen lives with her mother, who is a single parent, two younger brothers, and two younger sisters in a relatively small apartment in East New York, Brooklyn. This is a predominantly African American neighborhood where the median annual household income is $24,163, well below the national average (NeighborhoodLink 2010). Her mother told me that she was hard on Carmen because "I was a teenage mother. I had her when I was seventeen, you know what I mean, so there is a lot of things that I didn't accomplish, and a lot more that I want to accomplish, and if I can help it, if it kills me, she is not going to be that statistic." Originally from Queens, her mother told me that after Carmen was born, she stayed in high school and tried to finish. But she got pregnant again, and had another baby at the beginning of her senior year. Then, in November of that year, her father died (her mother had passed away when she was a year old). At this point, saddled with the responsibility of her late father's finances (her five brothers, she said, insisted that she take charge), as well as a toddler and a baby, she gave up on high school. This, she explained to me, was why she insisted on being such a strong female presence in her daughter's life, and on pushing her to succeed academically.

Carmen and Her Peers

Carmen involves herself in as many extracurricular activities as she can (in her mother's words, "She joins everything that will get her out of this house"), which leads her to make close female friends. Her junior year, she was involved in an after-school Community Service Initiative, facilitated by Ms. Meehan,[3] where students participated in after-school community service projects (there is also a school-wide community service initiative that sends students every Thursday during school hours to do community service work). Her sophomore year, she was closely involved in the school's music ensemble, which practiced twice a week, went on several field trips, and performed a number of times. In music ensemble, she became closer with Tracy, who is a grade below Carmen at school. By Carmen's junior year, the two were best friends. Carmen is also close with Destiny Jones, and with three other girls in her class.

When I interviewed Carmen after school, she asked if her best friend Tracy could come along for the conversation. I agreed, and the three of us walked to a nearby café. This interview was the most girl-talk-like conversation out of the eight student-shadowing debrief interviews. While Carmen is often quiet in her classes, occasionally engaging in whispered conversations with her close girlfriends, the conversation during the interview moved quickly without much inhibition on the part of the girls.

The conversation was about who was dating whom (Tracy wanted to date the freshman girl who had kissed Carmen; Carmen had a boyfriend who didn't go to College Prep), and who has a crush on whom (both girls confessed crushes on male teachers), but the girls also talked about what they had fun doing in school (trips and talent shows were among their top choices, as was moot court in Constitutional Law class), what their hopes for the future were (Tracy wanted to be a cosmetologist, and Carmen, much to her mother's chagrin, wanted to be a chef, not a lawyer), concern about teachers at the school seeming too stressed out and letting disrespectful students get to them, and how they saw gender, as well as race, functioning at the school and in the outside world (they told me that they had more fun in classes taught by male teachers, and didn't think teacher race mattered, but that they did notice that White people tended to take silly things way too seriously).

During our conversation, I noted how the girls talked about taking care of one another. I remember that during Tracy's freshman year at the school, many teachers saw her as a strong student and a social leader. Yet during her sophomore year, I overheard teachers talking about her cutting class and about her grades going downhill. I went to Carmen's house at the beginning of that year to interview her mother, and spoke with Carmen about what was going on with Tracy. Carmen told me that she was going to try to look out for Tracy, and was worried that she was "falling off." When I interviewed the girls in the spring of that year, I noted that Carmen continued to look out for Tracy and make sure that she excelled in school, even getting on the train at her own stop, then getting off at Rockaway (Tracy's stop) to pick Tracy up, and getting back on the train to go to school. Carmen stated, "I try to help her, like she had a good start, and then when I stopped picking her up from school she fell back down."

Tracy told me in our interview that she would describe Carmen as both ambitious and fun: she wants to do a lot of things, and she'll try anything. Yet clearly, there is more to their close friendship than that. Carmen values being a caretaker and giving support to those whom she loves.

Carmen and Her Family

When I interviewed Carmen's mother, she spoke with me at great length about how concerned she was about Carmen's younger brother, Malik.

Malik, she said, "gets entwined in . . . this little [housing] project over here, he wants to hang out with the boys over there." Although he was a freshman, he was already almost six feet tall. Ms. Fletcher told me that the year before, when he attended the neighborhood middle school, he had issues with the school's discipline systems. He was suspended five times for arguing with teachers. She expresses her frustration that the assistant principal of the school refused to work with her as a fellow community member to find an alternative to suspending Malik from learning as a punishment.

Ms. Fletcher wishes that she and her family lived in a community that better met their needs. She complains that no one even cares enough to organize a block party; when she grew up in Springfield Gardens, Queens, during the 1980s, children had respect for their elders.

> We all came together on the block—everyone—it's "Hi, Mr.
> So-and-So and Mrs. So-and-So." "Can So-and-So come out please,
> Mr. So-and-So?" Where around here, it's like, they'll see this older
> lady, and instead of calling her Ms. So-and-So, it's "Hi, Cookie!"
> And if they don't have that bond in the community, then they are
> not gonna get that, they are not gonna get the respect . . . the way
> I was raised, is the way I am raising my kids. They need to have
> respect for everyone, everyone, I don't care if it's the derelict on
> the corner who's got his dirty hands out begging for money, you
> understand, that you see him, it's "Good morning, how are you,"
> you know what I mean, someone speaks to you, you speak back to
> them, don't walk around with your head up in the clouds, it's all
> about respect, you know, and without that, these kids are doomed.
> These kids are doomed, and that goes anywhere, in school, at
> work, that's gonna be messed up, and so that's why I say, God bless
> my son Malik, because he is in his own world, and like I said, I am
> gonna do what I have to do if it kills me to keep him out these
> streets.

She told me that the only time the community comes together is around death; she spoke about the shootings of two young men in the neighborhood. This, she said, brought everyone together, but she also told me, "This community is not a community." She turned to Carmen and asked: "Is this a community around here, Carmen? Is there anything that they ever came together on around here that you can see? Besides if somebody get shot and die?" Carmen shook her head.

While Ms. Fletcher fears that she is losing her son to a community and to schools that don't have his best interest at heart, she has confidence in the ways both she and College Prep support Carmen. She told me that she gives College Prep "two thumbs up" because she feels that the staff does its best to reach out to her, and to challenge her daughter academically. The school's regular contact with her, she says, is more important than college matriculation. She says that she is a "very involved parent," and that she tries to get Carmen as engaged in community issues as possible, especially those that are designed to support women, like fund-raising for and participating in the breast cancer walk. She said:

> I try to keep her involved also 'cause I want her to see the seriousness
> of what's going on, you know, how bad women have it as a whole,
> it's not easy for us, it's not easy. It's more than walking around,
> being cute, and all the boys tell you how cute you are, it's more
> than that, you know, be active, it's more than what you do, you
> know, be mature about what you do.

She tries to be the female presence in Carmen's life that she didn't have in her own; she told me that if she had had more of a female presence in her life as a child, then she wouldn't have been a teenage mother.

Although she dropped out of high school with the arrival of her second child and her father's death, she got her GED after the father of Carmen's siblings left (Carmen has a different father). During Carmen's sophomore year, Ms. Fletcher worked full-time at a call center, but by the beginning of Carmen's junior year, she had lost the job and said that she was actively looking for something else. She consistently tries to reinforce the importance of education with all of her children, and uses herself as an example of why it is so essential to get a good education while one is young.

It is clear that Carmen respects and follows her mother's wishes in many ways. Through interactions with her peers and with teachers, and through her extracurricular and community involvement, she internalizes many of the values that her mother tries to teach her through words and action.

Carmen and Her Teachers

While Carmen maintains good relationships with the majority of her teachers, grades in her subject area classes often don't reflect these relationships. Carmen rarely gets into trouble at school; discipline records show that in the 2009–10 school year, she was written up for detentions a total of fifteen times, eight for lateness, five for dress code violations, one for verbally rude or disrespectful behavior, and one for disrupting the educational process. She is rarely the source of a disruption or discipline problem in class, but her mother explained: "She always seems to find a reason for not finishing the projects." At the end of her junior year, she had an average of 65 percent in all of her subject area classes, and during her sophomore year, I kept records of five phone calls that I made to her mother about grades that were below 70 percent in major subjects.

Because Carmen tends to blend in, teachers do not often target her as a student who is in need of extra help or who could do better if pushed. On the day that I shadowed her, I noticed that she spoke very quietly in class and that she raised her hand infrequently. She takes notes and pair-shares with her partners when asked, and she is prepared for class. Yet, she finds a way of slipping under the radar at College Prep, because she does not stand out for her academic weaknesses and resistant behavior nor for her academic strengths and disciplined behavior (as Destiny does). This is in direct correlation to Fordham's analysis of how young Black women are compelled to silence (1993); Carmen "gets by," and by most teachers' standards is "professional," but her transcript will not stand out in a competitive atmosphere beyond College Prep.

Carmen seems to work the hardest in classes where she is motivated by the topic and gets a lot of personal attention. She did well in her tenth-grade Social Studies class (85 percent average) and in her ninth-grade Science class (98 percent average), both of which she told me she enjoyed because of the content and her relationships with the teachers. She told me that Mr. Gonzaga, the science teacher, was her favorite teacher that year. "He's mad cool," she said. She elaborated:

> I get more help in Mr. Gonzaga's room than I do in Ms. Elliott's room. Like I get help there, but it's like Mr. Gonzaga will sit there and spend time with you until you get your work done, and Ms. Elliott has too many students, she has to walk around all the time.

> Mr. Gonzaga will walk around, but he makes sure that everybody gets help . . . like today in class, I was so confused in class today, about that whole balancing equations thing, but he helped me and now I somewhat understand it.

Sitting in Mr. Gonzaga's class with Carmen, I noticed that he approached her individually and explained how to solve an equation that she didn't understand. He told her at the end that she was "on the right track, but just needed to trust [herself] a little more." He reinforced her both personally and academically in this interaction; I could see why she classified him as "mad cool." I noticed the same pattern for each junior whom I shadowed in his class; he has a way of making sure that students who need extra guidance get the help and individual attention that they need. Students like Carmen, who may not display their need of help as openly as students like Destiny, thrive from more personal relationships with teachers.

It is telling to me that one of Carmen's best memories from College Prep was a field trip that we took as an advisory to Fordham University's Bronx campus. She told me that not only did she have fun "acting a fool" with her friends when they went on a campus scavenger hunt and had to interview some students (asking "college boys" the assigned interview questions about their academic and social experience was quite entertaining for her), but she also had the best time because "everybody was getting along." Carmen is a student who, although sometimes shy, learns best in settings where she is supported socially as well as academically. When I asked her over the summer to describe herself, she told me, "I am smart, and willing to learn at times; [it] depends on who [is teaching me]." Here we see the importance of giving students the opportunity to build more personal relationships with teachers. Although this may not be necessary for all students (for example, Destiny explicitly said that she does not need this: she prefers teachers who just "do their job"), there are some teachers whom Carmen learns from better than others. This is directly dependent on her relationships with them.

Carmen and Her Aspirations

When I asked Carmen how she viewed success for herself, she told me that she saw herself working in a restaurant, married, with a family.

Throughout the summer, and in our debrief interview after I shadowed her, she gave me detailed descriptions of the delectable meals that she cooked for her family and friends, and spoke about how much fun she had being creative in the kitchen. She told me that she appreciated the extracurricular and summer opportunities that the school offered. She wanted to go to college and major in culinary arts, and she was looking for a summer opportunity that had to do with this. She shared that she often felt bored in her classes. Yet this did not deter her from her excitement about college: she had just been on the school's over-night college trip, and told me that her favorite school was St. John Fisher.

Conclusions: Carmen

Carmen's overall life goal does not necessarily require a college degree, but because both her mother and College Prep push college as a non-negotiable, she sees college as one aspect of her future. Her mother's concern about her brother, Malik, as well as College Prep's push to op-portunities and college encourage her to take advantage of conventional possibilities for her future. While her mother's dream for her may be law, Carmen expresses that she has power over her own aspirations and dreams for herself. By only partially "buying into" what College Prep "sells," in other words, enacting her own critique of the narrative of college-for-all that is implied in the spectacle, she is skeptical about any future other than the one that she envisions.

Carmen's case study challenges young, Black, urban women's role in the spectacle in different ways from Destiny's. Ms. Fletcher, a single mother who had Carmen as a teenager, is a positive role model in Car-men's life who models community engagement and self-respect. Addi-tionally, while Carmen has experienced and internalized a great deal of trauma involving her loved ones, these experiences do not manifest in outwardly destructive ways. She has positive relationships both with her peers and her teachers, even though academically she slips under the radar at College Prep. The ethic of caring that Carmen demonstrates for her friends translates into what she needs from her teachers: she thrives from learning as a humanizing experience. Carmen's statements and demonstrations about how she learns best also trouble pedagogical meth-ods that rely on ostensibly impartial standards or scripted teaching; her case shows that teaching and learning are personal and intimate experiences, as opposed to an objective ones.

Case Study: Princess Smith

Princess's "Raised By" Poem

I was raised
By popping chicken
Grease on a Sunday
Morning, rice and
Beans, and from a
Screaming mom
Saying "hurry up
It's dinner time!"

I was raised
by morning cartoons
watching Barney
I love when he said
"I love you, you love
me."

I was raised in
"Spanish town," where all you
hear is people hollering
"¿hola, cómo está?"

I was raised by
Combs, brushes, wash
And blow dry every 2
Weeks, hot combs
Sizzling into my
Thick hair . . .

Princess is an attentive and hardworking student who has a love of pop culture, but at the same time incorporates her emerging identity politics into much of her schoolwork and actions. While she identifies ethnically as a "mixture, Indian with coarse hair," and is of Caribbean descent, one of her proudest moments as a College Prep student, she told me, was when she performed a poem that she wrote in my English class, "Black Girls." The poem is a critique of how Black women are portrayed in mainstream media, and Princess performed for a large student and staff audience at an after-school poetry slam. At first, Princess was only willing to recite the first lines of the poem: "Black girls / Shakin' what they momma gave them," in our class's poetry celebration. I had originally attributed this to shyness, but when I asked her about it in a follow-up interview two years later, she told me, "I wasn't shy; those kids in my class, I didn't think they deserved to hear my poem." At the poetry slam she said that her friends gave her the courage to get up in front of everyone and perform the poem in its entirety. "When I performed 'Black Girls,'" she said, "I wasn't really going to perform it, and it was getting to the end, but then, somebody gave me the courage . . . so many people were like 'do it!'"

When Princess got on the stage, she waited and waited, but there were some students who weren't paying attention. Most of these students, she noticed, were the popular girls who identified themselves as BOB. She stood up straight, took the microphone, and commanded "Hey BOB! Yeah, I see you. Listen up!" Staff and students laughed in nervous surprise; everyone knew how controversial it was at College Prep to even acknowledge the existence of BOB. Teachers were warned before the school year started by the deans of discipline to alert them immediately if we heard any mention at all of BOB, because, we were told, they were a "gang." Meanwhile, the girls who had been associated with BOB in the past all swore that the days of calling their clique "BOB" were over. Mentioning the acronym was close to sacrilege as far as the administration was concerned, and students and teachers knew this. Through her action in the slam, Princess demonstrated courage and self-assuredness in the face of her female peers, who were often seen as popular by students, and as bullies by staff; she also demonstrated that she had no fear of repercussions by staff, because she brought mention of the term from the margins to the center of school discourse at that moment.

Princess maintains an 85 percent average in her subject area classes, and is strongly supported both socially and academically at the school by her mother, Ms. Smith, who is heavily involved in the school's Parent Teacher Association. Ms. Smith maintains close relationships with Principal McCarren, as well as with Princess's teachers. Princess lives with her mother in Ridgewood, Queens, which is a predominantly Latino and White neighborhood. The median household income is $46,096 (NeighborhoodLink 2010), which represents a marked difference from the communities where Carmen and Destiny live.

Princess and Her Peers

Princess is close friends with Desiree Sutherland, who was only an occasional participant in the summer book club / cultural circle (which I discuss in the following chapter) because of a conflict with a summer program she participated in at Georgetown University. The two often socialize outside of school. Besides Desiree, Princess has a wide circle of friends in her class, both male and female. Despite this wide circle of friends, she is the kind of student who takes care of business in her classes before she is concerned about socializing. In fact, when I observed her in class, she rarely engaged in any side conversations, and often chose to engage academically with teachers, yet she managed, as far as I could tell, not to compromise relationships with her peers. Even when working in small, less-supervised peer groups, Princess typically made sure that work got done. In Ms. Elliott's class, for example, while students were supposed to be working in small groups on reading a literary critique of a novel, Princess voiced her resistance to the task, saying "This is boring" and "I don't want to do this, do you?" but she also offered her own summary of the first paragraph of the essay when her group didn't understand it ("I understand it—he's just giving background here"). The three girls assigned to her group then followed her lead and helped to interpret the essay as well.

At times, Princess expressed that she experienced some feelings of alienation from peers. Students related stories of calling Black teachers "White" or "oreo" because of the way they talk. The following conversation occurred in a summer book club meeting where we talked about the meaning of "Whiteness" and "Blackness" as it relates to teachers:

PRINCESS: They say I talk like a White girl. I don't care.
AB: What does that mean?
CARMEN: 'Cause White must mean . . . proper. And that's kind of a shame, if you think White is proper, then that makes Black . . .

DESTINY: And proper is more like etiquette and stuff like that.

PRINCESS: And that's good, you got manners, and I'm sorry, but my mommy raised me to . . .

AB: And that's not "White."

PRINCESS: Look at Obama! That's like being a person with manners.

DESTINY: I want to talk like that, and have public speaking and debating skills.

Princess is a relatively high-achieving student who has the reputation of being intelligent, a hard worker, and a good listener; she has many friends and maintains her standing in the context of the school's peer group structure, which, students tell me, in their class, doesn't really have set cliques (with the exception of BOB), but does have a word for the category of "lames" (also see Destiny's case study, above). "Whoever calls me a lame, they're a lame themselves, 'cause that word is lame," Princess asserted. She is a proud academic achiever who sees herself as successful beyond the labels that her peers might put on her at times and who sees herself as a developing leader.

Princess and Her Family

Princess's mother, Ms. Smith, is a common presence at College Prep. She preferred to be interviewed at the school, even though I offered to come to her home or to meet her at another location. When I thanked her for coming, especially since she wasn't in the neighborhood anyway, she shrugged. "It's my day off, and I like to keep my promises," she said, "that's why I'm here." But there was another reason why she chose to come to the school: she told me that she made sure that Princess's teachers knew who Princess's mother was. "If [parents] are always in there participating, if teachers always see them there, I think teachers give [students] a little more respect . . . and at the end of the day, teachers have the upper hand with my kids' education," she told me.

While all the students in my cultural circle had parents who were loving and supportive of their education, for Ms. Smith, this manifested in participating as much as possible in meetings and parent organizations at the school. She always attended the monthly meetings of the PTA

(I attended a PTA meeting where Ms. Smith was one of only eight mothers there), even though, she told me, at times Princess said that she was "too involved," and that other mothers were not as involved. When she heard this from Princess, Ms. Smith told me, she reminded her that this had always been the case—even when Princess and her two sisters were in elementary and middle school, she always went to the school activities, and when it was her children's birthday, she always took the day off. After she shared this with me, she told me that although Princess might complain, her middle daughter, one of Princess's older sisters, recently said to her, "Mom, you know what? I had a good childhood." Ms. Smith knows that although her children might express resentment at her involvement when they are teenagers, being a present and involved parent is of immeasurable value, especially when it comes to her children's education. She feels that every parent should be as involved as they can in order to demonstrate that they care.

Ms. Smith spent her childhood between Belize and New York City, where she attended mostly private Catholic schools. Contrasting her experience to Princess's, she told me that while she was impressed with College Prep, she felt that when she was in school, teaching and learning were much more "thorough." She looks over Princess's work frequently and wonders why teachers frequently give a grade without correcting all the grammatical mistakes. She wonders why teachers don't teach cursive or penmanship anymore, and she notices that everything seems rushed. Teachers seem too pressured, she said, to stick to a rote curriculum and timeline to prepare for tests, and she wonders what gets lost. She also notices that class sizes are much larger than when she was in school. This too, she said, takes away from much of the individual attention that students need. Another huge difference, she told me, between her own history of schooling and her daughter's was the push for college. "Before, we were pushed just to finish high school," she said. "It's not that anymore. It's your bachelor's and your master's. I heard a lady tell her daughter when Princess and I were doing a college visit, 'my job don't even look at associate's . . . you better go straight for your bachelor's and your master's.'"

Ms. Smith sees the truth in this at her own job as a counselor at Administration for Child Services (ACS) in New York City. When she got the job twenty years ago, she had only a high school diploma. All of her training was on the job. But now, she said, a bachelor's and sometimes a master's degree are required for new hires.

Because of the importance of a college education, she says, it's essential to prepare students for the SAT and for college starting from when they are very young. Here, too, she worries about the education that Princess is getting; she's aware that the school didn't do explicit SAT prep until Princess's junior year. This, she said, is too late to start. She is especially attuned to the fact that other schools that serve populations of more privilege start to prepare students much earlier, and that parents of more privilege can afford to pay for private SAT prep programs, like Kaplan. She worries about students, including her daughter, getting left behind through less preparation.

It is clear that Princess learns many lessons from her mother's work at ACS, and that this shapes the way in which she interprets problems that she sees or reads about in the world around her. As we discussed Sapphire's book *Push* (1996) in our cultural circle / book club (see chapter 6), Princess attributed Precious's mother's abuse to her background, in contrast to Destiny's analysis. Ms. Caldwell is a White staff member who elected to participate in some of our cultural circle meetings.

> DESTINY: I think, her father is sick and her mother is sick. Her mother is very sick and she is not doing nothing to stop it, I don't care if that's your husband, that's your daughter, you pushed her out, he didn't, and for her to let him do that to her, and then, to have let her do something disgusting to you, that to me, is even worse.
>
> MS CALDWELL: Yeah, I don't think I have a good—I was trying to put myself like a little bit in the mom's shoes to even be like begin to think like what's going through her head.
>
> PRINCESS: She probably wasn't loved when she was a child, the mother, and she's just, you know, giving her daughter the same treatment she was when she was little.

This is just one example of Princess's inclination to try to see the bigger picture behind people's actions, whether hurtful or helpful to those around them. This is a mind-set that she may have picked up from her mother and the stories that she brings home about children who are between homes or in the care of the system.

While Princess has a solid relationship with her mother, she has no relationship with her father, for whom she composed an elegy during the poetry unit in our English class. Based on what she wrote, he was present when she was a child, and then left her life with little explanation. She wrote in the poem, "I take away your name, Daddy . . . / you don't deserve to be called Daddy no more / Even though you're not gone / you're gone to me." While Princess's relationship (or lack thereof) with her father clearly causes her a great deal of pain, her mother does her best to be a meaningful and stable presence in her life.

Princess and Her Teachers

Although Princess, like Carmen, says that when she enters the school building she "count[s] down until she gets to go home," the effort that she puts into her academic work and her good relationships with her teachers reveal that her experience at College Prep is positive. Like Destiny, Princess was written up a significant number of times for disciplinary infractions (thirty-eight), but none of these infractions were a result of being directly oppositional to teachers or classmates; thirty-seven were for being late, and one was for coming to school out of dress code.

Princess played the role of a sort of cultural interpreter for Ms. Caldwell when she didn't understand references to popular or African American culture that students made in the book club. For example, when Princess made a reference to the TV show *Good Times*, Ms. Caldwell asked, "What's a 'good time'?" Princess gave Ms. Caldwell some background on the show, and while she was in a state of disbelief that Ms. Caldwell had never heard of *Good Times*, she was patient in her explanation and seemed glad to teach. The same thing happened as students discussed the upcoming *Precious* movie. Students said that Mo'Nique was going to be in the movie. Ms. Caldwell asked who Mo'Nique was, and again, Princess was the one who patiently explained where Ms. Caldwell might have seen Mo'Nique before.

Princess told me that sometimes the assignments that teachers give help her creative side. "I love doing projects," she said. "Fun projects. Like not, like, 'write a two-page essay.'" During Princess's junior year, I saw her do a presentation in her French class on fashion, where she presented a PowerPoint with pictures of herself wearing different outfits. She described what she was wearing in French. Although her pronunciation wasn't perfect, she clearly enjoyed her time in the spotlight. Following her presentation, her peers were complimentary of what she had done, both relative to the creative outfits that she had put together and to her efforts at speaking a foreign language in front of a large group.

Princess buys into school, and she expressed that even when other students resist school rules, she tends to abide by them. In our cultural circle / book club, when Destiny said that in the upcoming school year "dress down" (where students are permitted to come to school out of uniform) and "open lunch" (where students can leave the building to go get lunch) days would be for everyone at the same time and not just for a select group of students, Princess said that open lunch for everyone might be a bad idea because "nobody gonna come back"; however, she amended her statement to: "well, I'll come back." Princess most often gets positive feedback from and has positive relationships with her teachers.

Princess and Her Aspirations

Princess knows that she wants to be a performer, or to be associated with theater or television in some respect. While she told me in our summer cultural circle that she wanted to become an actress, I noticed that in the spring of her junior year in math class when students were doing research on potential college majors, rather than looking into theater programs, Princess did research on colleges that have majors in broadcasting. The previous summer, our conversation about the girls' aspirations took on a jubilant tone, largely as a result of Princess's aspiration to become a performer:

AB: What are you guys gonna major in in college?
DESIREE: Law.
PRINCESS: Theater. I want to be a Saturday Night Live improv person.
AB: We're gonna see you in ten years being like "Black Girls" . . .
DESTINY: Shakin' what they momma gave them!
DESIREE: When she make it big she gotta take me to the Oscars and I gotta be in the front row, and she gotta thank me in her speech and I gotta sit next to somebody big . . . like the—
PRINCESS: The New Boyz? [a hip-hop group]
DESIREE: Ooooh! If you sit me next to them, I . . .
DESTINY: While you sitting next to them, I might be representin' them!

CARMEN: And I just might be cooking for them! We all gon' be connected! She'll be on stage with them, she'll be cooking for them, she's managing them . . .

DESIREE: And I'll have my Versace dress on and my Gucci shoes, you know.

PRINCESS: Oooh all right! The lawyer!

At this point, Princess's aspirations, as well as a great deal of support from her friends and her mother, inspire her to continue to buy into school.

Conclusions: Princess

When I asked Princess about her opinion of professionalism at College Prep, she said that while she thought that professionalism points can at times be too strict because students are "just teens," they were in other ways a good idea. "Then again," she said, "[professionalism] prepares us for the real world." Her dreams for the future inspire her to form positive relationships with her teachers and to pursue extracurricular opportunities (like the summer program which focused on television broadcasting) that will give her more exposure and experience with her future career interests.

Like the case studies of Destiny and Carmen, Princess's case study also troubles the role of urban students in the political spectacle supported by College Prep and the media. Her self-confidence and emerging identity politics help to strengthen her voice, which she uses to critique stereotypes about young Black women. She also uses her voice to become a teacher to adults who are curious and willing to listen to her, like Ms. Caldwell. This is emblematic of the importance of dialogic pedagogies that valorize, rather than vilify or pathologize, students' knowledge or experience. It is also emblematic of the ways in which philanthropic or media discourses that construct students and their families as "problems" contradict the possibility for dialogic pedagogy or learning. If students and their communities are constructed as problems, then teachers or funders have nothing to learn from them.

Additionally, Princess's mother is present and extremely involved in Princess's education, defying stereotypes of urban families seen in films and some of the teacher narratives that are troubling in this chapter, as well as in chapter 4.

Concluding Thoughts

The young women profiled in the case studies above have varying outlooks on and relations to their peers, their families, their teachers, and their aspirations. All of their parents or guardians could be considered "working class"; that is, they don't hold a lot of power or freedom over terms and conditions of their employment, they do their jobs (if they are working) under close supervision, and they have little control over the pace or content of their work (Aronowitz 2003; Zweig 2004).

Destiny, the daughter of immigrant parents, is also encouraged by her family to pursue her dreams of academic and economic success in college. Destiny's father is well read and well educated, and encourages Destiny to read books at home that will engage and enhance her intellectually. Her academic interests supersede her social interests, although having good relationships with her peers is very important to her as well.

Carmen, the daughter of a single mother, while not as academically driven as Destiny or Princess, is driven to both community involvement and social justice thanks to her mother, who is deeply involved in her children's lives and decisions.

Of the three young women, Princess's mother is the most directly involved with her teachers and with school organizations, including the PTA. Princess does well academically, but is not interested in pursuing law as a career. Also thanks to a great deal of support from her mother, she is socially confident and is adept at seeing the bigger picture in relation to social injustices.

The case studies inspire a critique of the abstracted models of Black, urban adolescent girls that are perpetuated both by College Prep's marketing and by mainstream narratives about urban schools like *Freedom Writers* (LaGravenese 2007) and *Dangerous Minds* (J. Smith 1995). Unlike the youth in narratives that seem to beg mainstream White audiences for their pity, guilt, or money while simultaneously protecting privilege, the young people whom I profile all have extracurricular hobbies and interests, families that are supportive of education and upward class mobility for their children, and supportive communities of friends.

Family support exists regardless of a parent or guardian's direct involvement with the school. Although some of the students deal with some of the issues that are popularized in the school's marketing, as well as in Gruwell's and Johnson's books (absent fathers or neighborhood or community violence, for example), this does not make up the majority of their identities. While sometimes less conventional than others, these three students have a large network of support outside of the school, and a great deal of pride in their achievements, their Blackness, their intellect, their humor, and their femininity. Additionally, while College Prep's stereotype of girls' conflicts is prominent, peer networks of caring and support are integral to their confidence and success. College Prep and its corporate funders, as well as popular tropes about urban students, neglect this in dehumanizing and abstracted generalizations of urban "otherness."

The emergent identities of high school students are always couched in nuance and complexity. Dependence on profit and structures of privilege, in this case, serves to essentialize students' identities. In relation to urban, working-class, Black femininity, then, College Prep might ask itself what the model of the school is doing to talk back to harmful stereotypes about students and their families, which the school's Foundation perpetuates in its quest for corporate donations through the College Prep promotional film and the annual benefit, as well as many other fundraising events, media coverage, and promotional materials. In addition to finding more explicit ways of celebrating students' identities, families, and communities (the way these case studies strive to do), College Prep might explore ways to diminish the barriers between families who seek to be supportive of their child's education and the school, which, other than monthly PTA meetings, does not have a reliable or consistent system of family partnership. Also, finding ways (in addition to the school's Young Men's Association and Young Women's Association) to encourage peer networks of support and caring, rather than conflict or competition, is essential both for students' social well-being and for their academic achievement. Currently, parents or guardians are informed of their child's progress, but do not play an instrumental role, hand in hand with the school, in their child's education. The political spectacle in which College Prep participates requires that the school promote itself as the only positive influence in its students' lives. This essentializing logic may be effective to secure funding, but it furthers inaccurate stereotypes about students and protects the privilege of staff and funders.

The last two chapters have shown through case studies how College Prep teachers and students complicate mainstream tropes of the liberal or neoliberal savior. These tropes are an integral part of a political spectacle that the school's marketing supports, but students and staff members consistently trouble them. Chapter 6 explores my attempt at pedagogy of resistance to the school's spectacle, especially as it relates to the commodification and consumption of White and Black female bodies, and shows that the spectacle is not, as some might imagine, all encompassing, even in increasingly privatized spaces.

6

Critical Thinking

Reading Urban Fiction with Students

Thinking Critically at College Prep

Mr. Keating, a White teacher, in a conversation about teaching critical thinking, stated during a staff meeting:

> Where I learned to think critically wasn't in class, it was at the dinner table, or in the back seat of the car, seeing . . . debates that sustained me in the classroom. Many of our kids are not exposed to much of this, so we need to expose them and build in those critical thinking moments. [Students have an interest in] success [but] there is no interest in the process . . . there is no love for the process and no passion about learning. That needs to be built in.

Mr. Keating attributes behavioral issues and what he deems a lack of critical thinking skills or "college readiness" to students' peer groups, families, and communities. This resonates with some of Ms. Carr's comments about professionalism in chapter 3, which rely on a deficit discourse about students' families, homes, or communities that is based on a lack of knowledge. Some teachers conflate students' resistance to College Prep behavioral expectations with students' race and socioeconomic status, thus normalizing and upholding "Whitestream" (Grande 2000; Urrieta 2006) discourse,[1] and are unwilling to problematize the way in which the language of "helping" students masks their exploitation, and upholds the social order (see Edelman 1988, 72). Based in a similar logic, much of the school's relationship with donors was grounded in the idea that College Prep needed resources to continue to save or rescue "college-fragile" students from impoverished backgrounds or circumstances. Just as in the popular narratives that I described in the last two chapters, College Prep's spectacle markets students, their communities, and their families as "problems" and predominantly White female teachers as "saviors." Donors consume this narrative as they give (constructing themselves both as generous and as authorities on the problem), thus contributing to the maintenance of a racialized, gendered, and classed ideology. To some degree, as I demonstrate below, teachers and students consume this as well. Because of the tensions between what happens in front of and behind "the curtain," and because of students' critiques of College Prep's version of professionalism, I wanted to attempt a pedagogical intervention grounded in students' agency, identities, and literacies (Gallego and Hollingsworth 2000). I disagreed wholeheartedly with Mr. Keating's perspective about students' inability to practice critical thinking. Paulo Freire developed cultural circles as a generative approach to teaching literacy that honored participants' background and knowledge and moved them to *conscientização*, or critical awareness of transformative political action (Darder 2002). This method, grounded in participants' realities, seemed to be an appropriate response to some of the issues that plagued students and teachers at College Prep.

Theoretical Perspectives

At this point, contemporary U.S. manifestations of Freire's work tend to take place inside of classrooms, and focus on practices of questioning and tapping knowledge from students and their communities, as well as on forming a bridge to school-sanctioned curricula (W. Ayers 2001; Duncan-Andrade and Morrell 2008; Moll et al. 1992). Some work focuses on practices of democratic dialogue (Darder 2002) and on forging close relationships between teachers and students (hooks 2003). Outside of the classroom, Youth Participatory Action Research (Y-PAR) and activism (Cammarota and Fine 2008; Ginwright 2010) stem from Freirean philosophies. Yet, with few exceptions (Souto-Manning 2010; Williams 2009), researchers pay less attention to cultural circles, a method of Freirean pedagogy. Perhaps this is because Freire, wary of his methods being imported or exported, resisted providing a rote description of his cultural circles. He preferred that his pedagogy be reinvented in context (Boshier 1999; Darder 2002; Souto-Manning 2010).

For Freire, cultural circles are a way to generate critical conversations among "teacher-students" and "student-teachers" and can provide the motivation for critical consciousness and political action (1970). Both teachers and students learn from one another as their democratic dialogue provides a means to name and upend social structures of privilege and oppression. In the summer between the two academic years that I spent at College Prep, I decided to conduct a cultural circle with students in order to creatively contest the school's deficit-based marketing of its students.

In this chapter, I outline the goals and activities of our cultural circle, and the challenges that we faced. Through the cultural circle experience, we aimed to develop a critical, dialogic pedagogy through discussions and activities responding to student-selected urban fiction texts. I found that while the cultural circles garnered increased student motivation and critical engagement, participants also expressed ambivalence about critically engaging with literature and topics that were outside of school- (and spectacle-) sanctioned models of success, professionalism, and upward mobility. Data gathered from the cultural circles help us to problematize not only the school's ideals of professionalism, and the ways in which its narrative supports the construction and consumption of White and Black female bodies, but also to problematize the relevance of Freirean pedagogy in the context of school marketization and privatization.

While cultural circles were integral to Freire's methods, there are key differences between Freire's educational context (Brazil in the 1960s) and the context of the contemporary United States. While Freire's students were adults who came to cultural circles of their own volition to learn to read and write, students in the United States often may not see themselves as having a choice to attend school. Schools may not build on, and often may, in fact, attempt to rob students of the knowledge or skills grounded in their homes or communities (Valencia 2010; Valenzuela 1999), demonstrating what Freire calls a "banking style" of education, where students are seen as empty receptacles in which school-sanctioned knowledge can be deposited (1970).

As mentioned above, there is not a rote method for developing cultural circles; however, certain aspects are common across all cultural circles. Cultural circles often include a facilitator and a small group of participants. They revolve around a collaboratively chosen "generative theme" that is grounded in participants' lives. They follow a "problem-posing" approach to dialogue that involves or engages these generative themes, and that critical dialogue leads to some sort of political action

(Souto-Manning 2010). Often, cultural circles begin with the facilitator's ethnographic exploration of participants' community (Freire 1970). As meetings evolve, participants take on more ownership of the problem-posing dialogue, as well as the political action.

Cultural Circle Methods

Beginning with the Freirean idea of the teacher-as-ethnographer (Moll et al. 1992; Souto-Manning 2010) who moves to a place of solidarity with his or her students through more closely understanding their lives, struggles, and interests, I completed close to a full school year of teacher-research before I approached the idea of a cultural circle with the students in my English classes. Wanting students to participate of their own volition, I invited all the students in my English class to participate in my summer cultural circle during an open lunch meeting in April of 2008. Forty students (thirty-seven girls and three boys) came to this meeting, but only five students (all girls) participated in the end: Carmen, Desiree, Gabriela, Princess, and Destiny (see chapter 5 for case studies of Carmen, Destiny, and Princess). In interviews, all identified as Black or African American except for Gabriela, who identified as Latina (of Mexican descent). Wanting to hold the circles in a power-neutral space, we held some meetings in a Unitarian church willing to let us meet in an empty chapel, and others in an outdoor public space near the school.

I purchased composition books for the students in which they could summarize, critique, and question the texts that we read. That summer, we had a total of seven cultural circle meetings. At the beginning all five participants showed up regularly. Gabriela went out of town and stopped coming after the third meeting, and Desiree participated in a college-preparatory enrichment program for three weeks in July. Ms. Caldwell, a staff member who volunteered to participate, attended most of the cultural circle meetings through the month of July, and facilitated one meeting when I was out of town. In order to participate, students were required to provide consent forms signed by a parent or guardian. Consent forms stipulated that we would be reading and discussing the books students chose, and our discussions would be audio-recorded. I conducted a series of interviews with students during and after the cultural circle meetings, and conducted interviews with their parents after the cultural circle meetings. I met with each of their parents/guardians during the following fall and interviewed them about their impression of students' cultural circle experience, as well as their impressions of College Prep at large. In the summer of 2011, after students graduated from College Prep, we met again to discuss how the meetings impacted students throughout the rest of their high school experience, and how they felt the experience prepared them for their future educational goals.

Urban Fiction

When I first took each of my tenth-grade English classes into the school library in 2009, the first question from three of the four classes (all from African American girls) was whether the librarian had "those ghetto books." The librarian, as well as everyone in the class, knew exactly what this term meant. Some teachers and students whom I spoke with at College Prep worried about the impact of "urban fiction" on adolescent identity formation. They argued that these texts not only lack rigor and complexity, but perpetuate and reify sexist, demeaning images of people of color through depictions of violent crime, nonconsensual sex, and drugs (Chiles 2006). Others argued that what youth choose to read was not as important as the fact that they were reading (Marech 2003). Still others argued that these books provide a unique window into the challenges of U.S. urban life that is often ignored in the mainstream (ibid.). Many students whom I talked to recognized these perspectives. Nevertheless, College Prep community members saw students reading urban fiction under desks in class, in the cafeteria, and sometimes during school-mandated independent reading time.

While some students actively sought to incorporate urban fiction into the mainstream curriculum—for example, during school-mandated independent reading time, or in practice essays for the New York State English Regents examination—others were more skeptical or had mixed feelings about the genre. When I asked students during an informal interview early in the cultural circle experience what would happen if we read urban fiction books in English class, Carmen stated that students would be much more engaged with classroom reading, so much so that they would not be able to put the books down. I then asked students whether they thought that reading urban fiction books would prepare them for college. Desiree responded: "There's no vocabulary, there's no new words in [these books]; and there are typos in [them] too!" Princess, along with Destiny and Carmen, echoed her complaints. Interestingly, although these students were skeptical of the genre as a whole, when I asked them to create the syllabus for what we would read together over the summer, all the books that students chose would be classified as urban fiction: Teri Woods's *True to the Game III* (2008), Sister Souljah's *The Coldest Winter Ever* (1999), and Sapphire's *Push* (1996). The young women expressed interest in reading and discussing these books while simultaneously critiquing their lack of challenging vocabulary or thorough copyediting.

Cultural Circle Participants

All the students who participated in the cultural circle currently live in New York City. Based on information gathered at numerous staff meetings, as well as through informal conversations with teachers, cultural circle students have good rapport with College Prep teachers. All are friends and get along well.

In Table 1 give more information about the participants.

Creating a Curriculum

The list of books that students chose to read for the cultural circles was compiled from a longer list that tenth-grade students came up with during the initial voluntary meetings that I held to recruit participants. The protagonists of the books are all female and African American, and all live in urban areas of the United States. In all the stories, the main characters struggle against social, financial, and emotional difficulties to land on their feet and sometimes struggle to be in healthy romantic relationships, family relationships, and friendships. Both *True to the Game III* and *The Coldest Winter Ever* portray characters' struggle to reach economic security in the context of racial capitalism (Sweeney 2010); the characters are either involved directly in street crime or are romantically involved with men who are. *True to the Game III* ends as the main character, Gena, finally settles down with the drug dealer whom she has been in love with. *The Coldest Winter Ever,* however, ends with a different fate for the protagonist: Winter, the street-smart, beautiful, and materialistic main character, refuses to snitch on her boyfriend, who is a crack dealer. As the story ends, Winter is serving a fifteen-year prison sentence. *Push*

TABLE 1

Cultural Circle Participants' Demographic Information

PARTICIPANT	RACIAL/ETHNIC SELF-IDENTIFICATION	AGE/ GRADE LEVEL	HOME NEIGHBORHOOD	NEIGHBORHOOD MEDIAN HOUSEHOLD INCOME[1]	CUMULATIVE GRADE AVERAGE IN SUBJECT AREA CLASSES
Carmen	Black / African American	16/11	East New York, Brooklyn	$23,143[2]	65%
Desiree	Black / African American	16/11	Cambria Heights, Queens	$72,840	92%
Destiny	Black / African American	16/11	Brownsville, Brooklyn	$56,604	90%
Gabriela	Latina / Mexican American	16/11	Crown Heights, Brooklyn	$26,366	96%
Princess	Black / African American	16/11	Ridgewood, Queens	$46,096	85%
Ms. Caldwell	White / European American	23/ NA	Prospect Heights, Brooklyn	$67,650	NA

1 Source: NeighborhoodLink.com (2010).
2 At the time of my research, the national median household income was $56,604 (Neighborhood-Link.com 2010).

tells the story of Precious, an HIV-positive, illiterate teen mother of two who comes from an abusive home but struggles through an alternative school to become literate and to find beauty in herself and in her children.

During the first cultural circle meeting, after coming up with our initial list of readings, I asked students which generative themes (Boshier 1999; Souto-Manning 2010) they wanted our discussions to engage; themes, starting from issues relevant to participants' lives, serve as the starting point for cultural circle dialogue. This is supposed to move to collective problem solving and charting a course for political action, on a personal and a social level. Although I did not use the word "generative" when asking students to come up with themes, I explained to students that we would read the books, and then talk about them in relation to themes or topics of their choice. While Carmen suggested that we talk about race, Gabriela suggested power, and Destiny suggested power and gender. We decided to focus on all these themes.

We decided that we would take approximately two weeks to read and discuss each novel. After we read the assigned portion on our own, we would write a summary, an analysis, and questions in our composition books, focusing on the aforementioned themes. For the most part, we stuck with this, although conversations tended to be relatively informal, and topics of conversation were not restricted to the books.

Analysis

I coded interview data and field notes from the cultural circle based on our generative themes. The following section will describe students' conversations in relation to power. We engaged the idea of power especially in relation to oppression and social mobility. Destiny stated: "I think [the ability to think of the future] is sort of a luxury. People who are oppressed are just trying to keep up." Destiny admits that there are sometimes factors that are out of one's control that might contribute to whether one is oppressed. In other words, when one is "just trying to keep up," one may lack complete control of one's circumstances, and lack a means for social mobility.

Power, Oppression, and Individual Agency

As we began to read *Push,* the students came up with their own examples of power and oppression. We skimmed the back cover of the book together and Carmen noticed that the main character, Precious, is illiterate. Gabriela asked me what the word "illiterate" meant. I told her that it meant not being able to read or write. "I was like that," she said quietly. She spoke about her personal experience being teased, bullied, and treated "like I was stupid" in U.S. schools after spending most of her childhood in Mexico, because she did not speak English. She explained that she "didn't feel smart" but went to the library every day in order to improve her English literacy. "No matter whether it was raining [or] snowing, that didn't stop me," she said. "I went through struggles, 'cause I wasn't able to speak English very well. But now, like, I'm able to do anything." Here she makes a direct parallel between oppression and the lack of ability to speak one's experience. Both language and academics give her the power to "do anything."

This was also reflected in students' discussion of Precious's journey to literacy. During our last discussion of the book, after we struggled with Precious's decision not to emancipate herself from her mother, Destiny said, "In a way, I think Precious does emancipate herself. She gets stronger and freer from her writing and from the people around her." Here Destiny alludes to the possibility of the oppressed finding a sense of freedom and agency through language and community. Gabriela elaborated on her belief in the meritocratic ideal of working hard, despite obstacles, to get ahead. She shared that her family and her religious values give her the discipline to persevere in school and to someday (she hopes) excel in college. She stated that by working hard to overcome one's obstacles one can succeed. "In the future, I know that I'm gonna live the good life," she said. "In the end . . . it's worth it . . . no matter what, you don't have to feel bad or nothing, just keep going no matter how many times you fail . . . you got the power. You gotta think about yourself." Students frequently spoke about academic success (most specifically, college) as leading to power and agency. Students constructed themselves as intellectuals and academic strivers as they aligned, repeatedly, with the African American female characters in the books who displayed values of intelligence, groundedness, drive, and independence and against the characters who displayed ignorance, materialism, and greed. Students constructed themselves, their families, and their communities in opposition to the ways in which the school's spectacle constructed them: as unprofessional, uncritical, and in need of being saved.

Students' construction of their future selves often contrasted with feeling a lack of power in the present. For example, the power to control one's future, versus a lack of power in school and home contexts, is demonstrated through Carmen's statement: "I don't have power over nobody, not even my little brothers and sisters." Carmen spoke about how she felt no one listened to her. Gabriela, too, shared that in the beginning of our school year, she was frequently bullied by another student, and was quiet because she was afraid that people would laugh at her.

Frequently in our conversations, despite their own dedication and hard work in school, students displayed nervousness at not being able to attain academic success in college. Yet they repeatedly expressed that academic success in college would allow them to transcend other forms of oppression. As Gabriela said, "people can say whatever they want to say. I have no problem, because I am exceeding. If you don't get the grades, then you won't be accepted into college." Students recognized some forms of oppression in their present lives and in regard to the characters in the books. Yet students were not critical of grand narratives of color-, class-, and gender-blind meritocracy, and believed, regardless of their experiences with oppression, that agency grounded in education and ambition could trump social structure.

Students' nervousness at their academic preparedness shows that they are aware of College Prep's investment in its spectacle, much to their detriment. Teachers problematized this in a different way. While graduation and college matriculation rates are close to 100 percent for College Prep students, some teachers spoke about unsuccessful students getting "pushed out" in order to "keep the numbers up." As Ms. McGoldrick put it, "we are doing great with a lot of kids in terms of college readiness, but like what are we doing with the rest of them? And if you look at the [high] percentage of kids that are transferred out of our school, why did that happen?" She spoke about feeling that most College Prep students seemed "bored" in classes, and were "not learning anything." College Prep is practiced at supporting a political spectacle regardless of students' actions or investment.

Senior English teachers complained to me in interviews that they felt they were crossing the line between editing students' college personal statements and writing them for students. The college office keeps a file on each student, and, as one of the college advisors puts it, "holds students' hands" through the college application process—even if a student insists that he or she does not want to attend college, they are still mandated to apply to a minimum of six schools in the City of New York (CUNY) system. Ms. Goodwin, a White teacher, spoke about her suspicion about students' experiences when they got to college: "some of the brightest kids that we sent are really struggling [in college] . . . but they've had straight As the entire time through College Prep." Ms. Barnes, the college advisor, aware of College Prep's grade inflation, asked me, "what, are we going to put our best students in a room and say 'look guys, your 90 [percent], you know, not so much—your 90 is a kind of inferior 90'? No." In this sense, teachers manage the school's image to give the appearance of student motivation through its high college matriculation rate—but lament the discrepancy between the image and their own real-time observations in more intimate venues.

Intersections of Race and Gender

Within our cultural circle, we discussed gender and race intersectionally, often in the context of power and social mobility. For example, as we finished our discussion of *Push,* we read an interview with the author, Sapphire, who spoke about her reluctance to make a movie out the book, because, in her words, "Hollywood has done a disservice to Black people" (Keehnen 1996). As we deconstructed this comment, students immediately brought gender into the conversation, especially in relation to music videos that feature images of hyper-sexualized, materialistic Black women. Carmen worried that "Black people do a disservice to themselves in those videos, when they agree to be in them . . . but then sometimes, it's like a vicious cycle, because maybe you see all these images about yourself everywhere, and you actually start to believe them." Carmen's sentiment here is not only relevant to the ways in which Black female bodies are marketed and consumed in popular culture, it is also relevant to the ways in which College Prep students are marketed and consumed. At what level do College Prep students internalize the ways the school constructs them, and how does this impact their psyches?

Students also discussed the idea that Hollywood doesn't just do a disservice to Black people; it does a disservice to women in general. Students brought up White popular music star Hannah Montana (Miley Cyrus) who they said is a teenager who "dresses like she's grown," and, in their opinions, is too skinny. This, in turn, they said, sends messages to so many girls about the body types and clothes that they are expected to wear. Students felt that it is more common for White girls to get the message that they have to be skinny, versus Black and Latina girls, who get the message that it is okay to be "thick," because Black and Latino men like "thicker" women. Throughout our conversations, students recognized differing forms of sexed and gendered oppressions based on women's racialized identities.

Students saw racially differentiated expectations for body types in the context of the straight male gaze, but at the same time, saw the "right" kind of straight man as advocating for, and appreciating educated, confident, self-sufficient, independent, and community-engaged women. This was demonstrated by students' critique of the gender politics of *True to the Game III*. Destiny and Princess, in particular, struggled with the question of why Quadir, the main character, falls for Gena, whom students called a "hood chick," while rejecting Amelia, the beautiful doctor who is also in love with him. Destiny explained this by saying that "hood chicks" like Gena "are always in trouble, but bring excitement." Students also struggled with the question of why Amelia would risk her life and her career for Quadir, a "thug." Students use the racialized vocabulary of "hood chick" and "thug" to describe the ways in which characters represent gendered stereotypes; the "hood chick" represents an undereducated woman born in the stereotypically Black urban ghetto who may have street smarts, but may not have the drive, ambition, or opportunity to leave the "hood." The "thug" represents the "hood chick's" male counterpart; while he has street smarts, and perhaps power and money within the context of his urban surroundings, he makes his money through illegal means and may end up incarcerated or dead as a result. While students admitted that they are sometimes attracted to "boys from the hood," they explicitly differentiated themselves from the stereotype of the "hood chick"; they were college-bound and going to be independent, educated, and upwardly mobile.

Destiny shared that she was surprised at the end of the story, where Gena and Quadir end up getting married in the Bahamas. Not only did she think that the ending was improbable, she found it to be too sudden. "I thought Quadir was gonna choose Amelia over Gena," she said. "I guess true love does bring two people together, even though I don't think [in Quadir and Gena's case], that it was meant to be." Destiny said that Gena "doesn't have anything going for her, and is more dependent." This is a powerful statement, especially coming from Destiny, who prides herself on being more like Amelia than Gena: she and her family live in an area of Brownsville, Brooklyn, that some might construe as "the hood," where she said that they are banned from having block parties, perhaps due to violence, and where she once "walked into a shooting" because she had her headphones on. Yet rather than hanging out on the block like her brother does, which she says is "boring," she stays inside and reads, because, as I mentioned in the last chapter, she tells herself "I'm gonna go to college, and I'm gonna go for three different degrees."

Her choices aren't necessarily due to her parents putting extreme restrictions on her, she explained. Rather, it seems, she makes the choice on her own because of her goal of upward mobility through education in the context of a meritocracy.[2] Hanging out on the block does not bring her any closer to her lifelong goal of becoming a lawyer. Destiny guides her daily decisions to fit this goal. Her brother, on the other hand, has other goals, which affect what he chooses to do with his time in the present.

Destiny tells herself that if she works hard to attain her occupational and academic goals, other things (love, family, money, a stable living environment) will come. Yet, this novel portrays Amelia, a well-educated, beautiful, independent, financially stable Black woman, as the character who ends up lonely at the end of the story, because the man whom she loved (and whom she risked her job trying to save) went for the "hood chick" with no job and no conventional ambition. "I think when he left Amelia, I was just upset. Gena is a nice person, but she has nothing going for her, like she can't provide for him. What if he gets into debt? Amelia can provide for him," Destiny said. Here, Destiny's comment seems to incorporate issues of class and power as it relates to race and gender;[3] she portrays Amelia as upwardly mobile, and constructs Quadir as stagnant. In Destiny's view, Amelia has the potential to play the stereotypically feminine role of the caretaker through playing the less traditionally female role of the breadwinner, if Quadir would let her. Amelia is the real "catch."

The gender politics of the story's ostensible happy ending are unsettling to Destiny, who hopes to someday be academically on Amelia's level, not Gena's. To uncritical readers, the story could be construed as teaching that the Amelias of the world end up conventionally successful, but isolated, no matter what they do. As Destiny's analysis demonstrates, students did not necessarily take this away, as they continued to identify with Amelia, placing getting an education above "getting the guy."

This pattern continued as we read *The Coldest Winter Ever*. Sister Souljah places herself in the story as an activist radio talk show host. Students identified with the character of Sister Souljah in the story, as opposed to Winter. Students described Winter as "superficial" and a "spoiled brat who has everything taken away from her." According to students, Winter's behaviors are antithetical to her independence or survival. As a young woman, even though she is beautiful, she neglects a responsibility to herself, and negates the possibility of gaining any real respect from the people around her because of her promiscuous and materialistic behavior. Desiree described Winter as a young woman who "didn't have no standard, she just chose any sugar daddy!" Destiny agreed, saying: "she was too dependent on a man 'cause her father always gave her everything she wanted." According to Desiree, "what she wanted was money and clothes, not a job, not college, not housing—nothing." Destiny added, "and she didn't want somebody with a degree, she wanted somebody from the streets." While Carmen believed that Winter has low self-esteem, she didn't believe that even this is a viable excuse for the way Winter behaves.

Students saw Souljah as a character who tries to help Winter, and they grew frustrated with the fact that Winter disregards Souljah's attempts to get Winter to college and provide her with a place to live. When Winter decides to steal money from one of Sister Souljah's charity auctions, then to rob an old woman in a hotel parking lot in order to provide for herself, Desiree said, "she has no choice, it's like when you have no choice you'll do anything to survive." Destiny quickly countered: "she did have a choice, though, because Sister Souljah's going to help her enroll in college!" When Desiree responded that "[Winter] didn't want no help," Destiny concluded, "she's an idiot." As they did with Gena in *True to the Game III,* students explicitly constructed their identities counter to Winter's character in *The Coldest Winter Ever.*

Similarly, Princess declared that she "loved Sister Souljah," because she demonstrates values of community engagement and empowerment through her activist work, her charity work, and through her attempts to put young women like Winter on the path to education and independence. Destiny declared that she thought Winter was "jealous" of Sister Souljah, and Carmen agreed, stating that Souljah "has a [healthy and desirable] body, she's smart, and she's celibate." This, students said, was the reason that Souljah, and not Winter, is able to hold the attention of Midnight, the older male character in the book whom Winter is also attracted to. Destiny and Carmen agreed that from Midnight's point of view, women are "supposed to be strong and independent." Midnight, she said, "needed somebody to depend on if something went wrong." Desiree added: "And not a dumb girl like Winter." Destiny, on the other hand, said Winter was "just prostituting herself." Through these conversations, students explicitly brought sex into the conversation; in students' opinions, Winter demeans herself through her promiscuity, and disempowers herself through her drive to attain material goods rather than education.

When I asked students during the cultural circle what they took away from reading the book, Destiny said that she learned to "be more independent" and that she learned "not to depend on a man." Desiree said that she learned "not to be materialistic," and "not to mess with a boy who sells drugs." In critical cultural circle conversations about *True to the Game III* and the *Coldest Winter Ever*, students seemed to construct themselves in opposition to the idea of the "dumb" or "materialistic" young woman. Furthermore, they supported each other in constructing college-bound, upwardly mobile, raced and gendered identities. They constructed themselves against the trope that I problematize in chapter 5 of the Black, urban, adolescent girl who needs to be saved by the White liberal or neoliberal savior that I problematize in chapter 4. College Prep's spectacle depends on these tropes, but students demonstrate the ways in which they construct themselves as race conscious and proud, independent, and grounded in their families and communities, and simultaneously as able to build relationships with teachers.

Is Praxis Impractical? Recommendations and Implications

As I analyzed the data from the cultural circle, I found that the experience provided more questions than answers in regard to the relevance of Freirean cultural circles in this context. As we read the books students chose, Carmen commented that she enjoyed reading the nonstandard language of the books (which she called "AIM [AOL Instant Messenger] talk"), and that the books "made [her] think." Students engaged with and asked and answered difficult, critical questions about the texts (for example, from *Push*: Why doesn't Precious emancipate herself from her mother? From *True to the Game III*: Is money its own character in the story? Does it oppress the characters? From *The Coldest Winter Ever*: How is it possible to live in the projects and still place so much importance on material things?).

When the students and I met to discuss the cultural circle experience just after their high school graduation, we spoke at length about college readiness, and about how their experience at College Prep, as well as their experience in the cultural circle, prepared them. Carmen shared that it was fun, and that "a lot of people don't see the connection between what's going on and the stereotypes that we see all around us. We all just go about our business. It was good to actually read a book that relates to people and things I know and see." She seems to allude to the idea here that she enjoyed pushing herself to do the analytical work that many people don't do around urban fiction books. This was in great contrast to how she and Princess described, two summers beforehand, their feeling of boredom when they entered the school building.

At College Prep, college-readiness discourse often begins with the assumption that students are not "college ready" and that they are unprofessional, and that it is the unique role of the predominantly White college office staff members to prepare them for the "real world." The cultural circle experience showed me that students not only internalize the aspect of College Prep's spectacle about college-readiness and upward social mobility, but students also internalize the deficit discourse that the same spectacle depends on. Even after graduating from College Prep, students demonstrated a concern they may not have the skills to succeed in college. In a meeting just before most students left for college, Princess expressed that she felt woefully underprepared for the SAT, and Gabriela complained that she felt underprepared in terms of time management as well as organization. While all students expressed that College Prep was a good school for getting its students involved in extracurricular activities, and for making them "college eligible," they were concerned about whether they were socially and academically "college ready" (Zelkowski 2011). This demonstrates students' awareness of the discrepancy between College Prep's need to market them to funders as college bound and their actual preparation.

"College readiness," then, became synonymous with agency for students and with the ability to transcend systemic oppression. Desiree stated, in regard to the cultural circles: "I feel like we learned something . . . it was something new." Princess elaborated, saying, "I look more closely at race now." She notices internalized racism among her family and friends, or as she put it, "that even Black people can be racist." Carmen agreed, and they said that as a direct result of the discussions that we had, they voice protests to these forms of racism when they see them, even from their peers on Facebook. Carmen, after thinking for a few more moments responded:

> I think we should have read those books because they were of
> interest to us, but I think we also should have chosen harder
> books . . . We did good, we broke it down, we criticized it,
> we critiqued it, but we could have got some books that were more
> challenging, especially to get into college. We could have done
> better.

Although students reported that the cultural circle experience pushed them to become everyday anti-racist activists, and to be comfortable as Black and Brown female intellectuals, students, buying into College Prep's spectacle, were uncritical of meritocratic and mainstream models of success to overcome structural forms of oppression. There is a tension here between individual agency and social structure that represents a problem in regard to the school's narrative, but may also represent an impasse in Freirean pedagogy; in these cultural circles, students were able to identify and critique oppression, but did not use this knowledge to turn against the "superstructure." Rather, they turned to their belief in the power of individual agency and meritocracy (coinciding with College Prep's emphasis on the performance of professionalism) to reinforce their faith that their future selves will be untouched by systemic oppression (even despite their fear that they may not have what it takes to be "college ready"). They demonstrated that it is possible to experience and critique structural oppression, but at the same time hold on to a belief in individual transcendence. This tension and ambivalence bring up important questions and opportunities for further exploration in regard to the contemporary relevance of Freirean pedagogy. Critical educators and researchers might, in the future, grapple with the ways in which praxis, as Freire conceptualized it, is (or is not) practical in the context of dominant narratives of meritocracy and the power of individual agency at College Prep and in the United States, as well as with the ways in which perpetuating color-blind and meritocratic narratives discourage the possibility of developing and acting on a critical race or class consciousness.

Despite this impasse, I contend that the cultural circle served to humanize students' learning experience at College Prep, providing them with a means to critically construct positive self-identities with me and with one another. The cultural circle experience was explicitly not focused on image management for administrators or for funders; rather, it was grounded in knowledge construction, humanization, and intersubjectivity. In this respect, it represents hope for the possibility of following a very different model in the quest for a deeper and more solidarity-based way of teaching and learning in U.S. public schools. I am not advocating that urban fiction be brought into classrooms on a grand scale, but rather that teachers take the time to build a curriculum that is authentically grounded in where students are. This of course can only come from a genuine interest in, and solidarity with, one's students. Without this, I do not believe that it is possible to be an effective teacher.

I am also advocating for teachers to take the risk of making themselves vulnerable to students. Mr. Jackson told me that he often told his students that he was just the "highest-paid teacher in the room"—in other words, that everyone in the classroom was both a teacher and a learner. This mind-set, in my view, represents a much more human and grounded way of constructing knowledge. The urban fiction cultural circle was one way of doing this with students, but I believe that there are an infinite number of others.

Behind the Mask

Professionalism and Life after College Prep

We Wear the Mask

We wear the mask that grins and lies,
It hides our cheeks and shades our eyes,—
This debt we pay to human guile;
With torn and bleeding hearts we smile,
And mouth with myriad subtleties.
Why should the world be over-wise,
In counting all our tears and sighs?
Nay, let them only see us, while
We wear the mask.
We smile, but, O great Christ, our cries
To thee from tortured souls arise.
We sing, but oh the clay is vile
Beneath our feet, and long the mile;
But let the world dream otherwise,
We wear the mask!

—Paul Laurence Dunbar ([1896] 1993)

Drawing on Erving Goffman's theories (1963), lawyer, poet, and critical race theorist[1] Kenji Yoshino (2006) names "covering" what Dunbar (above) refers to as "wearing the mask." Yoshino defines the ways in which, in an era that is supposed to be "post-race," color-blind, or multicultural, oppression and hegemony continue to operate: "outsiders are included, but only if we behave like insiders—that is, only if we cover" (22). For Yoshino, covering is the civil rights issue of our time, for, he writes: "It hurts not only our most valuable citizens, but our most valuable commitments. For if we believe that a commitment against racism is about equal respect for all races, we are not fulfilling that commitment if we protect only racial minorities who conform to historically white norms" (23). Yoshino asserts that his stance against covering is not only about protecting "traditional" civil rights groups, but also about protecting those who might be viewed as "mainstream": all of us, he writes, have covered selves, and the struggle for civil rights is part of a larger project of human flourishing (25). This book contends that competitive logic in education, which dictates that schools should have to compete for corporate, philanthropic, or public resources, is deeply flawed. This logic, which is one facet of the spectacle supported by College Prep, depends on ideologies of inequity and dehumanizes people by making them into commodities that must "cover" to seem more deserving of the resources that should be equally available to everyone—in effect, furthering already existent inequalities.

When I conducted research in 2008–10 at College Prep, I told interviewees that I would solicit their thoughts and critiques when the manuscript was finished. Now, as I write in the fall of 2014, this has become a separate project that is still a work in progress. I have completed fifteen of, I hope, many more interviews based on this manuscript. This chapter describes the ways in which the participants in my study both interrogated and supported my main argument: that models of corporate or philanthropic charity in education ironically reify the race and class hierarchies they purport to alleviate. I describe and analyze participants' responses here.

Based on conversations with eleven teachers and four students whom I originally interviewed for the ethnography, as well as conversations with focus groups held with parents, students, and staff after a professional development in 2010, I share community members' critiques and questions and demonstrate how participants define their roles in the context of the political spectacle I critique, asserting themselves as agents, not props. This speaks to the importance and value of collaborative and innovative ways of writing ethnography, but also to the importance of anthropologists sharing the ownership of data and the stories we tell with the communities in which we work.

I argue that participants define themselves both within and against the spectacle. They used this ethnography to explain the frustration and difficulty of authoring professional identities in the context of conflicting discourses that essentialize students and teachers to gain resources in the name of students' upward mobility, but also label themselves as "social justice." Those whom I interviewed illuminate the tension between alleviating and perpetuating racial capitalism (Robinson 1983) and poverty in education through casting themselves as being both inside and outside the "total institution" of the school (Goffman 1961). Engaging in a critique of the tension between public and private interests in education inspires agency for participants and encourages them to identify, challenge, critique, or question the borders between private interests and the public good.

Besides positive or developmental feedback on the manuscript itself, what emerged most commonly from the interviews were themes of identity construction and agency, commodification and generosity, and humanization and solidarity. Before I share how the data gathered in the interviews articulate with my main arguments, I will briefly outline where some key participants "ended up" four years after the conclusion of the study.

According to College Prep's progress report on NYC.gov, 47.4 percent of the 2011 and 2013 cohorts at College Prep graduated, met the Regents exam, and met the SAT and/or course standards for passing out of remedial coursework at the City University of New York (CUNY). According to the same report, 69.3 percent of the students from the 2011 cohort persisted in college past the third semester. Six months after graduation, 81.6 percent of College Prep's students had enrolled in public service, a vocational program, or a degree program at a two- or four-year college. Eighteen months after graduation, 88.6 percent had enrolled.

In terms of the students I know, out of the 115 students whom I taught as tenth graders at College Prep, ninety-two remained on the roster as members of their class at the end of 2010, their junior year, when I left the school. Of the twenty-three who no longer appeared on the roster, some were held back and others transferred. In the fall of 2013 (two years after their 2011 high school graduation), out of these ninety-two students, I was able to connect with or track seventy-three on Facebook. I noted whether they had enrolled in two- or four-year colleges, as well as whether they had dropped out, were still in school, or had finished. From what I could tell, thirty-five listed themselves as not in college, while thirty-eight listed themselves as still being in two- or four-year programs (this equates to 52 percent, which is a bit less than the NYC.gov report I cite above, although the sample size is not the same). Fifteen listed themselves as having left their two-year programs (it was not clear whether they had graduated). Twenty students did not list themselves as having enrolled. Nine students listed themselves as still being in two-year programs, and twenty-nine were still in four-year college programs. I did not see any evidence of students who had started in two-year colleges having transferred to four-year programs.

Based on these students' online profiles, it seems that many of those who are in college are making friends and are involved in campus life. Yet for College Prep, a school that boasts such high graduation and college matriculation rates, I wonder what meaning we can make of the fact that two years after graduation, about half or just over half, according to the city's progress report, still seem to be in college. These statistics may be better than those from high schools that serve a similar demographic of students but do not have the resources that College Prep does. Yet I also cannot help but wonder whether more affluent or White high schools that boast similar graduation and college matriculation rates see similar longitudinal results with their graduating classes. In other words, do a larger number of students from more affluent or White high schools remain in, and graduate from, four-year colleges? These data beg the question of whether College Prep and schools like it truly contribute to the eradication of the social inequalities that college or career readiness for all students is supposed to solve. If students from schools like College Prep graduate from high school and enroll in college but do not complete it, are they able to attain the kinds of social and cultural capital and upward social mobility that College Prep's "social justice" model promises?

I caught up more intimately with all the students who had participated in the cultural circle. All of them, with the exception of Carmen, are still in school. These statistics are markedly better than those of the rest of their class. I don't think that the reason for this is their participation in the cultural circle, but rather, I attribute their success in college to strong networks of family, peer, and teacher support, and to strong academic foundations, all of which led to positive self-identity development. This ties explicitly into another aspect of my main argument: in addition to the idea that the goals and purpose of education are undermined through College Prep's use of people, professionalism criteria, and stock narratives as "props" in a political spectacle of charity, I also contend that support networks grounded in human connection and solidarity can provide a stronger foundation for teaching, learning, success, and critical thinking, and thus, for greater and more effective participation in civil society. Cultural circle participants' statistics are included in those above, but I outline them in more depth below.

Students

Carmen Fletcher

Carmen is not currently in college, but reports that she is applying. When I saw her during the summer after her senior year, she was planning on moving to Florida with her grandmother, and perhaps applying to colleges there, but she reports that she is now back in Brooklyn at her mother's apartment and is getting ready to apply. Although a strong writer when she was in my English class, she reports that she is not writing much these days, and is working at a frozen yogurt shop.

Gabriela Hernandez

Gabriela attends a four-year residential college in upstate New York. She is studying English and pre-law, and while she would like to become a lawyer, she is discouraged by the cost of law school and the job market, and is considering becoming an English teacher, either back in New York City or in Connecticut. She spoke to me about difficulties she had as an English major in college, as she realized the level to which her grades had been inflated at College Prep, and that her "grammar was not at . . . the level of a college student." Luckily, she said, she connected with an English professor who pushed and challenged her, and she feels more confident now. She also expresses interest in someday becoming a writer.

Desiree Sutherland

Desiree is beginning her junior year at a four-year liberal arts college in New York State. She reports that she is an English and communications major, and that she is the president of the school's multicultural association. She told me that she loves school, and is on the track to an on-time graduation.

Destiny Jones

Currently a junior at a historically Black university in the Southeast, Destiny is majoring in marketing and reports that she is working toward a career in the fashion industry. Over the summer, she was a marketing intern for a major fashion magazine, and reports that she is excited to obtain her degree. She is currently working in retail and doing a lot of freelance styling and PR. She continues to maintain the same ambition and drive that she displayed throughout high school.

Princess Smith

Princess currently attends a senior-level college in New York City and is studying communications. She is applying for internships in the entertainment industry. Also currently working in retail, she reports that life is stressful, but despite this, she still pursues her goals and connects with those around her with great energy and enthusiasm.

Teachers/Administrators

Barbara Meehan

Ms. Meehan left College Prep in 2011 to pursue a master's degree in experiential learning and social change at a university in New York City. She reports that she just accepted a job at a community college working with students on probation, and plans to work while she completes her thesis. She hopes to start a nonprofit organization that focuses on experiential or critical service learning.

Erica Caldwell

Ms. Caldwell left College Prep in 2009 to work for the New York City Board of Education, but then began a master's degree in teaching secondary English. She is in her second year teaching English in another New York City public school. She is involved with the New York City Coalition of Radical Educators, an activist, grassroots, left-leaning organization that supports New York City public school teachers and students; she continues to see teaching as a political act.

Frank Matthews

Capitalizing on his love of travel and exploration, Mr. Matthews left College Prep in 2012 of his own volition and took a job teaching humanities at a bilingual school in the Middle East. He reports that he still hopes to pursue his PhD and become a school administrator at some point in the future.

Howard Jackson

Mr. Jackson left College Prep in 2009. He finished his PhD, which focused on Black male teacher recruitment and retention, in 2014. While writing his dissertation, Mr. Jackson was a lecturer, research associate, and clinical teacher educator at a university in the Northeast, but after defending, he began a postdoctoral fellowship at a prominent research university in 2014.

Kathy Sands

Ms. Sands became the assistant principal of College Prep in the fall of 2012, and then in fall 2013 replaced Ms. McCarren as the principal. She reports that she will implement staff book clubs instead of traditional professional development meetings, so that staff, too, can see themselves as students and learners. She tells me that she is determined not to let the system pull her away from what she loves most about working in a school—that is, connecting with students.

La'Trice Williams

At the suggestion of Principal McCarren, Ms. Williams left the classroom in 2009 to oversee extracurricular activities for students at College Prep. In 2010, she left College Prep and took a job as the deputy director for an organization that runs legislative grassroots advocacy training and mobilization programs for parents of students who are in charter schools. The organization also helps parents navigate collocation and facilities allocation processes with the Department of Education (DOE), and sometimes serves as direct grassroots lobbyists for charter schools in the city. In 2014, she transitioned to another job at a national nonprofit dedicated to developing high-quality public schools.

Marie Carr

When I interviewed her, Ms. Carr had been on maternity leave for just under two years. She taught at College Prep until the day before she went into labor. The DOE allows four years off per child (the first three months of which are paid), and so Ms. Carr hopes to return to teaching, and maybe College Prep, when her son is four.

Martina McGoldrick

Ms. McGoldrick left College Prep of her own volition in 2011. Although she began her PhD in urban education, Ms. McGoldrick, who is married to Mr. Battle, is taking some time off to raise their two children. She plans to return to school to finish her PhD and is not sure whether she would like to go back to teaching at the high school level or at the college level when her degree is complete.

Tony Battle

Since leaving College Prep in 2012 at the suggestion of the administration, Mr. Battle is teaching special education and coaching soccer at another New York City high school. He is married to Ms. McGoldrick, and lives just outside of New York City with their two young children.

We Wear the Mask

I drove up to Boston on a summer day in 2012 to catch up with Mr. Jackson, who had moved there to begin research for his dissertation while his wife worked on her master's degree in education. As I noted above, he began a PhD program in education policy and social analysis in 2009 when he left College Prep. When I reinterviewed him, he was working as a teacher educator, training secondary English language arts teachers for Boston public schools, and said that he was interested in focusing his academic research on Black male teacher retention. When he worked in high schools, he had always been one of very few Black men on staff, and so he was interested in exploring the reason behind this pattern. He had also conducted some preliminary research in the high school at Rikers Island (New York City's main prison complex, located on an island in the East

River), and noticed that Black male teachers tended to demonstrate unique forms of caring and rapport building with their incarcerated male students. In his job as a teacher educator, he said, he was focusing on ways he could train the predominantly White women who were entering Boston's public school classrooms as teachers to better support their Black and Latino male students. He said that he had especially appreciated my chapter on White female teachers because of this, and noted that as one of the few Black male teachers at College Prep, he had "felt the weight of race less" in his interactions with Ms. McGoldrick and Ms. Meehan than with Ms. Carr and Ms. Elliott.[2] Pushing my findings further, he said "it would be interesting to juxtapose a sort of positive sense of self that students have that's derived in a class like Ms. McGoldrick's, as opposed to someone like Ms. Elliott's." Echoing my conclusions about cultural circle students' educational trajectory, here he seems to be referring to the importance of moving beyond the spectacle to the more human and solidarity-based forms of teaching and learning. Students had reflected his sentiment: one twelfth-grade student, during a focus group in the fall of 2010, asked to what degree being successful had to do with one's confidence, and a discussion ensued in which students agreed that confidence was intrinsic to success. To what degree, students wondered, did this come from relationships with teachers (many of whom had different methods of teaching or relating to students) and to what degree did this come from relationships with families, friends, or communities? They agreed that it was both.

As Mr. Jackson and I reflected on our experiences at College Prep, he referred to the poem printed in the epigraph to this chapter: Paul Laurence Dunbar's "We Wear the Mask" ([1896] 1993). As a graduate student, Mr. Jackson had conducted a pilot project about Black male teachers in public schools. He interviewed the four Black male staff members who had remained at College Prep after he left, and was surprised to find out how unhappy they were. He said that Mr. Battle, who had been one of the founding staff members of the school, seemed to be the most satisfied at College Prep. Mr. Jackson attributed this to the fact that he had figured out how to "cover" in Goffman's or Yoshino's terms, or "wear the mask," in Dunbar's—in other words, to participate in the school's spectacle in a way that was acceptable to those in power. Mr. Jackson reminisced about several Black staff members who had been told that they were "not the right fit"—who, in other words, were not as adept at "wearing the mask," by administrators' standards, and were asked to leave.

When I reinterviewed Ms. Williams, she expressed seeing this same pattern not only at College Prep, but also in her current job:

> A lot of the Black people that I meet doing this work get pushed out. They are deemed incompetent, or people say "oh, she just doesn't get it." Even when they are C-level people, they are pushed out. And I am like, "how the hell, if she is that incompetent, did she make it there?" . . . I've been growing increasingly frustrated with the absence of people of color in real, meaningful leadership positions.

She continued,

> I am not sure why, if you are a White kid from Nebraska, you are drawn to teaching in New York City in a way that's different from a Black kid in Oakland, right? Like I have not yet figured out why we are not entering the profession and why we are not staying and why we don't find this stuff interesting.

As she made this comment, I remembered her reluctance at leaving a teaching position to take on a staff position at the school. This had been partly due to a bureaucratic issue with transferring her teaching license from Texas to New York, but I recalled her bewilderment at the fact that former principal McCarren did not seem to rally for her to stay in the classroom, and then did not renew her staff position after one year.

When Mr. Jackson and I talked, all four of the teachers that he had interviewed were still at the school. Now, as I write this in the fall of 2014, two of the four are left; Mr. Battle left the school, according to him, not of his own volition, in the spring of 2013. He sent me a text message on his last day asking me to reinterview him for this project. The story of how and why he left the school was another, he felt, that needed to be documented. The school had moved him from teaching science to teaching physical education, although he was licensed to teach English and special education. When a special education teacher (a Black teacher who was certified as an administrator, but was, according to Mr. Battle, not given the opportunity to apply to be an assistant principal before Ms. Sands and Mr. Fulton were promoted to this position) left and a special education position came up at the school, Mr. Battle spoke with Principal McCarren about wanting the job. While he enjoyed teaching physical education, it was not his passion, and he was teaching out of license. Principal Mc-Carren discouraged him from applying for the other position, stating that she needed him to continue teaching physical education and that she would be forced to revoke his tenure if she transferred him to teaching special education. According to Mr. Battle, Ms. Sands, then an assistant principal, told him that there was a school in the Bronx she knew of that was looking for a special education teacher, and that she and Ms. McCarren thought he would be a "good fit" there. The two urged him to apply. "I had never really given any indication of the fact that I wanted to leave," he said, and continued:

> I loved College Prep, I just wanted to teach in my license at College Prep, and it was like, "no no and no," and finally it was like, there's this other school, and I was like, so seriously, you are not trying to retain me? Me, who started the school, and obviously was great with the kids—you wouldn't want me to come work with the kids? The kids that are "difficult to work with," so you say? . . . [I wasn't] valued [at College Prep].

Interestingly, when I spoke with Ms. Sands about this incident in our 2013 follow-up interview, she said she had believed at the time that Mr. Battle had wanted to transfer to the school in the Bronx since it was closer to his home. She was surprised to read that he interpreted the incident so differently, and she told me she wished he had been more forthcoming at the time about the fact that he did not want to leave College Prep.

It seems important that Ms. Sands and Mr. Battle have such different versions of this story. This speaks to another important facet of my argument: the challenges of finding reflexive, critical, empowering, and courageous ways of speaking about and listening to issues related to race, gender, and inequality in schools. When Mr. Mitchell stood up to White administrators, they saw him as someone who was "hostile" and who "bristled at authority" (chapter 2). He lost his job as a result. When Mr. Battle did not stand up to administrators, they were unaware that they were acting against his preferences. Either way, these Black staff members were no longer employed at College Prep.

In our follow-up interview, Mr. Battle stated, "I miss those kids so much . . . and it's a shame that the parting of ways was . . . in reality, that decision was made for me. That's really disheartening." Although it was Mr. Jackson's impression that Mr. Battle was a satisfied staff member who had succeeded in "wearing the mask" (a picture of Mr. Battle wearing a suit, teaching science, that ran along with an article in the *New York Times* praising College Prep's hardworking teachers still hangs in the main office), it seems that according to school administrators, he was another Black staff member whose image made the school look good, but was "not the right fit" in real life.

When I reinterviewed him, Mr. Battle elaborated on this:

> The first two years at College Prep, I'd say like once a month, there were people from the mayor's office, judges, prominent lawyers, newspaper reporters. Where do they go? My room. Hung out there, like, "Black science teacher! New York City public school!" But how many times was I asked to sit in on any roundtable with any of them? Not once! Not one time! When was it time to have an interview? Not once. But they were quick to put my picture out there. And that troubled me, too, you're quick to show me in a suit, doing this, doing that, but it's come time to—but I was never once invited, in the whole time I was there, to a fund-raiser.

In Mr. Battle's case, College Prep used him as a prop in the spectacle for very specific purposes. As Mr. Jackson put it, in a conversation about two Black former administrators at the school who had been asked to leave because they were "not the right fit," there is a certain type of leadership style that Black school leaders were expected to embody that is "almost a mammy-like figure . . . one that is not confrontational, that's not perceived as aggressive, that [would] make White teachers feel safe." Dunbar's poem seems to speak not only to Mr. Battle's and Ms. Williams's experiences, but also to the experience of students and staff members, who, by and large, are aware of the increasing necessity of image management in order to maintain resources, sometimes at the expense of their own agency or subjectivity.

As I spoke with Ms. Williams, she challenged me to push the analysis of this pattern in my follow-up conversations with students, saying that one thing she would like to see in the manuscript was [alumni] perceptions of how Staff Members of Color were treated and viewed by White staff members . . . because I think what you'll find is, aside from Tony Battle [who had not left yet], and aside from [parent coordinator] John Davis who had been there from the beginning but left two years ago now, for most of those kids there has not been a constant Person of Color in their schooling experience at College Prep.

Because of this pattern, and the relatively homogenous population at the school, Ms. Williams argued that most College Prep students don't think a lot about race vis-à-vis themselves and their White peers. They do think a lot about it, she stated, between themselves and their White teachers, who are in a position of institutional power. This is a dynamic that is worth problematizing further, especially in regard to the idea of positive self-identity development.

As this book shows, teachers are not the only ones who are expected to "wear the mask." As the school participates in the spectacle, those students who are most successful at this performance are put on display selectively for funders in much the same way that some Black teachers are. Ms. Williams developed this point in talking about her role in the College Prep film. While she played a prominent role in the film, the original had much more of her in it. Mr. Thomas asked the filmmakers to cut some of her, which Ms. Williams said she was fine with, because "[she] never wanted to be in the damn thing anyway." She went on,

So the pieces they kept were only the pieces about me having grown up in Watts—and me feeling like I wanted to give back to my community. But screw the other pieces about pushing kids to think critically and screw the pieces that were about the relationships I have with kids or with staff. All that matters is, here's a Black teacher who is from this place.

She spoke about there being fewer than ten Black teachers at the school, but even two years after she left the school, her name still appeared as a member of the Social Studies department on the school's website (my own was taken down as soon as I left the school). Two and a half years after she left, the image of her face was used on the cover of the materials at a conference presentation focusing on Black male student achievement that former principal McCarren and Mr. Matthews gave. "It's not because I'm great," she said, "and it's not because I stand out in any way. It's just over and over again, I have 'the look.' Over and over again, I say the right thing in a couple of sentences and you can boil that down to the best sound bites." The "right thing" in her case seemed always to have to do with her personal history or racial positionality, but not with her intellect or pedagogy, and certainly not with ideas that may have challenged the school's complicity in the entrenched power structure within and beyond its walls.

A weakness of the manuscript, she stated, was that while I emphasize to a great extent the critical race and class consciousness of some teachers, I don't do this to the same extent with the students. "You talk about people opting in and out of professionalism, and when and where and why they choose it, but I am not sure you talk enough about them feeling like it's a direct attack on who they are as Black and Brown kids." No one, she said, is engaging in this sort of conversation with students, who figure out very early on in their time at College Prep how to "turn it on and off" for funders. This is a key aspect of what I am trying to emphasize in this manuscript—that is, that every individual at College Prep is to some degree critically aware of the implications of their participation in the spectacle. Those who participate do so knowingly, ambivalently, and sometimes painfully. She continued:

> So it's like, to this person I should talk about the fact that my mom is a single mom. To this person, I guess I should talk about the fact that I am going to be the first person to graduate high school. The kids know that [funders] are peeking into their classrooms to see them do something that Black and Brown kids are not supposed to do.

In the revised introduction to this manuscript, I documented one of these conversations between Mr. Thomas and Kadeem, the student who was being considered for the NBC special with the Duchess of York, and tried to bring in more critical race analysis when it came to students' perspectives. As I speak with more of my former tenth-grade students, who are now alums, this is a conversation that I plan to approach to a greater extent and hope to explore in future publications.

Interestingly, Dunbar's poem puts the pressure to wear the mask in monetary terms: we wear masks to "pay our debt to human guile." To what degree do we convince ourselves that we have no other choice but to pay this "debt"? In the case of College Prep, or in the case of Mr. Battle, it may seem that our survival depends on it; we believe that we "owe" this debt to the funders who provide for us, or that we "owe" this debt to administrators, because our jobs are at their mercy. They may not overtly demand that we "wear the mask" (and may not even be aware of its existence); however, out of fear we comply with the image we think will most appeal to their generosity. We wear "masks" because we believe that this is what it takes to please those around us, sometimes disguising our disgust, sometimes our pleasure, sometimes our resistance. We disguise who we "really" are in the interest of a performance that we think is what others want to see. Mr. Battle's story, as well as the story that I tell about the dangers of image management at College Prep in general, teaches us that while we may accrue benefits from "wearing the mask," it may be instructive to consider what we sacrifice. Ironically, the sense that we have debts we must pay to human guile may lead to our self-destruction, and distract us from the real problems we must face: problems of continuing racial and class injustice and inequity, as well as dehumanization, at both the institutional and social/structural levels.

Reflecting on Identity Construction and Agency

As I sat across from Mr. Matthews in his empty classroom in 2012 (the year before he left the school to teach in the Middle East), I reminded him about a few of the topics we had covered during his first interview—he had been very positive about the mission of the school, and the direction in which it was going. He responded, pausing dramatically between each sentence: "I know. I just feel really jaded now. I have woken up." Although we both laughed at his dramatic pauses, the sentiment was very serious. Like other teachers whom I interviewed, Mr. Matthews came into College Prep inspired by the school's mission to send African American and Latino students from traditionally underserved communities to college, but after remaining at College Prep for some time, he became discouraged with how the school's participation in neoliberal saviorism contributed to the pathologization of students and their communities. Mr. Matthews and the other staff members and students remarked in my follow-up interviews that they were appreciative of the critiques that I was making and were interested in deepening them.

When I asked Mr. Matthews to describe his role at the school, and whether it had changed at all since our last interview, he mentioned that he had taken on more responsibility—he took over for Mr. Jackson in leading the young men's empowerment group at the school, which took up many of his evenings and weekends, and he was teaching ninth-grade history. "I have to manage [the young men's group] and teaching," he said. "What is expected of teachers here is interesting in terms of your critique of the school and the business model . . . this place . . . [has] somewhat unrealistic expectations for [what] adults in the building [should] produce." He mentioned that reading critiques from other teachers helped him to further define his life plan, which was to move toward becoming an administrator and then start his own school for young men. He added,

Reading the critiques from other teachers in terms of "it's not sustainable to work here" so there is a large number of teachers especially this year who, since you were here, have grown in the sense that they have a family, different responsibilities and priorities and they are like "I am not going to sacrifice."

Mr. Matthews's critique was echoed by other staff members whom I spoke with—it seemed that for staff, reading the ethnography affirmed their discomfort with the idea of being cast as the "savior teacher." They used the manuscript to define themselves against this trope.

Pushing this point further, Mr. Matthews added,

I don't even feel like the school mission is something students are supposed to believe in and uphold. To me it's like, [the mission is] something that the adults at the school who donate money believe in. So it feels good that I am donating to some, you know, "underprivileged" or "underserved" kids—which is a crock as well because . . . there are a ton of salaries that parents make, all the way from six-figures to living in a shelter . . . but [the mission is] going to continue to allow the school to make money. I feel like in terms of the people that New York City schools attract, and it could be College Prep in terms of we feel like we can save—or why specific people work here . . . we feel like we are going to save this child.

Drawing on Althusser (1971), Hall and Du Gay (1996) explain identity construction as a point of "suture" or temporary attachment between, on the one hand, discourses that interpellate subjects, and on the other, subjects that invest in the position. Mr. Matthews expresses discomfort at being interpellated as a neoliberal savior by the institution, because this identity position automatically both essentializes and ascribes a deficit to students. He tried to invest in the identity position of an asset-based pedagogue who strives to recognize the diversity of the student body, as well as scaffold students to take pride in their communities and identities. Yet he recognizes that the hierarchical model of the institution and its spectacle depended on interpellating teachers, students, and their communities in an essentialized way in order to ensure the comfort of the predominantly White, elite funders and corporate philanthropists who contribute money.

Mr. Jackson and Ms. Sands echoed this concern in a different way, both critiquing what they called the "hero" mentality of some staff members. "There can only be one great white knight," said Mr. Jackson, in agreement with my racialized critique of the school's participation in a market-oriented spectacle. Ms. Williams commented that College Prep, like many other New York City schools, does not respect the expertise or experience of parents. Both she and Mr. Jackson felt that the issue of pushing parents out worked in tandem with the school's reliance on funders' generosity, as well as with the construction of the White neoliberal savior.

Students who participated in the cultural circles felt that I had written an accurate portrayal both of them and of their families. Carmen stated, "reading about what Destiny said, I felt like I was at home; I could hear her mother's accent. And you told the story of my life, losing friends, losing my Dad, living in East New York." Princess said that reading the manuscript made her feel "a little famous." Students appreciated their stories being told in this format, and overall said that the manuscript was accurate in terms of portraying both the opportunities that some students are given at College Prep as well as the difficulty that some teachers have in building relationships with students and in maintaining discipline in their classrooms. While Desiree felt that she was able to develop her "pizzazz" at College Prep, Carmen and Gabriela seemed skeptical that College Prep had done enough to prepare them for the SAT or for academics, organization, or time management in college.

Parents were concerned, in looking at the school-wide questionnaire (appendix B), about students' impressions of professionalism, and how many students have negative opinions of it. They also brought up concern regarding the job of a parent versus the job of a teacher. Should it be a teacher's role to talk with students about their problems? How should teachers best connect and form relationships of solidarity with students and their communities? The manuscript seemed to create, for parents, teachers, and students, a welcome opportunity to deeply consider the ways they constructed their identities in relation to the institution, as well as a way to problematize and interrogate people's ambivalence about the institution's participation in the spectacle.

Reflecting on Commodification and Generosity

Overwhelmingly, when they looked back at their experience, the students whom I had a chance to reinterview were appreciative of the resources and extracurricular opportunities available to them at College Prep. That said, the students I interviewed were those who participated in my cultural circles, and were often the ones who were chosen to participate in the school's extracurricular activities. Perhaps, as I get the chance to connect with more alumni, my findings might be different.

Teachers tended to have different opinions about the school. Mr. Matthews's concern and construction of self in resistance to the school's interpellation of him was heightened by how he saw the money from donors being used: "It's a game. I feel like . . . it's a game [played] especially with Black and Brown children that we are going to experiment with your child." Ms. Williams, in her interview, agreed: "[Donors] are funding an experiment." As an example, Mr. Matthews spoke about a nearby public school whose theme and curricula were centered around boating:

> Who needs to know how to—like, really? If I want to think about a school mission, and about how we want to educate students who are low-skilled, are not performing at grade level when they enter the ninth grade, why am I taking you on a sailboat so you can figure out how to navigate a ship? Why am I giving you scuba lessons and that's what your class is during the day? I understand there is a need for extracurricular activities, but I need to see the results, like what are the results? I feel like you are just playing

around; it's like we are throwing money at you and we are throwing money at the problem, but we are still keeping you in your place, because we are not giving you the tools you need to really function [at the college level]. You know how to cruise a boat, and then you'll maybe go to [City College] and get your associate's degree. But put that in [a donor's] child's school? No. Why isn't my child taking an advanced math class or something like that? SAT prep. Don't give my child scuba diving.

Mr. Matthews sees this ideology of experimentation and the need to get instant results or move on to the next experiment as being an overtly racial project (Omi and Winant 1994). It is racist because it links essentialist representations of race with social structures of domination; although these "innovations" are named as reforms, they are actually experiments on racialized bodies that function to maintain a racially hegemonic spectacle.

The fact that these experiments are funded by charity reinforces the hierarchical racial and class project of the institution. Mr. Matthews said:

We as a school expect that once a child graduates and they go to college the family and the student is forever indebted to the school in terms of "look what we did for your child," as opposed to "look what your child did for himself or herself" . . . [when I was in high school], it was like, my parents always congratulated me, it was always intrinsic, you know, that I was motivated and I wanted to do this, and I never felt indebted to my school. And I think it was maybe just my understanding of public education is that everybody deserves it. This is my right. And I was like, I can thank you, but I don't feel like I need to thank you because everybody should get this regardless.

Portraying the school and its funders—as opposed to the student, the family, or the community—as holding the primary responsibility for students' acquisition of social and cultural capital and upward mobility is tied in with the school's branding; this is one way in which College Prep portrays itself as both needy and deserving of funders' generosity. Students and their families are expected to thank the school for "saving" them, and in turn the school thanks the funders who continue to provide, even though it is under essentializing and commodifying conditions.

I asked Mr. Matthews how he was able to reconcile his deep critique of the institution and its interpellation of him and his students with coming to work every day. He said, "It's like, you don't want to bite the hand that feeds you." Mr. Jackson echoed this sentiment, stating that while he was critical of the institution's racial and class project, he recognized that he was an active participant. Mr. Matthews told me that he had conversations with former principal McCarren about his problems with the school's construction of students and teachers for the purpose of enhanced marketability. "It seemed like she agreed," he said, "but I don't even know if she even knows how to go about making these changes—or she agreed, but not publicly, because she doesn't want to lose her support amongst the staff, so I think it's kind of been like, what can you do, right?"

Mr. Battle and Ms. McGoldrick also made critiques of the tension between the fight for equity and the school's racialized spectacle. Mr. Battle stated,

> It's not so bad to try to get these donors, but it's how you try to solicit the donors and it's how you try to change the image of kids to get the money. People should be trying to give money to the school because they are helping out a school that shows promise, but promise is not always just, "I am going to take the ten most articulate kids and put them in a room" . . . The image part, for donors should be, well, don't you want to just help out a school? Is [the problem] privatization, or is it the underlying racism? Is the privatization underlying the racism?

While Mr. Battle problematized the relation between privatization and race, Ms. McGoldrick concisely remarked that in her opinion, having "all these rich people giving to all these poor kids is . . . ignoring the bigger problem of education in the city, and why most of the schools are so crappy." She added, "We shouldn't have rich people coming into the school. The system should work for itself." While the students who have those opportunities are grateful, Ms. McGoldrick plainly states that these opportunities should be available to *all* children, whether at College Prep or outside. Ms. Carr and Ms. McLeod also echoed this statement in our follow-up interviews, both in regard to resources and extracurricular opportunities. As I have argued in this book, a school model that is dependent on commodification and generosity seems to inhibit this possibility.

Reflections on Humanization and Solidarity

What might counter the inequalities that come about as a result of a spectacle of commodification and generosity? Students communicated to me when I reinterviewed them that they most valued those teachers who both "didn't play"—in other words, had high expectations—and were also able to "connect" with them. Students emphasized that there was no rote or scripted method for doing this; the best teachers, they said, accomplished this in very different ways. By and large, students named the teachers whom I reinterviewed for the afterword as being especially adept. These teachers seemed to agree that humanizing pedagogy and deep connections between teachers, families, and students can trouble the race and class hierarchy furthered by the influence of charity and commodification. In other words, College Prep's model makes it easy to give without really "seeing" those whom one is giving to, but it is impossible to teach effectively if you refuse to "see" those who are in front of you.

Some teachers connected professionalism at College Prep to the influence of charity and marketization, aligning it with yet another way in which teachers do not "see" their students. When I reinterviewed Ms. Caldwell, the White teacher who participated in our cultural circles, she said,

> The thing that is so interesting about the White teachers chapter is that the choices to build relationships with kids seems to be the primary difference [between them] . . . The teachers with a more color conscious or whatever consciousness they have—with more of a critique of Whiteness—they are just more critical in general and they build tighter relationships with kids. [It seems like] there are two ways of building relationships with kids [at College Prep]. It's like you build relationships with them, or you determine how professional or unprofessional they are.

She added that this is why many of the more critical teachers at College Prep leave:

They are caught in the middle of like—they have close relationships with students because they are critical, and one of their values is in building relationships with kids, and no one ever leaves because of the kids, but they also can't stay . . . it seems like the school is a little bit imploding on itself. What are students' realities, and what is the reality that is being pushed by the school? And like those two things don't match up . . . For a teacher to feel like their job is fulfilling, then those things need to match.

When I interviewed Ms. Meehan, she seemed to echo this sentiment as she communicated her reasoning for leaving the school. She gave a year's notice before she left, and stated, "I decided I was gonna leave but it was very difficult for me to make sense of why the school just wasn't feeling right to me . . . Part of me knew that if I was a student there, I wouldn't be happy . . . it's this idea that students are supposed to feel so grateful to be there." This, she expressed, inhibits the human give-and-take that has to happen between teachers and students for real learning, connection, and communication to take place. In other words, she said, "Some people say that they are not comfortable engaging with students on social or emotional level. You kind of have to be comfortable with it." Teaching and learning cannot occur otherwise.

Even in regard to teaching SLANT (which I mentioned seeing in Mr. Rodino's class in chapter 2), Principal Sands said, "On its own it's not so bad—it's not a terrible thing to teach someone to sit up, listen, ask questions, nod their head." She elaborated, "It's when you teach it like it's an inhuman thing . . . to tell someone, I am listening to you, and so if I'm not listening to you, I shouldn't be doing it." If one is really listening, she said, one asks questions, one nods one's head. One demonstrates these nonverbal cues. "Instead," she said, "it gets, like, it's so processed out that by the time somebody gets it it's like robotic, you do it all the time. Well no, you don't do it all the time, and now we've not even taught them what was meant initially." The performance takes away from the possibility of a more human, and a much more satisfying and real, solidarity. Participants overwhelmingly agreed that humanization and solidarity between and among teachers, students, funders, and parents counter the oppressive aspects of masking or covering oneself in the interest of a political spectacle. I detail this point further in the afterword, which discusses the implications of this research, as well as future recommendations.

Beyond the Spectacle

I reinterviewed Ms. Sands in the fall of 2013. When I taught at the school, she was the chair of the English department, but the year after I left, she was promoted to assistant principal. When I caught back up with her to reinterview her, she had replaced Principal McCarren, who left the school to lead one of the nonprofit networks with which the school was affiliated. Principal Sands, too, spoke about the complicated relationship that she felt she has to maintain with the board. We need more resources, she explained, because there is so much more work to be done at the school. She expressed her critique of the spectacle by saying that she does not want to impress funders, she said, by "putting shininess" on everything, but because it's real:

> I want people to invest in this school because they are like, wow, people in this school are doing really thoughtful work and loving kids, you know . . . and in my conversations with board members so far I have not been able, I have not been allowed almost to go down that path . . . it's very much, "How are you going to maintain the mission of the school? How are you going to maintain the excellent college going rate? How are you going to maintain funding?" It is not all about my children. I realize it needs to be done and I am grateful. I am so incredibly thankful to the people that are giving their money . . . because they believe they are doing something good . . . but it's weird that we send a child to India for six weeks and they have never really seen the face of the person that makes that possible for them . . . and I think what the people funding our school miss is being able to see it visibly change. And then I'm wondering: do they care? Is it important to them? Is that kind of outcome important to them, or is it more to keep the quantitative data outcome looking good?

Here, Principal Sands critiques the school's spectacle on two fronts: both because it takes the humanity out of students and staff because funders rely on quantitative data, rather than on qualitative gains in students' educational experiences, but also because it takes the humanity out of the funders for students. In other words, the spectacle is based on irony, distance, and self-aggrandizement for funders, and explicitly *not* based on a model of agonistic solidarity (Chouliaraki 2011), which is grounded in an awareness and appreciation for diversity of experience as well as a common sense of injustice at human vulnerability, inequality, and oppression.

As Ms. Sands said when I reinterviewed her, in order to be an effective teacher, one has to thoughtfully engage with children. As principal, she hopes to develop College Prep into a school where this can take place. At this point, she said,

> We settle for this sort of shinier version of things—we settle for
> "give me the script for how I should interact with [the name of one
> of the funders] when I go to the Firm," and the student is like, "I
> feel armored now." They've got their armor on. And the funder
> feels like they've got their armor on . . . I think it would take some
> work to get us to a place where Ms. Elliott took her armor off and
> the children took their armor off, or in this case, really, the board,
> the funders, and had an open dialogue. I don't even know what
> our funders would do if they heard a child tell them their real
> story. I would love to see what happens in that moment.

Ms. Sands seems here to be voicing a wish for the possibility of moving beyond the spectacle to a point of agonistic solidarity, without using this term. This may, according to Ms. Meehan, be a more realistic goal than many think. Because of her work in the Foundation, Ms. Meehan worked very closely with many of those employed by the Firm; there were some funders who were also invested in "dropping their armor" and in forging real relationships with students. "I get the sense," she said, "some of the funders were engaging on a level that was more than just giving monetarily." Some of the funders, she said, came to the school, and engaged students in extracurricular activities. She mentioned that other funders had worked with her on building curriculum, and had volunteered their time to have lunch with groups of students as well as to present to groups of students about the work that they were doing. One wealthy White male funder, she said, gave a presentation to students and then facilitated a dialogue about how his work was helping to fight racism. Having observed the presentation, she noted that it seemed he felt really comfortable doing that. "The much bigger challenge," she said, "is to get everyone who has money to engage on that level." She elaborated,

> I come from a lot of privilege, and I have to believe that I can play an authentic and integral and worthwhile role in this struggle. So if I said something like, for wealthy people to be funding education or any other kind of issue like that's inherently problematic, then that would not be reflective. I wouldn't be owning my own stuff, and I would be wanting to feel better than other privileged people or people who have a little more privilege than I do. I would be distancing myself from that group. So I want to believe that wealthy people can be movers and shakers, but it's like anyone who wants to be effective has to be a part of this critical reflective dialogue.

Real relationships between people can occur across levels of privilege and power, and can make change. However they cannot be only about superficial performance, guilt, or sympathy for the "other."

Mr. Battle and Principal Sands both emphasized the fact that teachers' jobs become much easier and much more empowering when they are aware that teaching and learning are about human connection. She stated, "If you're not doing the work for this reason, then maybe you should consider doing it for this reason. You might find—you might find—it's easier. It's actually a lot easier if you do it with different motivation." The best teachers do not see themselves as heroes, she said. Instead, effective practitioners recognize that they are one person in a child's whole world of people who are offering support. The best teachers, she said, figure out how to be guides whose messages work in concert with the messages that children are getting from other places in their lives; they are those who value solidarity. Teachers and funders, she said, make a grave error when they participate in a spectacle that casts them as a lone savior figure. She said:

> We are taught by the world. Privatization, we are taught to put ourselves first, right, we are taught to go after what you want and get it and it doesn't really matter. I don't think that that works in

teaching. If you are here for that stuff, then you are not going to last very long . . . If you want to do this work, I think you really have to do it because you want to help children do whatever it is they want to do—you know, if this is the path they want to take you want to help them do it, you know, you want to help them have good guide. And a thoughtful one.

Mr. Battle expressed this same mentality in terms of how he related to students, regardless of the content area that he was teaching in. Even in teaching sports, he said, he taught students "ways to look at the world and try to change the world and themselves within the world." He elaborated:

> I reach kids on a level that has nothing to do with sports at all, and it's like the conversation that they need to have, like you have to prod them to get them to have it with you, but that they are so happy that you take the time to listen to them and that you actually see . . . there is nothing more important in the classroom than to stop and learn to reach the kids on that level, to stop and hear what they say, because quite honestly, that is to know them.

Unknowingly reflecting Ms. Sands, he said, "They are twenty years younger than me, they are in a different world! Nonetheless, they are pretty cool little individuals trying to figure out who they are in the world. My job is to help and guide them through that process." In relation to his students, he said, "I am gonna need you in the future . . . Eventually I am not going to be able to take care of myself, and you guys are the future voters and you are the decision makers. The ones that are going to take care of me, and my future." This knowledge undergirds the connections that Mr. Battle forms with students. He knows that his students are in his hands, but also that before long, he will be in theirs. Thus, he envisions this relationship of care and trust as lasting long beyond the classroom.

Concluding Thoughts

In our discussion of the manuscript, Mr. Jackson remarked, "When I read your first chapter, what came to mind was chapter 1 of *Invisible Man* . . . Black bodies on show for the White elite—for [Whites'] enjoyment. For their own pleasure [and] to reify, in their mind, the social order." The scene in Ellison's book (1952) that Mr. Jackson refers to involves the protagonist of the story, the young, Black, "invisible man," who has just finished high school. He is the chosen speaker for his high school graduation and is subsequently invited to give a speech for the wealthy White patrons of his town. Politically, he aligns himself with Booker T. Washington, and is thrilled at the prospect of giving the speech for such an important audience. Yet when he arrives, instead of giving the speech, he is forced, along with a group of other young Black men in the town, to participate in a battle royal as the town's White citizens watch. The young men don boxing gloves and, once in the ring, are forced to watch the gyrations of a naked White woman with an American flag painted on her stomach. They are then blindfolded and are forced to fight one another. After the fight, the blindfolds are removed from the last contestants standing and they wrestle on the ground for bills and coins (later, the protagonist finds that these are valueless brass tokens) scattered across a rug, which participants discover is electrified. The narrator, who gets shocked himself, watches in horror as his peers' bodies stiffen from the intensity of the shocks. He is finally permitted to give his speech. He quotes Booker T. Washington at length. The White citizens laugh and talk over him. At one point in the speech, the protagonist substitutes the words "social equality" for "social responsibility." The audience balks and protests, and he tells them that he actually meant "social responsibility." He is allowed to continue the speech, and at the end, the White patrons give him a briefcase. Its contents, they tell him, will help determine the fate of his people. It contains a scholarship to a state college for Black youth. The narrator juxtaposes his impressions of scenes from the battle royal with his impressions of the White audience laughing, eating, smoking cigars, and catcalling.

The implications of this violent raced and gendered scene are clear: not only does the power structure stay the way it is, but those who are in positions of privilege actually gain enjoyment and entertainment from a spectacle that humiliates and dehumanizes the oppressed. The White audience members are incapable of seeing or hearing the humanity of the narrator and his peers, and the Black participants are not only blindfolded but are blind to the true politics and intentions of the White audience's ostensible goodwill and concern. "Social responsibility" equates to the maintenance of the status quo.

Mr. Jackson elaborated,

> In order for me to have my position (as the former head of the
> Young Men's Association), in order for me to do my work, there
> almost has to be this sort of bastardizing of the experiences of,
> you know, poor Black and Brown kids and so it becomes hard
> to . . . It is a dog and pony show . . . it was a story that brought in
> money, you know, these students, they don't have, and we need
> you people who have a lot to give it to them.

Just as White patrons construct themselves against the dehumanized
Black youth in the battle royal, Mr. Jackson argues that College Prep's
participation in a political spectacle of philanthropic generosity and fundamental inequity helps the funders of the school, and in some cases, the
teachers, to construct themselves against a monolithic and essentializing
narrative about students. In *Invisible Man,* as well as in Dunbar's poem
and at College Prep, masks and/or blindfolds—whether literal or meta-
phorical—prevent self-reflexivity, social critique, or humanization.

This is a story that Ms. Williams told in a different context, having
recently accompanied her boss to a fund-raiser for KIPP (Knowledge
is Power Program) charter schools in Newark, New Jersey. Arianna
Huffington was the keynote speaker. The evening started with a cocktail
hour where an elementary school choir performed, followed by a middle
school drum line. Then, the founder spoke about the organization's growth,
and potential funders watched films about the school. "I was right back at
College Prep," Ms. Williams said. She continued:

> And then it was time to raise the money. And you can now text
> your pledge, so they put up a screen and you text your pledge
> and you can see the screen. The starting pledge was twenty-five
> thousand dollars for their new elementary school. And they said,
> "we need six new classrooms," and just like that, texts went up.
> And they raised, I think over half a million dollars that night . . .
> the idea that I am sitting next to people who can text to pledge
> twenty-five thousand dollars—it's crazy to me. So that part of the
> program is over, so you go out, more cocktails, and you come back
> in and it's time for dinner. And they put a teacher and a student at
> each table. The teacher—White woman, from northern Michigan.

The student—Black kid from Newark. And all over again, I'm remembering College Prep, but now I'm on the other side. Now this teacher thinks I am someone who can text to pledge twenty-five thousand dollars. And so she's like trying to sell to me why she does this work and why she loves it so much. It makes my blood boil!

Cory Booker was the next speaker, and Ms. Williams remembered him saying to the room full of mostly White funders that it was their generosity that made the evening possible. "Your generosity," Ms. Williams repeated, shaking her head, "your generosity, your generosity." She continued:

And then I remembered being a high school kid and sitting in a room and hearing everyone talk about me like I wasn't there. And hearing everyone talk about how messed up my life was. And how I needed them to save me. And I looked across the table at this girl who is in the eighth grade and I was like, "I remember being you, and I still feel like you in these moments." And every single kid in that room was checked out. They were totally checked out. They were either on their phones, or talking to each other, or trying to go to the bathroom together . . . because any part of the presentation that talked about the need to save them from Newark talked about them in a way that made them feel uncomfortable in middle school. And they gotta sit through those things because they are chosen over and over again. They choose the same kids, over and over again. They've gotta sit through those presentations over and over again, and all they keep hearing is, it's not their hard work that makes a difference, it's not their parents that makes the difference. It's these White folks who are giving them twenty-five thousand dollars a pop who make their lives possible.

Like Mr. Jackson, and many of the teachers whom I spoke with for this project, Ms. Williams is pained by the implications of students' and teachers' involvement in selling a story in order to enforce funders' self-aggrandizing narratives of generosity.

Mr. Jackson remarked that in his mind, "I don't think people at the Foundation knew that students were aware of how to play this game. You know, I don't know. I am very conflicted over it. Because I played the game too, in some ways." Mr. Jackson brings us back to Principal Sands's meta-

phor of armor. Everyone plays the game, but few find pleasure or fulfill-
ment in it. Most are ambivalent, some try to resist. Perhaps, said Ms. Meehan, there might be an alternative possibility: "Is there a way for people
who have resources to give . . . to think of themselves in solidarity with the
people that they are sharing with, as opposed to feeling so good about
themselves for sharing or giving?" While she said that she did not know
how to create this, she thought it might be a worthwhile consideration.

Some believe that competition in education inspires innovation, and
that success in the world outside can only come from continued exposure
to a competitive and "professional" environment. In other words, we
cannot change the reality of the world, with all its inequities. Students,
they feel, should learn to navigate that in a "socially responsible" fashion.
While it may be true that competition can inspire people to try harder, it
is more important that we cultivate the ability to deeply connect with and
learn from others. All students—not just a few—should enjoy access to
the resources that are available at College Prep as a result of the Foundation and the Firm—or the resources that are available to students in more
elite schools as a result of property taxes, alumni donations, or branding.
I have demonstrated here how altruism can prevent us from truly "seeing"
other people. A gift of resources does not make up for a theft of humanity,
or for the continued maintenance of stark social inequities. The participants with whom I conducted follow-up interviews seem to align with the
idea that we might work against dependence on problematic philanthropic relationships, but that where they exist, we might work toward making
them more humanizing, proximate, and engaged (Richey and Ponte 2011),
and capitalizing in better—and more equitable—ways on donors who
may genuinely have the best of intentions.

Principal Sands stated, "I really do think it is about love. It's about loving the children as people and it's about loving them so much so that you
want what's best for them. And what's best for them so often doesn't look
like what your track was." Building on this in a discussion of how I dealt
with race in the manuscript, she said,

> I think it's more than just what you've written. I'm never going
> to say it's not about race because it's always about race. But I do
> really think I've come to believe that it's about loving other people
> and about loving them really well . . . you put other people before
> yourself . . . you put your children before yourself.

Ms. Sands was open about not feeling like she had the answers, but that she wanted to continue to think reflexively about how to create a more humanizing school model. Maybe someday, she said, "I feel like I'll have the Foundation—I feel like I'll have it figured out. So I'll be able to tell you this is actually what's wrong with this model, and what could be done to make it right." Other teachers whom I spoke with suggested that a more viable model might be for donors to give to education in general, taking out the marketing piece while working for equity. Still others suggested that we do away altogether with models of philanthropy in education. Others think that there is possibility in working toward solidarity by developing more human relationships with donors.

The agency and critical perspectives of those whom I profile in this study demonstrate that educators, administrators, and policymakers might shift the focus of school reform away from quantitative results and competition for private resources and toward deepening the possibility for human connection and agonistic solidarity (Chouliaraki 2011). Participants agreed that the best teaching and learning happen when those who teach and those who learn are willing to experience vulnerability and growth, to drop their masks and take off their armor. This study tells a story that is important for funders, teachers, parents, and students to engage; that is, that along with good intentions, it is essential to have the self-awareness to continue to ask questions, and to reflect on one's role in relation to stock narratives about power, difference, need, and generosity. It is my hope that these conversations will continue and that this book might contribute toward an unwavering investment in equity and liberation in the context of an increasingly privatized and polarized world.

Producing Knowledge through Qualitative Research Methods

When I teach qualitative research methods, three of the central questions I explore with students are: (1) What counts as solid evidence for knowledge claims about the human world? (2) What are the strategies and techniques researchers use to produce that knowledge? And (3) How does researcher positionality influence claims to knowledge and serve to maintain or contest social structures of privilege and oppression? This book is an exercise in knowledge production that operates on the premise that there is a relationship between ontology (what actually exists in the world) and epistemology (how we gain knowledge about what exists) (Maxwell 2013). While I assume that there is a knowable "real world" out there, the strength of qualitative research is that it allows for a relativist ontology that throws the idea of "epistemological sovereignty" (Lather 2004), in other words, the idea that the mission of social scientists should be to explore an objective and generalizable "truth" about human communities, cultures, societies, or traditions, into question. Rather, I engage in what Demerath calls the "science of context" (2006). In this appendix, I explore the "culture" concept as it was employed at College Prep and then explain in greater depth the methods that I used to conduct research and construct knowledge given the context and culture of this school. I emphasize the value and importance of qualitative research methods beyond anthropology.

Ontological standardization, Demerath writes, can have damaging implications for those who attempt to understand social processes at local levels, and to understand how people make meaning of their lives (2006). On the other hand, it is important to remember that there is a system and a structure for what qualitative researchers do in the field—we go beyond a kind of "deep hanging out" and engage in a "systematic and improvisational hanging out" (ibid.) that is informed by a long tradition of theory and method (Behar 1996; Denzin and Lincoln 2011; Glesne 2011; Maxwell 2013; Spindler and Hammond 2006). The ethnographic narrative in this book is a construction that is informed by the localized and context-based nature of human interactions at College Prep, as well as by a genealogy of research methods and theoretical frameworks that are foundational to the discipline of anthropology. This manuscript is a written exploration of how people make meaning of their world within (and beyond) the institutional setting of College Prep.

My findings emerged from an iterative process in which my data continually refined my research questions as well as the study's theoretical framework, and vice versa (Charmaz 2011; Glesne 2011; Goulding 2005). I did not embark on my field research with the goal of writing a qualitative critique of the political spectacle and inequities that are encouraged and exacerbated by philanthropic or altruistic relationships. Rather, I had hoped to document how teachers in a contemporary U.S. public school were rewriting Freirean or critical pedagogy in context. Yet when I began my teacher research at the school in 2008, rather than finding the wealth of critical pedagogues that I had hoped to, I found that teachers and students were extremely conflicted about the school's marketing project. They knew that they were performing for funders, and were conscious of the tension between needing to maintain critical resources and "selling" a story that reified social hierarchies of class, race, and gender. In Gramscian terms, they were like organic intellectuals who were both critical and had a vested interest in their community (in this case, the school), but were frustrated because of the seeming inability to enact a radical praxis in the face of the school's political spectacle.[1] Through learning and using the tools of qualitative research, but also from prior exposure in graduate-level anthropology classes to the various manifestations of hegemony and neoliberalism, I formed a critique of how hegemony and neoliberalism were manifesting for students and teachers at College Prep. The relationship between the Firm, the Foundation, and the ways in which teachers taught and students learned, I found, was inseparable from how people created "culture" in that setting. I didn't leave Freire behind (as we see in chapter 6) but integrated him into a larger and more contextually relevant question about the effects of privatization and marketization on public school students and teachers.

"Culture" Outside and Inside College Prep

Debates around the "culture" concept form the foundation for much of the heuristic in anthropological fieldwork (Harrison 1992, 1998; Hartigan

2005; Liss 1998; Stocking 1974; Visweswaran 1998). Anthropologists use research methods to study culture, but what does this mean? How does the culture concept resonate with U.S. public schooling, especially when it is often portrayed as the gateway to upward class mobility?

Through the late nineteenth and early twentieth centuries, anthropologist Franz Boas pioneered the concept of "cultural relativism" (1887; Stocking 1974). Prior to Boas, many Western anthropologists held an "evolutionary" concept of culture, which championed the scientific rationalism of industrial England, and defined culture as a bounded, static list of elements that were often biologically based or conditioned. Boas changed the way in which anthropologists worked and the methods that we used, because he rejected the evolutionary view of culture, arguing that there is no culture that is inherently superior to any other. He also argued that culture is contextually and habitually learned. Boas laid the groundwork for anthropology becoming a science of context (Demerath 2006).

Despite Boas's arguments for cultural relativism, as I point out in chapter 3, New York senator Daniel Patrick Moynihan (1965) popularized explaining the causes of poverty with "culture" through his racist ideas about urban, African American families. Academics took Moynihan to task, pointing out that not only does he essentialize Black families, but he also "blames the victim," not taking into account larger socioeconomic structures that reproduce and exacerbate inequality (Akom 2008; Briggs 2002; Kelley 1997; Pierre 2004).

The ways College Prep staff members defined culture seemed to resonate with more static and classed conceptions of the term. For example, during the homecoming focus groups, teachers questioned College Prep alums about difficulties they encountered in their colleges, or about differences that they noticed between what they saw in college and what they had encountered at College Prep. As alums mentioned that they had difficulties when it came to the mechanics of academic writing, and that their peers seemed to be much more competent in terms of study habits, teachers asked what they could do at College Prep to better prepare our students for college. Clinton, an African American alum and the former president of the senior class, who now attends a small liberal arts college in the Midwest, remarked,

> You gotta build an atmosphere. A lot of times, it's not like everyone is there for the right purpose. You gotta have leaders, people

that let you know that this is not a game. On campus, we know we have to get our work done. In the hallway, you see people studying, people put peer pressure on you—you need to have leaders, you know, that 10 percent or whatever.

Former principal Cohen, a bit jokingly, asked how to create that culture. Yet underneath her sarcasm, there was a hint of seriousness, voicing a concern that there wasn't necessarily a "culture" among students of academic rigor, of seriousness, or of community spirit.

Teachers were often troubled by what they called the "culture" of the school, and spoke to me about how it didn't reflect the visions or ideas that they dreamed of, or that it didn't reflect the culture of the high schools that they had attended. Sometimes, comments about issues with school culture were framed in terms of pointing out what they noticed about "these kids'" culture, or about what students were or were not getting at home.

For example, Mr. Kipp, a twenty-seven-year-old White man originally from a rural area of New England, who coached cross-country track for the school and conducted the school's music ensemble, expressed his frustration to me one day in the copy room about how easily many students gave up on competition in track meets, and got discouraged. "Cross-country running is for people who grow up with trails around them," he explained. "It's just not in these kids' culture to run long distances. The only time that they run is for the bus." On another occasion, Mr. Kipp expressed to me the importance of integrating music and dance into the classroom. "It's such an important part of our kids' culture that we ignore," he said. I found his comments to be provocative. While not necessarily ascribing a deficit to students or to their communities, using the language of "culture" he makes a subtle comparison here between norms of kids who grew up the way he did (running on trails, and in classrooms that use more "traditional" pedagogical methods), and "urban" classrooms. Based on the reaction to cross-country meets and music ensemble from students, he constructs, under the guise of culture, a generalization about students as a group that may or may not be true, implicitly differentiating "us" from "them."

Most teachers were subtle about their reading of students' culture. Sometimes, without using the word *culture,* statements about students' backgrounds and about what they needed in order to become successful critical thinkers belied teachers' impressions of the home habits, life-ways, and customs of College Prep students. While I argue that culture is created at College Prep, it seems based on staff conceptions of student "culture" that is opposed in some ways to staff members' ideal (but not yet realized) version of "school culture." It also may be based on students' impression of the fact that their histories, identities, and perspectives are not included in staff members' vision and purposeful cultivation of a certain kind of "culture." This idea was validated through a series of "culture meetings" that took place among staff in the spring of 2010 in the interest of changing or reshaping "school culture." The conception that culture can be, in some sense, choreographed by those in positions of power is limiting in that it negates the agency of those who collaboratively create culture through everyday, spontaneous actions. This idea is what I strive to highlight in this work through my research methods, as well as through centralizing the voices of students, parents, and staff at College Prep.

Educational anthropologist Mica Pollock (2008b) argues for a deep cultural analysis of educational settings. Rather than attributing certain behaviors to certain "cultures," she argues that educational anthropologists need to document and analyze how larger patterns in U.S. education are produced by actions in "real time," accounting for diversity and variation of behavior patterns across groups of people, and looking closely at everyday behaviors and interaction patterns that occur between actors (including but not necessarily limited to parents, teachers, and students) in school settings. Pollock defines studying culture as "the organization of people's everyday interactions in concrete contexts." In the context of education, culture affects larger achievement patterns over time.

It is important to remember that culture is neither static nor shallow; it is not a set of behaviors or traditions. Rather, Pollock reminds us, culture is a verb, it is something that we continually "do" and dynamically create. It is learned, fluid, malleable, and shared. Ethnographic research methods find a way to construct a theoretically informed narrative of how people create culture. Educational researchers Margaret Sutton and Bradley Levinson (2001) argue the importance of sociocultural policy analysis that links the normative practices of educational institutions with larger social structures of governance and law. Research in education, they state, needs to move toward ethnographic documentation of how people engage with macro-level policy and politics. Through methods that helped me to document how people affiliated with College Prep make (and define) school "culture," I articulate how culture both makes and is made by the political economy (the relationship between structures of capitalism and everyday agency) at College Prep.

It is crucial, as Gramsci reminds us, to remember that we cannot effectively analyze culture without keeping in mind the reality of cultural hegemony:

> An order in which a certain way of life and thought is dominant, in which one concept of reality is diffused throughout society in all its institutional and private manifestations, informing with its spirit all taste, morality, customs, religious and political principles, and all social relations, particularly in their intellectual and moral connotation. (cited in Takaki 2000, vii)

Studying how people create culture at College Prep gives a particularly vivid window into concrete manifestations of cultural hegemony, since the main purpose of educational institutions is to explicitly prepare students to enter into the realities of a larger social power structure outside of school walls. Culture at College Prep (which includes the political spectacle that the school engages in to maintain good relationships with its funders, as well as what actually goes on in classrooms, hallways, and bathrooms) is a verb that is informed by both the structural and unequal dimensions of power and the agentic, everyday acts of individual subjects in a mainstream educational setting. How people create culture is never separate from the creation of gender, social class, race and racial meaning, and, importantly, the ways in which researchers study how people create culture is never separate from our own personal identities and histories.

Positionality and Getting Hired at College Prep

As a White teacher, my racial positionality is representative of a majority of New York City teachers; the city's teaching force is 60 percent White (E. Green 2008). Citywide, the student demographic is very different from the teacher demographic: according to 2009 data, 30.8 percent of students identify as Black, 39.9 percent identify as Hispanic, 14.6 percent identify as Asian, and 14.3 percent identify as White (schools.nyc.gov 2011).

Originally from a college town in central Pennsylvania, I attended a large, predominantly White public high school where students were tracked into classes based largely on socioeconomic status. My father, a retired clinical psychologist, has his PhD, and my mother has her master's and works for the university as an academic advisor. Growing up, I had the impression that we were solidly middle class. In my high school, I remember being tracked into advanced humanities classes along with the sons and daughters of the town's academics and entrepreneurs, while noticing that many of the school's poor and working-class White students who lived just outside of town in more remote areas, or who lived in the town's trailer parks, were tracked into the Center for Applied Technology to work on car engines or in the wood shop. Most of the teachers at my high school came from my town, or from somewhere close, and most stayed at the school for the duration of their careers. For me, when I became a New York City teacher, it took both time and curiosity to get accustomed to the differences and similarities in what teaching and learning meant in a setting very different from the one where I grew up.

After joining the New York City Teaching Fellows program in 2003 when I was twenty-three years old, I noticed that many of my colleagues were as young as I was and were, like me, from places outside of New York City. Many were unsure about how long they would stay in teaching. The majority of my teaching fellows cohort was White,[2] and all of us were teaching in what the Fellows program called "high need," racially segregated urban schools. Because of this, I became especially interested in how teaching and learning occur when classroom teachers come from different backgrounds than their students, which influenced my decision to leave the classroom for PhD coursework in anthropology in 2006–8.

When I interviewed for a tenth-grade English position at College Prep in April 2008, I was still in the process of completing my doctoral coursework in Texas. College Prep was situated between two public housing projects and shared a building with an elementary school. This was the same neighborhood where I began my teaching career in 2003, although at a different public school, and I knew it well. When I came for my interview and demo lesson, I stayed with a former colleague who lived within walking distance from the school. On my way that cold morning, walking past bodegas and liquor stores, through gray slush between parked cars, beneath the roaring, trembling el of the expressway, I ran into one of my favorite former students. Now seventeen, he had been in my class five years beforehand when I taught eighth-grade English. After a hug, we caught up, and he informed me that he was starting at community college in the fall. I felt, at that moment, as if I was coming home, in a sense—to a self, a life, and a routine that, while never easy or predictable, was comfortable, and was at times painful or challenging and at times joyful. After arriving at College Prep's building, I was ushered into a ninth-grade class to do my lesson. Following the lesson, the students voted to hire me.

Unlike other schools where I had applied to work, College Prep required a portfolio (including lesson plans, student work, and assessments) in addition to a demo lesson and an interview. After turning in my portfolio, I interviewed with Claire Cohen, the thirty-two-year-old, New York City–born, White principal, then with a panel of three teachers. I was open about my research project with Ms. Cohen during the interview, and told her that it would supplement my full-time teaching. Based on my experience, and my successful interview and demo lesson (as well as my colleagues' recommendations; see below), I was hired on the spot to begin my teaching and research the following fall.

By the fall of 2008, when I began my teacher-research at College Prep, the school had moved, and Kelly McCarren, a forty-five-year-old White woman originally from the West Coast, had replaced Ms. Cohen as the principal. As I mentioned in the introduction, the school was now located in a renovated building in a different, more affluent neighborhood, close to quite a few bus and subway lines, stores, restaurants, and public buildings. As I described above, the school had resources that seemed incomparable to those at the other two New York City public schools where I had previously taught, where photocopiers, overhead projectors, and working computers were unavailable or limited, and chalk was the only teaching tool distributed freely. College Prep's new location had four working copy machines, unlimited paper supplies for teachers, interactive whiteboards and LCD projectors in almost every classroom, computers for teachers and students, and overhead projectors available for teachers who wanted them.

From teaching in two other New York City schools previously, as well as from coming into teaching through the New York City Teaching Fellows program, I found three familiar faces on staff: thirty-three-year-old Kathy Sands, a White English teacher and former teaching colleague from 2003–5; Ralph Fulton, a thirty-year-old White math teacher and colleague from 2005–6 (both were originally from the midwestern United States); and thirty-two-year-old, New York City native Martina McGoldrick, also White, who taught with Mr. Fulton and me in 2005–6. Ms. Sands had taught at the school for the previous two years, and Mr. Fulton and Ms. McGoldrick had been there only the year before. I applied (and I believe was hired at the school) based largely upon their recommendations to Ms. Cohen. For the two years that I worked at the school, I remained close with all three.

Soon after arriving at the school, I was informed that I would be sharing a classroom with La'Trice Williams, who is African American and was a history teacher. We would both teach tenth grade, and while we would teach the same students, our classes would meet at alternating times in the same room, where both of our desks would be located. Originally from Watts, Los Angeles, Ms. Williams had just moved to New York from Austin, Texas, where she taught at a public high school. That year, Ms. Williams and I also developed a close personal friendship, sharing in many of the joys and challenges that came with our first year at this school.

Gaining Acceptance at College Prep

I worked to become a trusted community member of this school in as fluid a manner as possible, building relationships with staff, students, and parents/guardians. During the first year of my project, as a full-time tenth-grade English teacher, I developed close working and personal relationships with colleagues and was open in telling staff and students that I was simultaneously doing research for my dissertation, mostly by recording daily field notes, photocopying student work, doing preliminary interviews with teachers, and collecting school memos and documents. The first year I worked at College Prep, I focused more on my teaching than my research, which felt somewhat natural given that I had been in the classroom for three years prior to training as an anthropologist. I was incredibly busy that first year, and often exhausted from planning, teaching, and grading for a full course load of American literature to 115 tenth graders, as well as planning and teaching an "advisory" (social and academic support) class of eighteen students. I made regular and frequent phone calls to parents/guardians about trips, grades, or behavior. I attended frequent official staff and planning meetings, less frequent parent meetings and disciplinary mediations, and frequent unofficial happy hours and parties with my colleagues. I regularly stayed up until midnight or 1:00 a.m. that first year to type field notes, or record them as audio files if I was too tired to write, only to wake up again at

6:30 the next morning to shower, eat, put on teaching clothes, and repeat the process.

Partly because I was so overwhelmed by the volume of work involved in teaching full-time my first year at a new school, and partly because I wanted to be careful to develop strong relationships before further developing my researcher identity, I did not start the interview process with staff until April of my first year. The school had a shortened schedule on Wednesdays so that teachers could meet in their grade teams (all the ninth-grade teachers met together, all the tenth-grade teachers met together, etc.). After meeting with Principal McCarren and gaining her initial support to talk about my project and solicit interviews from staff at meetings, I began with my grade team, the tenth-grade team, and then moved to other grade teams.

Teacher interviews, which were anonymous and confidential, took approximately one hour each, and took place at locations convenient for the teachers, either on or off campus. I talked with teachers during a common planning period during school, before school, after school, or on weekends. Interviews were audio recorded and later transcribed. I told teachers that I saw them as co-researchers rather than as subjects or informants, and I informed them that I would ask for their perspective on the completed manuscript. I wanted to get as rich, nuanced, and full a perspective as possible of teacher stories in this space.

Interviews were semistructured (Glesne 2011; Oliver, Serovich, and Mason 2005; Spradley 1979) and, despite the recorder and the consent form, felt more like friendly conversations than interrogations. After interviews, several staff members told me that they had fun talking with me, or that they were glad that I was initiating conversations about teachers' experience with race, gender, and academics at the school. Although I had a list of potential questions, I told staff members that they could feel free to ask me any questions that came up for them during the process, and they often did. In the interviews, I often commiserated or celebrated with teachers, sharing my own stories and experiences in response to theirs. I was conscious through this whole process that ethnographers often expect those whom we interview to reveal everything about themselves while we remain closed and distant under the guise of "neutrality" (Behar 1996). Despite being empowered in the interview context through my privilege (my Whiteness, middle-classness, recorder, questions, consent form, and ownership of the project), I tried to play up my strong relationships, insider status, and priority to highlight the voices of my "co-researchers" in this context. I tried to let interviewees tell their stories as naturally as possible, while I gently guided the process.

At opportune moments, informal interviews with teachers took place—for example, on the subway ride home, over the phone, in the teachers' office, at Friday happy hours, or in chats after meetings. I found that teachers were continually reflective about the school, their teaching, and their relationships with students and their families. These informal conversations often provided me with opportunities to get critical perspective from teachers on my ideas. The process was one of continual conversation, reflection, and reevaluation. I continued to type or record daily field notes through the end of June 2009 when the school year ended. My field notes continued during 2009–10, my second year at the school.

It was important to my project not only to get teachers' perspectives at the school, but also to get students' perspectives. The summer following my first year, in order to explore a more critical or humanizing pedagogy that resisted the school's deliberate and racialized "interpellation" (Althusser 1971; Hall and Du Gay 1996) of students as marketable subjects, I held the weekly "cultural circle" book club (Freire 1970), which met outside of the school with five former students.[3]

My second year at the school, I served as a part-time mentor/assistant to two teachers, which allowed more time for data collection. I also served as the school's cheerleading coach. This gave me excellent insight into school culture, achievement, school spirit, and students' gendered relationships to the school's "extracurriculum." I continued to gather documents and memos, attend after-school meetings, and pay a great deal of attention to how the school marketed itself to funders. I attended the school's fourth annual benefit, a private evening function that solicited donations from individual and corporate funders. Following Anne Ferguson's model (2001), I wore the school uniform and shadowed students for an entire school day, in the interest of getting a fuller perspective on the experience of being a student, as opposed to a teacher. I collaborated with teachers in choosing eight students to shadow and interview: three young men and five young women, all African American.

During the fall and winter of the second year, I began interviewing parents. Since I was required to call the homes of all of the students in my advisory every three weeks about grades and progress reports, I already had close relationships with many of the parents of the eighteen students who were in my advisory the year before. Out of the eighteen advisory homes that I called, I interviewed eight parents. In addition to reaching out to parents within my advisory, as well as to parents of students that were in my summer cultural circle book club, I also asked our parent coordinator and a few staff members whether there were any parents they could recommend that I interview. Out of these recommendations, I found three more parents who were willing to talk with me. Semistructured interviews with parents took place in a location of their choice: sometimes at their home, sometimes at the school, and sometimes at a restaurant or café. Sometimes their children were present for all or part of the interview, and when they were present, they participated in the interview process as well. Most interviews were with mothers, but one was with a student's grandmother. For one, both parents were present. Parent interviews were audio recorded and transcribed later. In the end, combining advisory parents, cultural circle parents, and parents who were recommended by other staff members, I interviewed a total of fourteen parents, all Black, and either U.S.- or Caribbean-born.

To learn more about College Prep and college readiness, I interviewed fourteen alumni from the school's two graduating classes: seven young women, all Black and all U.S.-born, and seven young men, five Black, one Latino, and one who identifies as mixed White/Latino. One was born in the Caribbean, and the other men were U.S.-born. I approached many of them at the school's homecoming day, which took place over college winter break. Alumni were recommended by College Prep's parent coordinator, staff from the college office, or from the enrichment team, who had close academic and personal relationships with these former students. Sometimes staff members introduced me to the alums before I approached them about an interview, and sometimes, I approached them on my own. I explained that I would ask them about their experiences at College Prep, as well as about their experiences at their college or university. Many were happy to talk with me, and most of our interviews either took place at the school, or at a café behind the school. In one case, I went to an alum's home and we walked to a nearby doughnut shop where we sat and talked.

As I stated in the introduction to this book, in total, over two years I interviewed forty-five members of the school staff (including administrators, security guards, guidance / college office staff, and deans of discipline), fourteen alumni, fourteen parents/guardians, and ten students. I also collaborated with teachers and students on authoring and disseminating a school-wide questionnaire (appendix B) about students' home life, school life, personal interests, and aspirations. At each grade-team meeting, as well as at the enrichment team / college office meeting, I showed staff members an initial list of questions. Because I was interested in exploring the "culture of achievement" at College Prep, this was developed largely from Demerath's school-wide questionnaire in his ethnography, *Producing Success* (2009), but was greatly expanded and revised with feedback from students and staff members. I also elicited student feedback on the questionnaire by asking a pilot group of students to take the survey and give me their comments and questions. Their feedback helped me to time the survey (which took about thirty minutes) and to make the language and format more student friendly. At Principal McCarren's invitation, I returned to the school in October 2010 to present the questionnaire results and facilitate a community dialogue with teachers, students, and parents/guardians about what the College Prep students' feedback means for teaching and learning.

From 2011 through 2014, I began to conduct follow-up interviews with some of the students and teachers who participated in the study. Some of the interviews were face-to-face, and others were over Skype or Google Hangout, depending on our respective locations. I spoke with eleven of the teachers and four of the students who worked at or attended College Prep during the time of my study and who were prominently featured in the ethnography, and they offered their critiques and opinions on the manuscript. I integrated many of their suggestions and I detail their thinking to a greater extent in the afterword to this book. These interviews were also semistructured, audio recorded, and typically lasted between one and two hours. I transcribed each of them. Especially as I conducted follow-up interviews, I was quite aware of the desire to maintain participants' trust and confidence. Writing is always a political act, and ethnography depends on relationships of trust and openness. My first responsibility remains to those who participated in my study at College Prep (Glesne 2011). Thus, I sought feedback from participants on this manuscript. Because I was, in many senses, an insider in the school community, I established relationships of trust with its members that I hope to maintain. This trust, as Ruth Behar has stated, is complicated by the fact that

feminist ethnographers have found themselves caught inside webs
of betrayal that they themselves have spun; with stark clarity, they
realize that they are seeking out intimacy and friendship with
subjects on whose backs, ultimately, the books will be written
upon which their productivity as scholars in the academic
marketplace will be assessed. (1996, 297)

For me, Behar's critique is especially ironic given that, in some ways, I am
critiquing one educational marketplace in order to establish my credibility
in another. I am not interested in constructing this credibility "on the backs"
of those who gave me their time or their thoughts, or even "on the back" of
College Prep. Rather, I'm telling what I, and many members of the community at College Prep, feel is an important story for an academically and
educationally engaged audience. It is my hope that I will continue to maintain acceptance as a member of the College Prep community, and also
maintain trust and rapport with the members of that community.

In 2013, I spoke with Kathy Sands, who had by then become the new
principal of the school. After reading my study and giving me her perspective, she invited me to come back to the school anytime, to "just
hang out" or to gather more data, and expressed interest in co-writing
with me at some point in the future. This invitation and interest were
some of the highest compliments she could have paid me; despite the
somewhat critical lens I took, Ms. Sands expressed that as a critical eth-
nographer, I still had the school community's trust and respect.

Race, Gender, and Identity at College Prep

As I mention above, my positionality as a White, straight, middle-class,
able-bodied teacher and researcher is inextricably intertwined with the
ethnographic narrative that I construct here. The politics of this positionality sometimes led to my acceptance within the networks of College
Prep, and other times served to limit my acceptance.

Race relations among the staff, I think, are well encapsulated using
anthropologist John Jackson's conceptual framework of "racial paranoia"
(2008). Jackson notes that while it is no longer acceptable to be explicitly
racist, society still operates on a framework of racist logic and is in fact,
still quite racially segregated. While people no longer feel comfortable
engaging in racist talk explicitly out of fear that they will be persecuted

or stigmatized for this, explicit racism manifests in more intimate or "safe" settings. Thus, seemingly innocuous interactions between people are not "good faith" interactions. Repressed racism still bubbles up at times, but may seem less overt or obvious. This leads to a state of "racial paranoia," the knowledge that racism is still very much present in the ways in which people engage with one another, but can sometimes operate in ways that are much more difficult to call out.

I noticed early on that there did seem to be a clear racial divide among the staff: that is, there was a clique of predominantly White staff who often socialized together, and there was also a clique of predominantly Black staff who socialized together. I did my best to socialize with both. I noticed, in comparing outings with both groups, that race, as well as critique of Whiteness and White privilege, was a much more frequent topic of conversation and humor among Black staff than among White staff. Additionally, on several occasions, I was advised by Black staff members to document moments of racial tension among the staff in my study. I remember in my second year at the school a happy hour hosted by Frank Matthews at his house in Crown Heights, Brooklyn. I had a close personal and professional relationship with Mr. Matthews, especially since he had also moved to the school from Austin, Texas, and we had a few connections in common at the University of Texas at Austin. Ms. Williams (with whom I shared a classroom) was there with her sister, Susan. John Davis, the parent coordinator, and Francis Mitchell, the twelfth-grade college advisor, were there. Three of Frank's African American friends were in attendance. Mr. Sandler (one of the deans of discipline), Mr. Horowitz (a special education teacher), and I were the only non–African American guests there at this point.

It was getting late, and we were standing around the kitchen table, playing a drinking game with playing cards called "Ring of Fire." At one point in the game, Susan had to make up a "rule" that the rest of us had to follow. "White people, drink!" she said, laughing. As the rest of the room erupted in laughter, and Mr. Sandler and I raised our glasses, Mr. Horowitz protested: "First of all, I do not identify as White; I am Jewish-American, not White!" This led to a protest from many of the people around the table, including me. Weeks before, Mr. Horowitz had left a Black colleague's (Mr. Battle's) house, quite intoxicated, with an open container of beer in his hand to wander by himself around Bedford-Stuyvesant, a historically Black Brooklyn community. He was stopped by the police for his violation of open-container laws, but instead of being arrested, or even given a ticket, the officer told him to finish his beer, and let him walk away. Mr. Matthews, Ms. Williams, and Mr. Davis refused to let Mr. Horowitz live this down; they saw the whole incident as Mr. Horowitz naively flaunting his White privilege, and getting away with it. In juxtaposition with Mr. Horowitz's public and somewhat serious denial of his Whiteness in this context, the protests were fierce from all around the table. As we tried to get Mr. Horowitz to be more self-reflexive, Ms. Williams leaned back and motioned for me to do the same. Behind the backs of the rest of our friends who were yelling at Mr. Horowitz, she said pointedly, "Are you taking notes on this? This has to go in the book." This happened frequently, both in and outside of school. Mr. Davis, Ms. Williams, and Mr. Matthews would frequently vent frustration at explicitly racial or racist incidents that occurred among staff and among students that seemed to go unmarked or unrecorded. In this sense, as a result of close personal relationships of trust as well as of the fact that I was engaging race in my study, some staff members were open with me about what they saw as "critical race moments," and engaged in a dialogue that in some sense tried to shed light on the experience of "racial paranoia" among the staff at College Prep.

In the same vein, I believe that White female teachers were more open with me about their experiences with (and many times shame around) race because they saw me as sharing a race and gender positionality— and thus, common experience and understanding—with them. Many thanked me after the interview process was over, and said that our talk had been not only helpful but necessary for them in terms of processing their racial positionality in the context of College Prep. When we talked, they saw themselves in a "safe" (and racially and gender-segregated) space where they could discuss their experiences and be a bit more forthcoming than they may have been had we not shared this positionality. This comfort, too, is a manifestation of "racial paranoia"; it is demonstrative of the problematic fact that we continue to struggle to engage race comfortably in racially diverse settings, thus remaining quite stagnant when it comes to upending racialized forms of oppression.

There were other moments when teachers tried to interpellate me explicitly as their friend or colleague and not as a researcher, which at the same time always marked their awareness that I was not just a teacher or a friend, that I was also an anthropologist. This complicated our relationships and our social interactions. While out at a birthday dinner with one teacher, several colleagues, and some of our former students, the teacher began to tell a story, then stopped, looked at me, and said, "you're not collecting data now, are you?" I shook my head no, we all laughed, and her story continued.

When it came to students, my positionality influenced my level of acceptance, but also seemed to lead to a nuancing of the definition of race that I did not see with teachers. In April of 2010, for instance, I wrote in my field notes about a classroom activity in Literacy, the class that I co-taught with Mr. Rodino. That spring, we had a student teacher in the class, Ms. Moss, who had designed a project that asked students to research and present to the class about a real-life hero of their choice. As the class brainstormed their heroes, Aneisha, one of the African American students in the class, suggested Afeni Shakur. Neither Mr. Rodino nor Ms. Moss knew who this was, and three of the students in the class explained to them that she was rapper Tupac's mother and that she was a former Black Panther. The teachers in the room asked about the spelling of her name, and students struggled with this, and so I interjected. Another student suggested Madame C. J. Walker, and when Ms. Moss expressed her unfamiliarity, the student asked for my help in explaining her importance.

I sat with Aneisha as she worked on her Afeni Shakur presentation, and I asked her whether she expected that most people in the class would know who Afeni Shakur was when she suggested her as a possible hero. She said she expected that most of the students would know, but that the teachers would probably not. I asked her why she didn't think the teachers would know, and she said, "Because they are White." I asked her whether Black teachers would be more likely to know about Afeni Shakur. She responded affirmatively, then added, "but I knew you would know, Ms. Brown, because you act Black."

This was not the first time I had heard this from a student. Since I look phenotypically "White" by U.S. standards, and am usually read as such, I would often follow comments that challenged my Whiteness (as well as comments that challenged other teachers' racial identities) with a question like "What does that mean?" Aneisha responded that she thought I "acted Black" because I "read urban books" and "know a lot about Black history and culture." At other times, when I asked students who remarked that I "acted Black" what they meant, they said that it was because I was "cool." Tracy, another African American female student said, "Ms. Brown, you are one of us" when I interviewed her and her best friend Carmen at a café close to College Prep. When I asked her what she meant, she laughingly held her arm close to mine, and noted that our skin colors weren't really that different. She then became more serious, and responded that I "don't get mad about stupid little stuff."

The ways that students identified each other, as well as their teachers, seemed to highlight the fluid and arbitrary character of racial categories. Black students sometimes classified other Black students or teachers as "White" to me in interviews, because of the way they spoke or dressed, or based on where they were from. Some Black teachers spoke in interviews about the experience of being called "White" by students. Yet some White teachers, including me, experienced being called "Black" or "not White" by Black students. One male teacher, Ron Esparella, who looks phenotypically White but whose father is Latino, discussed students' reaction to finding out that he was "half Spanish"—"Oh! So that's why you're so cool!" Interestingly here, phenotypically White teachers seem to enjoy the privilege of some sort of racial ambiguity or fluidity (one might argue that this is one way White privilege works in this space), and some Black teachers seem to be caught in a bind of being racially tokenized (Kanter 1977) by White colleagues while simultaneously being judged by students as being "not Black enough" or even "White."

Sometimes, teachers called "not White" by students seemed to be the ones whom students connected with the most. But teachers were also racially classified by body type (non-Black female teachers, including myself, who had wide hips or a big rear end were sometimes told that they had a "Black body" by female students, usually, but not always, jokingly). This is not only about race, but also about gender (I never saw or heard of a White male teacher being told that he had a "Black body") and about sexuality.

Patricia Hill Collins (2004) places the sexual objectification of parts of Black women's bodies in hip-hop culture and the mainstream media since the early 1990s into the context of the slave auction block under chattel slavery. In hip-hop, Collins cites songs like Sir Mix-A-Lot's "Baby Got Back" and the video for 2LiveCrew's "Pop That Coochie" as examples of the specific objectification of Black women's rear ends. She connects this to White European men's fascination with the buttocks of Sarah Baartman during the late eighteenth and early nineteenth centuries. Also known as the "Hottentot Venus," Baartman was born a slave, but was forced to display and gyrate her unusually large naked rear end at European high-society functions. Collins critiques the fact that this practice that began as a construction of White racism is now celebrated uncritically among Black people in hip-hop culture (129). Despite the fact that I am White, my rear end genders and sexualizes me in the eyes of some of my students, and marks me in some sense as not completely "White," due to popular and problematic hypersexualized mainstream marketing and commodification of Black femininity.

College Prep community members threw racial boundaries into question in other ways. One parent spoke to me of her surprise at realizing on open school night that Ms. Sands was White; based on how much she called home and her strict discipline policies in the classroom, this parent had assumed, they told me, that she was African American. On another occasion, I witnessed students policing racial boundaries differently: in Mr. Rodino's ninth-grade English class, he once jokingly used the word *ghetto* to describe students immediately after several members of the class had jokingly described themselves that way in unprompted journal entries that they shared with the class. As soon as Mr. Rodino said the word, though, the laughter stopped, and two students immediately said "you can't use that word" [because you are White]. While Black students marked their group membership through employing a pejorative term problematically associated with low-income Black communities in racist mainstream discourse, they reinforced their collective identity here by marking who belongs and who does not (Carter 2003).

My Openness about the Study

When asked, I spoke openly about my project, including about the fact that I was interested in studying the construction of race and gender at College Prep. I found, for the most part, that teachers were supportive of my project (although some were more eager to have me in their classrooms, and to talk about my project, than others). Many were curious, asked how my work was going in passing, and told me repeatedly that they were interested in my findings. Many offered to help in any way they could, opening their classrooms to me for observations, and taking the time to interview with me during their busy days, evenings, and even occasional weekends. I took copious notes at meetings, and often my raw field notes were close transcriptions of conversations that had taken place. After staff meetings, I often shared these notes with those who were at the meeting as "minutes" in a gesture of reciprocity. Especially in ongoing meetings about school culture, or about student rights versus privileges, staff members told me that these were quite helpful. After I took notes at these meetings, at home I wrote memos and expanded these transcriptions into full field notes.

As my research questions evolved to be more about the effects of the school's political spectacle on the construction of race, class, and gender, I continued to be open with staff and students about how my research questions were evolving. Because of this, staff members suggested that I observe in the college office, that I attend various extracurricular activities, or that I attend school benefits or events where sponsors or funders would be present. They let me know about opportunities when they came around, and made efforts to connect me with the staff member or administrator in charge, if necessary.

I was open about my study with students and parents as well. They knew that I was writing a book, and that I was interested in race, class, and gender. Besides seeing me observe in their classrooms, students were especially involved in the aspect of my study where I focused on urban fiction and cultural circles, and so they were also aware that I was interested in literacy and in politicized and dialogic conversations about books. Since I sought parent permission before holding the cultural circle, some parents were quite aware of this aspect of the study too. When I interviewed parents, I told them that I was interested in their experiences with and involvement in College Prep as well as in their opinions of College Prep in regard to their own child's education, edification, and college readiness.

When I authored the student questionnaire for the study (appendix B), I went to each grade-team meeting and to each administrator and sought each person's advice on revisions. I also sought a pilot group of students to complete the questionnaire and offer their revisions. I asked administrators for their advice on which group of students I might pilot the study with, and one mentioned that the group of students sitting in detention might be the perfect group. Detention was held after school, and grades nine through twelve were in a classroom together. Students were not assigned any work in detention, and it was often run as a silent study hall. I approached the deans of discipline, who supervised the detention, with this idea, and they were fine with it, so I piloted the study with approximately fifteen students who were sitting in detention. Students took the survey, which took them about a half hour to complete. We then held a roundtable discussion of any items that they suggested I change or revise. Teachers, administrators, and students were forthcoming in their suggestions for the questionnaire, and I incorporated all the revisions that they suggested before I facilitated giving the survey out to students. As a result of the process being participatory and collaborative, students and staff engaged wholeheartedly with the results of the questionnaire in 2010 when I presented them in classes and after school. I presented the results to members of the Parent Teacher Association (PTA) as well, and although parents had not been instrumental in revising and disseminating the questionnaire, they were quite interested in the results and what they suggested for ways College Prep might improve. Since I was a College Prep community member, a spirit of openness and collaboration provided the basis for my research methods.

Teaching/Observing at College Prep

Being both a teacher and a researcher at College Prep inevitably affected the collection of my data. Teachers, I think, were more apt to have me in their classrooms as an observer because I was their peer and colleague. I was not an "outside" researcher coming in. In interviews, we were "on the same page." They saw me as an equal because I was expected to work the same hours they did, adhere to the same policies, and work with the same students, parents, and administrators. Having completed a master's degree in education, and having sat through innumerable professional developments as an educator, I am well aware of teachers' skepticism at advice from people who have little to no classroom experience, of the instant rapport that is created between educators because of a common understanding of the expectations and demands of the work, and of the resiliency, commitment, and patience that it takes to become a master teacher.

I tried as much as possible to minimize my presence in classrooms, and thus to minimize students' awareness of me as a researcher when they were in other teachers' classes. In several of the classrooms where I was observing repeatedly over a period of time, I believe that I became less noticeable, which was evidenced by the fact that students stopped remarking on me being there. The fact that students and teachers were already used to my presence in the building, I like to think, helped me to blend in a bit more. When I was observing in classrooms, sometimes teachers asked me to sit next to students who needed a bit more help so that I could lend support if they needed it. Other times, teachers let me have free rein, in which case I would sit in a less noticeable location. I always handwrote notes while I was observing, and at home later in the evening typed these raw notes into full field notes. Often, students would get excited when they saw me observing in their classrooms. At times, they would exclaim that they were going to be in my book, and a few asked me whether, when I wrote about them, I would use their real name instead of a pseudonym (I did not, in accordance with my Institutional Review Board protocol).

The fact that I was a teacher made connecting with parents and alumni a bit easier, I think. I did not interview parents while their children were in my classes, but I did interview many when their children were no longer in my classes. As a teacher, I called students' homes frequently in order to maintain consistent relationships with parents. At times, these calls were grade or behavior related, but other times they were just to check in. Because I had already established rapport with parents, many were open to talking with me about their experience at College Prep. It is important to note that parents indubitably saw me as a (White, female) employee of the school; even if I wasn't in a relationship where I was grading their child, I was still a representative of the school in some sense. Inevitably, this affected the data that I gathered in interviews, and affected the trust and the rapport I was able to cultivate with parents.

On Autoethnography / Narrative Style

I chose to study the effects of privatization at College Prep from the vantage points of both an observer and a participant. This text could be framed as "observant participation" (Vargas 2006) in some sense, because during my fieldwork, I considered myself first and foremost a teacher. In this sense, because I was a complete participant in the social world of College Prep, my study is autoethnographic in nature (L. Anderson 2006). While I was in some sense a complete participant, I differed from members of the College Prep community, because I am also a member of the social science community (Strathern 1987). I was both an insider and an outsider who made a methodological commitment to being both analytic and self-reflexive about my presence in that space, and I made myself vulnerable here through writing (Behar 1996).

Autoethnography involves more than exposing one's identity through one's writing: it implies a political commitment to an epistemology that connects the self with others; it implies a social world and places that social world into a larger context (Denzin 2006). It recognizes that meaning is always co-constructed. At the same time, it is possible to make an ontological commitment to learning more about a "real world" that exists beyond co-constructed truths (Maxwell 2013), and to considering alternatives. Autoethnography recognizes that the researcher is never separate from the knowledge that he or she produces (Glesne 2011; Haraway 1988; Peshkin 1988). As scientists, it is crucial for us to state where the knowledge we choose to construct comes from.

Speed (2008) emphasizes an approach to anthropological research that equally privileges a final written ethnographic product and the research process as sites that allow one to collaborate with subjects and address critiques. Through this process, both the research and the interpretation of data are grounded in partnership and dialogue with College Prep community members. In this way, my critique of larger social, economic, and political structures is informed by the agency of that community.

The act of listening is crucial to the anthropological and ethnographic sensibility (Jackson 2013). As ethnographers, Jackson says, we must commit, through paying close attention, to understanding how people organize their worlds in very different ways—ways which often diverge greatly from our own. Our training teaches us to rediscipline ourselves to listen more carefully to others, even when (and especially when) their perspectives or worldviews might be dissimilar to ours. In some sense, anthropology is a search to see through the eyes of our interlocutors; ethnographic fieldwork is about deeply committing to human relationships. This is especially challenging, Jackson notes, in a world where we learn to be more invested in talking, and in winning arguments, than in listening. For dialogue to begin, we must look at ourselves. We must examine closely (and be open about) who we are and what our agenda may be, and we must be cognizant of the various ways the research and writing we produce may be operationalized. Then we move toward listening openly and empathetically to people's individual and localized worldviews, and consider the ways in which worldviews (those of ourselves and of others) might articulate with structures of power, privilege, and oppression. Once we are able to see through the eyes of those whom we listen to, we might, in a more politically engaged sense, consider dialogic interventions that unsettle how social exclusions are reproduced. This book is one that I tried to forge in dialogue, first through being open about my own agenda and positionality, then through being open to dialogue and exploration with my participants, and finally through writing an ethnography that seeks to give credence to the stories that they told me.

I reinterviewed Ms. Meehan in the winter of 2011. She spoke about the manuscript as being one that she believed could inspire important kinds of dialogue and growth among College Prep community members. She said,

> Your manuscript was so awesome . . . I think you are bringing up things that people are too busy to look at or don't want to look at—and I would be really interested in other people's responses to it. Because I don't think you are ripping anyone a new one, you know? I think you are bringing up issues that are so valuable for this community. And I think when you present them, you are making yourself so vulnerable. So I think that maybe the shared vulnerability will help something to happen. Even in the [Ms. Elliott] case study, you keep saying that [she is] really effective. You say that over and over again. And it's true. People who have grown a lot, and have become better and better teachers.

Importantly, she sees the research that I tried to build in dialogue with the study's participants as having the potential to create even more dialogue and growth. I hope that she is correct, and that this study is useful and provocative in and beyond College Prep.

Conclusions

In an era of school reform that emphasizes quantitative data, standards, and accountability (Demerath 2006), it is critical that researchers, pre- and in-service teachers, students, and funders develop the tools to ask questions and conduct research that nuances and supports or refutes claims about power, justice, equity, and choice in education. How might some political spectacles further class, racial, and gender hierarchies, while shaping consent through a language of justice or reform? How might other agendas further a more critical, community wealth–based or funds-of-knowledge approach? Most important, how do funders, teachers, students, and communities rearticulate or resist oppressive spectacles in everyday practice?

Tickle (2001) as well as Yogev and Michaeli (2011) highlight the importance of training teachers to become Gramscian "organic intellectuals" who care, are involved with communities, evolve knowledge, are committed to self-esteem, and are committed to public political action. Yet there are more people who are deeply involved with schools than teachers. Instead, perhaps all those who have a stake in schools—teachers, students, parents, board members, and funders—might consider how the findings and tools of qualitative research might help to refine teaching, learning, and giving practices so that they move toward eradicating rather than ignoring or supporting inequality. Flyvbjerg (2006) argues that it is through cases that people can learn and become experts in their fields—in other words, people engage in authentic learning through hands-on, real-life, prior experience. Learning and knowledge production is context-dependent, and learners need experience to develop from what he calls "rule based beginners" to "virtuoso experts." Learning from real-life cases and dialogue encourages people to form the sorts of critical qualitative lenses that can potentially talk back to present-day inequities that are wrought through privatization and political spectacle in educational settings. Qualitative research methods help us to construct knowledge within the discipline of anthropology, but our questions and our methods are often shaped by the problems and contradictions that we all face every day. Qualitative research can help us to critique the ways problems are constructed, and see "behind the curtain." As we see in this ethnography, taking note of these problems and contradictions is not unique to anthropologists. Qualitative forms of thinking and research can help us all to scientifically and collaboratively construct knowledge in context, tying localized forms of agency to structures of power, and, if we are willing to listen, can teach us unique and humanizing ways of learning from those we engage with.

2010 College Prep Student Questionnaire

You are being invited to complete a questionnaire that will ask you some personal and demographic questions. This will take about 30 minutes of your time. Please answer as honestly as you can. The survey is anonymous (your answers will not be tied to your identity). Once compiled, the results of the survey will be organized by Ms. Brown and shared with students, staff, and administrators to try to make learning a better experience for you at College Prep.

I. Background and Home

1) Grade (*please choose one*):
   - ⊗ 9
   - ⊗ 10
   - ⊗ 11
   - ⊗ 12

2) Age: _____

3) Sex (*please choose one*):
   - ⊗ Male
   - ⊗ Female

4) Ethnicity (*please choose all that apply to you*):
   - ⊗ Black / African American / Caribbean American
   - ⊗ Asian American
   - ⊗ European American
   - ⊗ Hispanic/Latino
   - ⊗ Other (please specify) _____

5) Did you or your parent(s)/guardian(s) immigrate to the United States from another country or countries?
⊗ Yes
⊗ No

6) If so, from where? (*List all that apply*) _____

7) Primary language(s) spoken at home (*list all that apply*):

_____

8) Whom do you live with at home? (*Please choose the most accurate*)
⊗ One parent
⊗ Both parents
⊗ Guardian(s)
    Relationship(s) to you _____
⊗ Other (please specify) _____

9) Mother / female guardian's occupation: ⊗ I don't live with a mother / female guardian _____

10) Mother / female guardian's educational history (*choose highest level completed*):
⊗ Did not complete high school
⊗ High school
⊗ 2-year college (associate's degree)
⊗ 4-year college (BA, BS)
⊗ Master's or professional (MA, MS, MBA, JD)
⊗ Doctorate (PhD/MD)
⊗ Don't know

11) Father / male guardian's occupation: ⊗ I don't live with a father / male guardian _____

12) Father / male guardian's educational history (*choose highest level completed*):
⊗ Did not complete high school
⊗ High school
⊗ 2-year college (associate's degree)

⊗ 4-year college (BA, BS)
⊗ Master's or professional (MA, MS, MBA, JD)
⊗ Doctorate (PhD/MD)
⊗ Don't know

13) How many people live in your house? _____

14) How many siblings do you have? _____

15) How many of your siblings live with you? _____

16) Are you often asked to care for a younger sibling / family member?
_____

17) Do you have any siblings in college?
⊗ Yes
⊗ No

Please answer the following as accurately as possible:

18) Which TV programs do you typically watch on Tuesday night?
_____
_____
_____

19) Which TV programs do you typically watch on a Saturday night?
_____
_____
_____

20) When you read independently or do homework, do you like
⊗ quiet
⊗ background music
⊗ to get up and move around a lot
⊗ to be doing many other tasks at once (like watch TV or talk on
   the phone at the same time)

21) If you like background music, what kind of music helps you focus?

_____

22) About how many hours do you spend on the Internet **on an average school day / night**?
- ⊗ 0–1
- ⊗ 2–3
- ⊗ 4–5
- ⊗ More than 5 hours

23) About how many hours **per week** do you spend reading for pleasure outside of school?
- ⊗ 0–2
- ⊗ 3–5
- ⊗ 6–8
- ⊗ More than 8 hours

24) What time do you usually go to bed on a **school night**?

_____

25) What time do you usually go to bed on a **weekend night**?

_____

26) What time do you usually wake up on a **weekend day**?

_____

27) What time do you usually wake up on a **school day**?

_____

28) How important do you think it is to be on time to school?
- ⊗ Very important
- ⊗ Somewhat important
- ⊗ Not very important
- ⊗ No opinion

29) If you are late to school, what factors contribute to you being late? (*You may choose more than one*)
    ⊗ Oversleeping
    ⊗ Dropping off a sibling to school
    ⊗ Public transportation
    ⊗ Stopping for breakfast on the way
    ⊗ Illness
    ⊗ Other (please specify) _____

30) Are you a person who is good at doing many tasks at once (like watching TV while doing homework and talking on the phone)?
    ⊗ Yes
    ⊗ No
    ⊗ Sometimes

31) What are you reading when not in school? (*For each category, check the box that most accurately applies to you*)

	OFTEN	SOMETIMES	ALMOST NEVER
Catalogs/shopping (online or print)			
Magazines			
Instruction manuals / information books			
Maps / bus schedules			
Research papers / newspaper articles			
Biographies/autobiographies			
Religious books			
Music lyrics / poetry			
Comic books / graphic novels			
Novels / short stories			
E-mail			
Websites			
Facebook/MySpace/Twitter			
Letters/notes			
Other (please specify) _____			

32) Which genre(s) of fiction do you like best? (*e.g., historical fiction, urban fiction, mystery, sci-fi/fantasy, graphic novels ...*)

_____

33) How many hours **per week** do you spend writing for pleasure outside of school?
- ⊗ 0–2
- ⊗ 3–5
- ⊗ 6–8
- ⊗ More than 8 hours

34) What are you writing when not in school? (*For each category, check the box that most accurately applies to you*)

	OFTEN	SOMETIMES	ALMOST NEVER
Journal/diary			
Music lyrics / poetry			
Graffiti or tagging on paper			
Directions/instructions			
Comics			
Grocery / shopping list			
Stories			
Letters or notes			
E-mail, chat, blogs			
MySpace/Facebook/Twitter			
Other (please specify) _____			

35) Do you have a job?
- ⊗ Yes
- ⊗ No

36) If so, how many hours a week do you work?
- ⊗ 1–5
- ⊗ 6–10
- ⊗ 11–20
- ⊗ 21–40

37) What is your hourly wage?
    $_____ per hour

38) Do you receive an allowance from a parent or guardian?
    ⊗ Yes
    ⊗ No

39) If so, how much is it?
    $_____ per (*week or month?*)

40) How much do you trust that your parent(s) or guardian(s) know what is best for you?
    ⊗ Very much
    ⊗ Somewhat
    ⊗ Not really
    ⊗ No opinion

41) Should your parent(s) or guardian(s) be stricter with you?
    ⊗ Yes
    ⊗ No

II. School

1) If you went to an academic competition in math and science where you were competing against other College Prep students, how do you think you would do?
    ⊗ Very well
    ⊗ Somewhat well
    ⊗ Not very well
    ⊗ No opinion

2) If you went to an academic competition in math and science where you were competing against other students from all over the United States, how do you think you would do?
    ⊗ Very well
    ⊗ Somewhat well
    ⊗ Not very well
    ⊗ No opinion

3) If you went to an academic competition in English and history where you were competing against other College Prep students, how do you think you would do?

⊗ Very well
⊗ Somewhat well
⊗ Not very well
⊗ No opinion

4) If you went to an academic competition in English and history where you were competing against other students from all over the United States, how do you think you would do?

⊗ Very well
⊗ Somewhat well
⊗ Not very well
⊗ No opinion

5) Is it important to you that you do better than others academically?

⊗ Yes
⊗ No

6) Estimated GPA (grade point average) for all classes:

⊗ A = 4.0 (90 or above)
⊗ B = 3.0 (80 or above)
⊗ C = 2.0 (70 or above)
⊗ D = 1.0 (60 or above)
⊗ F = 0 (below 60)

7) What kinds of general competition are there at College Prep? (*e.g., academic, sports, popularity, between boys and girls, between girls, etc.*)

_____

_____

_____

8) What, in your view, is a successful person? (*e.g., a person who makes a lot of money, a person who is a good parent, a person who gives back to the community, a person who has a stable job, etc.*)

_____

_____

_____

9) Are you an "involved" student? (*Do you get involved in opportunities and extracurricular activities offered through College Prep? Do you participate wholeheartedly in your classes?*)
⊗ Yes
⊗ No

10) Do you think your teachers give you enough opportunities to earn extra credit?
⊗ Yes
⊗ No

11) Is extra credit important to you?
⊗ Yes
⊗ No

12) If yes, why?

_____

_____

_____

13) Do the grades you receive influence how much you like your classes? (*i.e., do you like a class better if you are getting a good grade in it?*)
⊗ Yes
⊗ No

14) Do the grades you receive show how much you are learning? (*i.e., are you more likely to get an A in a class where you are learning a lot?*)
⊗ Yes
⊗ No

15) Do you think College Prep has enough ways of recognizing students for good achievements?
⊗ Yes
⊗ No

16) How much freedom does College Prep give you?
⊗ Not enough
⊗ Just enough

⊗ Too much
⊗ No opinion

17) Would you consider yourself a confident student?
    ⊗ Yes
    ⊗ No

18) If yes, where does this confidence come from? (*e.g., family, friends, teachers, older role models, celebrities*) If no, how have you come to be not very confident?

_____

_____

_____

19) How many hours do you spend on homework on **an average school night?**
    ⊗ 0–1
    ⊗ 2–3
    ⊗ 4–5
    ⊗ More than 5 hours

20) How many hours do you spend on homework **over the weekend?**
    ⊗ 0–1
    ⊗ 2–3
    ⊗ 4–5
    ⊗ More than 5 hours

21) Please complete the following simile:
College Prep is like a
    ⊗ University
    ⊗ Corporation or business
    ⊗ Private school
    ⊗ Party
    ⊗ Prison
    ⊗ Second home / family
    ⊗ Typical NYC school
    ⊗ Other (please specify) _____

22) How does your experience at College Prep compare with the experiences of your friends/siblings who don't go to College Prep (*i.e., College Prep is more academic, more strict, more wild, out of control, easier or harder work, better or worse teachers, better or worse students, etc.*)?

_____

_____

_____

23) What advice would you give a new student who is just starting at College Prep?

_____

_____

_____

24) How often do you feel stressed out?
   ⊗ All the time
   ⊗ Frequently
   ⊗ Infrequently
   ⊗ No opinion

25) If you answered "All the time" or "Frequently" to the above question, which of the following stress you out the most? (*please rank: 1=most stressful, 6=least stressful*)

	1 (VERY STRESSFUL)	2	3	4 (SOMEWHAT STRESSFUL)	5	6 (NOT VERY STRESSFUL)
Schoolwork						
Social life / relationships with friends						
Things at home / family						
Extracurricular activities						
The future / reaching aspirations						
Other (please specify) _____						

26) If you do often feel stressed out, how do you cope with it?

_____

_____

_____

27) Do you sometimes think that you know better than your teachers what or how you ought to learn?
⊗ Yes
⊗ No

28) Can you explain or give an example?

_____

_____

_____

29) How much do you trust that your teachers know what is best for you?
⊗ Very much
⊗ Somewhat
⊗ Not really
⊗ No opinion

30) Do your teachers make an effort to connect to you and your interests?
⊗ Very much
⊗ Somewhat
⊗ Not really
⊗ No opinion

31) Do your teachers make an effort to connect to your community or neighborhood?
⊗ Very much
⊗ Somewhat
⊗ Not really
⊗ No opinion

32) Can you think of a time when you thought you were treated unfairly by one of your teachers?
⊗ Yes
⊗ No

33) What happened?

_____

_____

_____

_____

_____

34) How often do you see students cheating on assignments at College Prep? (*i.e., copying other students' HW or classwork, plagiarizing, cheating on tests*)
- ⊗ Every day
- ⊗ About once a week
- ⊗ A few times a month
- ⊗ Never
- ⊗ No opinion / not sure

35) How common do you think drug use is among College Prep students?
- ⊗ Very common
- ⊗ Somewhat common
- ⊗ Not very common
- ⊗ No opinion / not sure

36) How common do you think alcohol use is among College Prep students?
- ⊗ Very common
- ⊗ Somewhat common
- ⊗ Not very common
- ⊗ No opinion / not sure

37) How common do you think cigarette smoking is among College Prep students?
- ⊗ Very common
- ⊗ Somewhat common
- ⊗ Not very common
- ⊗ No opinion / not sure

38) Outside of your classes, from your entire time at College Prep, what have been the most helpful programs/activities/ASLAs at College Prep in terms of your:

A) Self-confidence / overall well-being:

_____

_____

B) Academic success:

_____

_____

39) For what purposes do you mainly use the Guidance Suite?
   ⊗ To talk about my problems with a social worker
   ⊗ As a place to go when I am sent out of class for a discipline issue
   ⊗ To get a pass to the nurse/library
   ⊗ To avoid going to class
   ⊗ To avoid going to lunch
   ⊗ Other (please specify) _____

40) Is College Prep a multicultural community?
   ⊗ Yes
   ⊗ No

41) Why or why not?

_____

_____

_____

42) If not, what could be done to make it one?

_____

_____

_____

43) How often do you use College Prep's library?
   ⊗ Almost every day
   ⊗ About once a week
   ⊗ About once a month
   ⊗ Less than once a month
   ⊗ I only go when my class is visiting
   ⊗ I have never been to College Prep's library

44) If you do go to the library at College Prep, what do you use it for?
   ⊗ Independent reading
   ⊗ Research for school
   ⊗ To get on the Internet
   ⊗ As a quiet place to study
   ⊗ To hang out with friends
   ⊗ Other (please specify) _____

45) What plans do you have for your future (*career-wise, family-wise, location-wise*)? Please be as specific as you can.

_____
_____
_____

46) Are you planning on going to college?
   ⊗ Yes
   ⊗ No

47) If yes, how are you preparing yourself to gain admission to the college of your choice?

_____
_____
_____

48) If you can, list three colleges that you are interested in attending:
   1)
   2)
   3)

49) Which major(s) are you interested in?

_____
_____
_____

50) Based on your grades, what do you think your chances are of being accepted to a college of your choice?
   ⊗ Very likely
   ⊗ Somewhat likely
   ⊗ Not likely

51) What do you expect to be the most valuable part of your college experience?

⊗ Learning / knowledge / becoming a better thinker
⊗ Cultural diversity
⊗ Diploma/degree
⊗ Making connections with people who can help me succeed

52) How important will cultural diversity be to you in your college experience?

⊗ Very important
⊗ Somewhat important
⊗ Not important

53) What factors contribute the most to getting into the college you want? (1=most important, 3=least important)

	1 (MOST IMPORTANT)	2 (SOMEWHAT IMPORTANT)	3 (LEAST IMPORTANT)
Internships			
Pre-college programs (like College Now)			
Extracurricular activities (ASLA, sports)			
Test scores (PSAT/SAT scores)			
Grades			
Contributing to family income by working and/or taking care of siblings			

54) Are you familiar with the term "professionalism"?

⊗ Yes
⊗ No

55) If so, can you define the term as if you are writing to someone who has never heard of it?

"Professionalism" is:

_____

_____

_____

56) When did you first learn about professionalism? Who taught you?

_____

_____

_____

57) What is your opinion of professionalism / professionalism points at College Prep?

_____

_____

_____

III. Outside of School

1) Do you think you could use more adult presence in your life?
   ⊗ Yes
   ⊗ No

2) Why or why not?

_____

_____

_____

_____

3) How important are the following influences in determining one's future? (*1= most important, 3= least important*)

	1 (MOST IMPORTANT)	2 (SOMEWHAT IMPORTANT)	3 (LEAST IMPORTANT)
Individual effort			
Parents' background			
Social support			
Quality of education			

4) Has your life changed since the election of President Barack Obama?
   ⊗ Yes
   ⊗ No

5) If so, how?

_____

_____

_____

_____

_____

6) If you have a serious problem, whom would you most likely want to talk with about it? (*Please check the most accurate option: 1= most likely to turn to, 3=least likely to turn to*)

	1 (MOST LIKELY)	2 (SOMEWHAT LIKELY)	3 (LEAST LIKELY)
Friend			
Parent/guardian			
Sibling/relative			
College Prep teacher			
College Prep counselor or social worker			
College Prep support staff			
College Prep administrator			
Other (please specify) _____			

7) Do you belong to a public library?
⊗ Yes
⊗ No

8) If yes, what do you use it for? (*You may choose more than one*)
⊗ Independent reading
⊗ Research for school
⊗ To get on the Internet
⊗ As a quiet place to study
⊗ Other (please specify) _____

9) When you need to find something out / get information, how do you usually do it? (*You may choose more than one*)
⊗ Ask someone
⊗ Internet
⊗ Library
⊗ Other (please specify) _____

10) Do you have your own bedroom at home?
⊗ Yes
⊗ No

11) Do you have a working computer with Internet at home?
⊗ Yes
⊗ No

12) On average, how many times **per week** do you have dinner together with your family?
⊗ 0–1
⊗ 2–3
⊗ 4–5
⊗ 6–7

13) How many hours on average do you spend alone at home during a **typical school day**?
⊗ 0–1
⊗ 2–3
⊗ 4–5
⊗ 6 or more

14) How many hours on average do you spend alone at home during a **typical weekend day**?
⊗ 0–1
⊗ 2–3
⊗ 4–5
⊗ 6 or more

Thank you for sharing your thoughts. When you are finished, please turn in your survey to your advisor.

Notes

Introduction

1. Of the 458 students enrolled in the school, grades 9–12, 73 percent are female and 27 percent are male. Students and staff often hypothesize that this atypical imbalance is due to the school's lack of a football team, as well as to the school's theme, which they assume is more popular with young women.

2. In this book, I elect to capitalize the racial markers "White," "Black," and "Brown" to emphasize the centrality of race to my analysis, as well as to draw attention to the importance that this study's participants placed on race as a sociohistorically constructed way of giving meaning to bodies with real material consequences, as well as a mode of identity construction. I also capitalize "Color" when used as a racial marker. In this book, I also use ethnic markers, such as "African American" or "Latino," which sometimes, but not always, overlap with racial markers in the United States. See Collins (2004, 17, 310) and Vargas (2006, 249) for related discussions.

3. The Robin Hood Foundation is a nonprofit philanthropic organization that was founded in 1988 by hedge fund manager Paul Tudor Jones. The Foundation is seen as a pioneer in using venture philanthropy to solve social problems. The stated mission of the organization is to end poverty in New York City (Robin Hood Foundation 2013).

4. In accordance with the Institutional Review Boards at the University of Texas at Austin and the University of Pennsylvania, all interviews were held in confidentiality, and the names of all participants in this study, including interviewees, have been changed by mutual agreement.

5. Here I am drawing on Donna Haraway's ideas of "situated knowledge" and "feminist objectivity" in science (1988).

6. Also see Gregory's (1998) ethnographic portrayal of political culture and activism in Black Corona, Queens, for a critique of mainstream discourse that conflates race, class, and place by classifying Black urban communities as "socially disorganized."

7. But see Lipman (2004) for an exception; she demonstrates the problematic role of market- and standards-based "reforms" in education, using Chicago as a case study.

8. See, for example, Gibbs (2005), Hass (2009), and Pérez-Peña (2010) for mainstream media documentation of private and corporate philanthropy in U.S. public schools.

1. A Mind Is a Wonderful Thing to Invest In

Epigraph: Qtd. in Nasaw (2006).

1. In fact, Rogers notes that only 20 of the approximately 1,011 billionaires in the world are women, about 2 percent. Approximately half are American (2011, 376).

2. For example, the Bill and Melinda Gates Foundation gave over 112 million in grants between 2000 and 2009 to organizations providing education-related services, not including grants made to the Fund for Public Schools, and the Robin Hood Foundation reported contributions of 133 million and program expenses of 94 million in 2006 (Schwartz and Steifel 2011).

3. According to an April 7, 2011, *New York Times* article, Mayor Bloomberg asked Ms. Black to resign three months after her appointment due to her unpopularity and incompetence. He replaced her with deputy mayor Dennis M. Walcott (Barbaro, Otterman, and Hernandez 2011, A1). State Commissioner David Steiner, who gave Black the waiver to be chancellor without any background in education, resigned as well.

4. Although it is important to note that Black's and Steiner's resignations were due largely to pushback from local public and school leaders, and from the teachers' union, they demonstrate that this logic is contested, and is not all-encompassing.

2. The College Prep Look

1. See Sanjek (1991) for a discussion of the "ethnographic present."

2. See Kailin (1999) for a discussion of White tokenization of Black teachers in U.S. educational institutions.

3. This is reflective of a "culture of poverty" discourse that traces back to Oscar Lewis's (1959) and Daniel Patrick Moynihan's (1965) deficit-based arguments. The idea of a "culture of poverty" continues to be heavily contested in the social sciences, because it tends to "blame the victim," and lacks any structural critique. For example, see Foley (1997), Good and Eames (1996), and Valencia (2010) for critiques of the recycled "culture of poverty" in anthropology and education.

4. In a 2014 follow-up interview, Ms. McLeod and I spoke at length about my use of the term "worthy" here, and what the term signifies about the agency and politics of the adults who worked in the Foundation's office. She stressed that she worked to advocate for kids who were not deemed "worthy" in a mainstream sense, nor, at times, by College Prep teachers and administrators, of extra-curricular opportunities. From her perspective, she was passionate about her work for the Foundation because she felt that every school should have someone in her position—someone who could ensure that every student had access to learning and opportunities for edification beyond the school day. She valued equity, but was doing what she saw as her best in a fundamentally inequitable and competi-tive system. This is important to note in terms of College Prep community mem-bers' ambivalent and sometimes resistant agency. While some College Prep staff members (unlike Ms. McLeod) felt that certain students were not "worthy" of certain opportunities, my use of "worthy" here indexes a long history of some of the poor being deemed "worthy" or "deserving" of help by those in power (see Carnegie 1889; M. Katz 2013).

5. In an attempt to preserve anonymity, I do not cite the articles I discuss here.

6. Former Principal Cohen left the school to work for a charter school start-up organization.

7. In order to preserve anonymity, I do not include a reference for these articles.

8. In order to preserve anonymity, I do not include a reference for this article.

9. Every student at College Prep has an advisory class, which is supposed to give students social and academic support.

10. Although we did not know it then, Principal McCarren would ask Assis-tant Principal Humphries as well as Ms. Williams to find new positions at the end of the 2009–10 year. In the 2012 school year, Mr. Battle, the gym teacher and a founding teacher at the school (who was not licensed to teach gym, but rather to teach English and Special Education), was pressured to find another position. Their dismissals further support a patterned practice of pushing out African American staff members.

11. In 2009–10, the merit/demerit point system was changed to an eligible/in-eligible list. If a student had three or more unserved detentions for discipline in-fractions, he or she was marked "ineligible" and prohibited from attending field trips, dances, after-school, or extracurricular activities.

12. African American Vernacular English or "AAVE," is also known as Black English Vernacular, or "BEV," by Labov (1972), as "Ebonics" by Smitherman (2001), among many others, and as "African American Language" or simply "African American" by DeBose (2005).

4. Waiting for Superwoman

1. The article also states that 8 percent of U.S. teachers are Black, 6 percent Hispanic, and 1.6 percent Asian, while 40 percent of public school students are minorities.

2. See J. Elspeth Stuckey's (1990) critique of the "violence of literacy" that ascribes failure and pathology to groups of "illiterate" students.

3. I discuss Ms. McGoldrick's skill at creating intellectual professionalism as a norm in chapter 3.

5. Girl Drama

1. Interestingly, when I searched for the word *boys* in my inbox, 36 e-mails appeared, and when I searched for *young men*, 150 e-mails appeared. When I searched for *girls,* on the other hand, 110 e-mails appeared, but when I searched for *young women*, only 45 e-mails appeared. The imbalanced nature of these linguistic choices reveals differences in student and staff perceptions about boys' and girls' behavior, and hints that young women are typically viewed as more dramatic, insecure, and emotionally immature as compared to their male counterparts. It may also reveal what Ferguson (2001) terms the problematic "adultification" of Black male youth.

2. The first "Raised By" poem was written by Kelly Norman Ellis, and is actually entitled "Raised by Women" (2007). It moved Linda Christensen (2007) to create a series of lesson plans around this poem that would inspire high school students to write their own "Raised By" poems as a tribute to their families and communities. I owe my own inspiration for this assignment to Ellis and Christensen.

3. See chapter 4 for a case study of Ms. Meehan.

6. Critical Thinking

1. This term was originally used by Grande (2000) to refer to "the cultural capital of Whites in almost every aspect of society." Urrieta (2006) refers to Whitestream as "the official and unofficial texts used in U.S. society that are founded on the practices, principles, morals, values, and history of White Anglo American culture, i.e. White cultural capital." He emphasizes that any person actively promoting White models as "standard" furthers Whitestream ideals. Here, I am using this term to emphasize how Whiteness is normalized in the spectacle of "college readiness" at College Prep through the school's emphasis on meritocracy, as well as the ways in which "college readiness" for minority youth is framed as a deficit discourse.

2. Interestingly, her emphasis on upward mobility connects not only to College Prep's mainstream definition of *success,* but also to Marcus Garvey's racial uplift efforts in the early twentieth century; see Hill (1983).

3. Thanks to an anonymous reviewer at the University of Pennsylvania's *Perspectives on Urban Education* for pointing this out.

7. Behind the Mask

1. In the 1970s, lawyers, activists, and legal scholars who were interested in studying and transforming the relationship between race, racism, and power developed critical race theory, synthesizing the disciplines of critical legal studies and radical feminism. Critical race theory questions the foundations of liberalism and takes as its basic tenets the ideas that (1) racism is ordinary, foundational to, and not aberrational in the United States; (2) White supremacy serves important psychic and material purposes, insulating and protecting those in positions of racial power and privilege; (3) race and races are social constructions with real material consequences; (4) all identities are intersectional and no person has a single or unitary identity—that is, while someone may be privileged in terms of gender, he or she might be oppressed in terms of race, social class, gender, sexuality, or other social categories; and (5) voices of Color have unique and different histories and experiences with oppression, and in this sense have a privileged competence in comparison to White voices when it comes to telling stories and teaching about race and racism (Delgado and Stefancic 2001).

2. Ms. Elliott left College Prep in 2011 and moved out of New York City. She did not respond when I e-mailed her for a follow-up interview.

Appendix A

1. Thanks to Douglas Foley for pointing out this important idea.

2. New York City Teaching Fellows, which make up 20–25 percent of teachers in New York City, are making an effort to recruit higher numbers of Black and Latino teachers. In the 2006–7 school year, 32 percent of the Teaching Fellows were Black or Latino, and in 2007–8, 37 percent were (Green 2008).

3. See chapter 6 for an in-depth exploration of the cultural circle.

Bibliography

Adams, Vincanne. 2012. "The Other Road to Serfdom: Recovery by the Market and the Affect Economy in New Orleans." *Public Culture* 24, no. 1: 185–216.

Ainsworth-Darnell, James, and Douglas B. Downey. 1998. "Assessing the Oppositional Culture Explanation for Racial/Ethnic Differences in School Performance." *American Sociological Review* 63, no. 4: 536–53.

Akom, A. A. 2008. "Ameritocracy and Infra-Racial Racism: Racializing Social and Cultural Reproduction Theory in the Twenty-First Century." *Race, Ethnicity and Education* 11, no. 3: 205–30.

Alim, H. Samy. 2006. "The Natti Ain't No Punk City: Emic Views of Hip Hop Cultures." *Callalloo* 29, no. 3: 969–90.

Althusser, Louis. 1971. "Ideology and Ideological State Apparatuses (Notes towards an Investigation)." In *Lenin and Philosophy and Other Essays*, translated by Ben Brewster, 121–76. New York: Monthly Review Press.

Ancess, Jacqueline, and David Allen. 2006. "Implementing Small Theme High Schools in New York City: Great Intentions and Great Tensions." *Harvard Educational Review* 76, no. 3: 401–16.

Anderson, James. 1988. *The Education of Blacks in the South: 1860–1935.* Chapel Hill: University of North Carolina Press.

Anderson, Leon. 2006. "Analytic Autoethnography." *Journal of Contemporary Ethnography* 35, no. 4: 373–95.

Annenberg Institute. 2011. The Annenberg Challenge. http://www.annenberg institute.org/challenge/sites/nynsr.html.

Apple, Michael. 2001. "Comparing Neo-Liberal Projects and Inequality in Education." *Comparative Education* 37, no. 4: 409–23.

———. 2006. *Educating the "Right" Way: Markets, Standards, God and Inequality.* 2nd ed. New York: Routledge / Taylor & Francis.

Aronowitz, Stanley. 2003. *How Class Works.* New Haven, Conn.: Yale University Press.

Ayers, Rick. 2010. "An Inconvenient Superman: Davis Guggenheim's New Film Hijacks School Reform." *Huffington Post,* September 17. http://www.huffing tonpost.com/rick-ayers-/an-inconvenient-superman-_b_716420.html.

Ayers, William. 1996. "A Teacher Ain't Nothin' but a Hero: Teachers and Teaching in Film." In *City Kids, City Teachers: Reports from the Front Row*, edited by W. Ayers and P. Ford, 228–40. New York: The New Press.

———. 2001. *To Teach: The Journey of a Teacher*. New York: Teachers College Press.

Baldacci, Leslie. 2004. *Inside Ms. B's Classroom: Courage, Hope, and Learning on Chicago's South Side*. New York: McGraw-Hill.

Baldwin, James. 1993. *The Fire Next Time*. New York: Random House.

———. 1996. "A Talk to Teachers." In *City Kids, City Teachers: Reports from the Front Row*, edited by W. Ayers and P. Ford, 219–27. New York: The New Press.

Balibar, Etienne, and Immanuel Wallerstein. 1991. *Race, Nation, Class: Ambiguous Identities*. London: Verso.

Baltodano, Marta. 2012. "Neoliberalism and the Demise of Public Education: The Corporatization of Schools of Education." *International Journal of Qualitative Studies in Education* 25, no. 4: 487–507.

Barbaro, Michael, Sharon Otterman, and Javier C. Hernandez. 2011. "After 3 Months, Mayor Replaces School Leader." *New York Times*, April 8.

Behar, Ruth. 1996. *The Vulnerable Observer: Anthropology That Breaks Your Heart*. Boston: Beacon Press.

Bettie, Julie. 2003. *Women without Class*. Berkeley: University of California Press.

Bishop, Matthew, and Michael Green. 2009. *Philanthrocapitalism: How the Rich Can Save the World*. New York: Bloomsbury Press.

Bloom, Howard, Saskia Levy Thompson, and Rebecca Unterman. 2010. *Transforming the High School Experience: How New York City's Small Schools Are Boosting Student Achievement and Graduation Rates*. New York: MDRC.

Bloom, Howard, and Rebecca Unterman. 2012. *Sustained Positive Effects on Graduation Rates Produced by New York City's Small Schools of Choice*. New York: MDRC.

Boal, Augusto. 1979. *Theatre of the Oppressed*. London: Pluto Press.

Boas, Franz. 1887. "Museums of Ethnology and Their Classification." *Science* 9, no. 589: 612–14.

Bomer, Randy. 2008. "Miseducating Teachers about the Poor: A Critical Analysis of Ruby Payne's Claims about Poverty." *Teachers College Record* 110, no. 2: 2497–531.

Bonilla-Silva, Eduardo. 2014. *Racism without Racists: Color-Blind Racism and the Persistence of Inequality in the United States*. 4th ed. Lanham, Md.: Rowman and Littlefield.

Boshier, Roger. 1999. "Freire at the Beach: Remembering Paulo in the Bright Days of Summer." *Studies in Continuing Education* 21, no. 1: 113–26.

Bourdieu, Pierre. 1977. *Outline of a Theory of Practice.* Cambridge: Cambridge University Press.

Bowles, Samuel, and Herbert Gintis. 1976. *Schooling in Capitalist America: Educational Reform and the Contradictions of Economic Life.* New York: Basic Books.

Brayboy, Bryan, Angelina Castagno, and Emma Maughan. 2007. "Equality and Justice for All? Examining Race in Education Scholarship." *Review of Research in Education* 31: 159–94.

Briggs, Laura. 2002. "La Vida, Moynihan, and Other Libels: Migration, Social Science, and the Making of the Puerto Rican Welfare Queen." *Centro Journal* 14, no. 1: 75–101.

Brown, Amy. 2012. "A Good Invesment? Race, Philanthrocapitalism and Professionalism in a New York City Small School of Choice." *International Journal of Qualitative Studies in Education* 25, no. 4: 375–96.

Brown, Keffrelyn. 2010. "Is This What We Want Them to Say? Examining the Tensions in What U.S. Preservice Teachers Say about Risk and Academic Achievement." *Teaching and Teacher Education* 26, no. 10: 1077–87.

Burch, Patricia. 2006. "The New Educational Privatization: Educational Contracting and High Stakes Accountability." *Teachers College Record* 108, no. 12: 2582–610.

———. 2009. *Hidden Markets: The New Education Privatization.* New York: Routledge.

Cammarota, Julio, and Michelle Fine, eds. 2008. *Revolutionizing Education.* New York: Routledge.

Carnegie, Andrew. 1889. "The Gospel of Wealth." In *Andrew Carnegie: The "Gospel of Wealth" Essays and Other Writings,* edited by D. Nasaw, 1–12. New York: Penguin Classics.

Carter, Prudence. 2003. "'Black' Cultural Capital, Status Positioning, and Schooling Conflicts for Low-Income African American Youth." *Social Problems* 50, no. 1: 136–55.

———. 2005. *Keepin' It Real: School Success beyond Black and White.* New York: Oxford Univeristy Press.

Charmaz, Kathy. 2011. "Grounded Theory Methods in Social Justice Research." In *The Sage Handbook of Qualitative Research,* edited by N. Denzin and Y. Lincoln, 359–80. Thousand Oaks, Calif.: Sage.

Chen, David W. 2011. "Charter School Cries Foul over a Decision to Close It." *New York Times,* January 12.

Chiles, Nick. 2006. "Their Eyes Were Reading Smut." *New York Times,* January 4.

Chouliaraki, Lilie. 2011. "'Improper Distance': Towards a Critical Account of Solidarity as Irony." *International Journal of Cultural Studies* 14, no. 4: 363–81.

Christensen, Linda. 2007. "Raised by Women." *Rethinking Schools* 21, no. 3: cover story.

Chubb, John E., and Terry M. Moe. 1990. *Politics, Markets, and America's Schools.* Washington, D.C.: Brookings Institution Press.

Codell, Esmé R. 1999. *Educating Esmé: Diary of a Teacher's First Year.* Chapel Hill, N.C.: Algonquin Books.

Collins, Patricia Hill. 1990. *Black Feminist Thought: Knowledge, Consciousness and the Politics of Empowerment.* New York: Routledge.

———. 2004. *Black Sexual Politics: African Americans, Gender, and the New Racism.* London: Routledge.

Compton, Mary, and Lois Weiner. 2008. "The Global Assault on Teachers, Teaching and Teacher Unions." In *The Global Assault on Teachers, Teaching and Teacher Unions,* edited by M. Compton and L. Weiner, 1–9. New York: Palgrave Macmillan.

Cook, Philip, and Jens Ludwig. 1998. "Weighing the Burden of 'Acting White': Are There Race Differences in Attitudes towards Education?" *Journal of Policy Analysis and Management* 16, no. 2: 256–78.

Coons, John E., and Stephen D. Sugarman. 1978. *Education by Choice: The Case for Family Control.* Berkeley: University of California Press.

Corcoran, Sean, and Henry Levin. 2011. "School Choice and Competition in the New York City Schools." In *Education Reform in New York City: Ambitious Change in the Nation's Most Complex School System,* edited by J. O'Day, C. Bitter, and L. Gomez, 199–224. Cambridge, Mass.: Harvard Education Press.

Cornuelle, Richard. 1965. *Reclaiming the American Dream: The Role of Private Individuals and Voluntary Associations.* New Brunswick, N.J.: Transaction Publishers.

———. 1983. *Healing America.* New York: Putnam.

Craven, Wes, dir. 1999. *Music of the Heart.* Hollywood, Calif.: Craven-Maddalena Films and Miramax Films. Buena Vista Distribution.

Crenshaw, Kimberlé. 1995. "Mapping the Margins: Intersectionality, Identity Politics and Violence against Women of Color." In *Critical Race Theory: The Key Writings That Formed the Movement,* edited by K. Crenshaw, N. Gotanda, G. Peller, and K. Thomas, 357–83. New York: The New Press.

Crew, Rudy. 2010. "More Than Managing 'Assets.'" *New York Times,* November 10.

Cucchiara, Maia. 2013. *Marketing Schools, Marketing Cities: Who Wins and Who Loses When Schools Become Urban Amenities.* Chicago: University of Chicago Press.

Cucchiara, Maia, Eva Gold, and Elaine Simon. 2011. "Contracts, Choice, and Customer Service: Marketization and Public Engagement in Education." *Teachers College Record* 113, no. 11: 2460–502.

Darder, Antonia. 2002. *Reinventing Paulo Freire: A Pedagogy of Love*. Boulder, Colo.: Westview Press.

Davies, Bronywn, and Peter Bansel. 2007. "Neoliberalism and Education." *International Journal of Qualitative Studies in Education* 20, no. 3: 247–59.

DeBose, Charles. 2005. *The Sociology of African American Language*. New York: Palgrave Macmillan.

Delgado, Richard, and Jean Stefancic. 2001. *Critical Race Theory: An Introduction*. New York: New York University Press.

Delpit, Lisa. 1998. "The Silenced Dialogue." *Harvard Educational Review* 58: 280–98.

Demby, Gene. 2013. "New Ads Still Warn a Mind Is a Terrible Thing to Waste." *Code Switch: Frontiers of Race, Culture and Ethnicity*. http://www.npr.org /blogs/codeswitch/2013/06/14/191796469/a-mind-is-a-terrible-thing-to.

Demerath, Peter. 2006. "The Science of Context: Modes of Response for Qualitative Researchers in Education." *International Journal of Qualitative Studies in Education* 19, no. 1: 97–113.

———. 2009. *Producing Success: The Culture of Personal Advancement in an American High School*. Chicago: University of Chicago Press.

Denzin, Norma. 2006. "Analytic Autoethnography, or Déjà Vu All Over Again." *Journal of Contemporary Autoethnography* 35, no. 4: 419–28.

Denzin, Norma, and Yvonna Lincoln, eds. 2011. *The Sage Handbook of Qualitative Research*. 4th ed. Thousand Oaks, Calif.: Sage.

Diamond, John. 2013. "Despite the Best Intentions: The Persistence of Racial Inequality in 'Good' Schools." Paper presented at University of Pennsylvania Graduate School of Education Visiting Faculty Scholars of Color Lecture, October 1, 2013, at University of Pennsylvania Graduate School of Education.

Diamond, John, Amanda Lewis, and Lewis Gordon. 2007. "Race and School Achievement in a Desegregated Suburb: Reconsidering the Oppositional Culture Explanation." *International Journal of Qualitative Studies in Education* 20, no. 6: 655–79.

Dillon, Sam. 2010. "Administration Outlines Proposed Changes to 'No Child' Law." *New York Times*, February 1.

Domanico, Raymond, Carol Innerst, and Alexander Russo. 2000. *Can Philanthropy Fix Our Schools? Appraising Walter Annenberg's $500 Million Gift to Public Education. Case Studies: New York City*. Washington, D.C.: Thomas B. Fordham Foundation.

Dunbar, Paul Laurence. [1896] 1993. "We Wear the Mask." In *The Collected Poetry of Paul Laurence Dunbar*, edited by J. Braxton. Charlottesville: University Press of Virginia.

Duncan-Andrade, Jeffrey, and Ernest Morrell. 2008. *The Art of Critical Pedagogy: Possibilities for Moving from Theory to Practice in Urban Schools*. New York: Peter Lang.

Du Preez, Paul. 1980. *The Politics of Identity: Ideology and the Human Image*. New York: St. Martin's Press.

Dyrness, Andrea. 2011. *Mothers United: An Immigrant Struggle for Socially Just Education*. Minneapolis: University of Minnesota Press.

Ealy, Lenore. 2014. "The Intellectual Crisis in Philanthropy." *Society* 51, no. 1: 87–96.

Edelman, Murray. 1988. *Constructing the Political Spectacle*. Chicago: University of Chicago Press.

Education Law Center. 2013. *Campaign for Fiscal Equity: A Project of ELC*. http://www.edlawcenter.org/initiatives/campaign-for-fiscal-equity.html.

Edwards, Michael. 2011. "Impact, Accountability and Philanthrocapitalism." *Society* 48: 389–90.

Ellis, Kelly Norman. 2007. "Raised by Women." In *Coal Black Voices: The Poets*. http://coalBlackvoices.com/poets/kelly/index.html.

Ellison, Ralph. 1952. *Invisible Man*. New York: Random House.

Fabricant, Michael, and Michelle Fine. 2012. *Charter Schools and the Corporate Makeover of Public Education: What's at Stake?* New York: Teachers College Press.

———. 2013. *The Changing Politics of Education: Privatization and the Lives Left Behind*. Boulder, Colo.: Paradigm.

Fanon, Frantz. 1965. *A Dying Colonialism*. Translated by H. Chevalier. New York: Grove Press.

Farb, Peter. 1991. *Man's Rise to Civilization: The Cultural Ascent of the Indians of North America*. New York: Penguin Books.

Ferguson, Ann Arnett. 2001. *Bad Boys: Public Schools in the Making of Black Masculinity*. Ann Arbor: University of Michigan Press.

Fine, Michelle, Lois Weis, Linda Powell Pruitt, and April Burns. 1997. *Off White: Readings on Race, Power, and Society*. New York: Routledge.

Fine, Michelle, Lois Weis, Susan Weseen, and Loonmun Wong. 2003. "For Whom? Qualitative Research, Representations, and Social Responsibilities." In *The Landscape of Qualitative Research*, 2nd ed., edited by N. Denzin and Y. S. Lincoln, 167–207. Thousand Oaks, Calif.: Sage.

Flyvbjerg, Bent. 2006. "Five Misunderstandings about Case-Study Research." *Qualitative Inquiry* 12, no. 2: 219–45.

Foley, Douglas. 1997. "Deficit Thinking Models Based on Culture: The Anthropological Protest." In *The Evolution of Deficit Thinking: Educational Thought and Practice*, edited by R. Valencia, 113–31. London: Falmer.

———. 2008. "Questioning 'Cultural' Explanations of Classroom Behaviors." In *Everyday Antiracism: Getting Real about Race in School,* edited by M. Pollock, 222–25. New York: The New Press.

———. 2010. *Learning Capitalist Culture: Deep in the Heart of Tejas.* 2nd ed. Philadelphia: University of Pennsylvania Press.

Foley, Eileen. 2010. *Approaches of Bill & Melinda Gates Foundation–Funded Intermediary Organizations to Structuring and Supporting Small High Schools in New York City.* Washington, D.C.: Policy Studies Associates.

Fordham, Signithia. 1993. "'Those Loud Black Girls': (Black) Women, Silence, and Gender 'Passing' in the Academy." *Anthropology and Education Quarterly* 24, no. 1: 3–32.

———. 2008. "Beyond Capital High: On Dual Citizenship and the Strange Career of 'Acting White.'" *Anthropology and Education Quarterly* 39, no. 3: 227–46.

Fordham, Signithia, and John Ogbu. 1986. "Black Students' School Success: Coping with the "Burden of 'Acting White.'" *The Urban Review* 18, no. 3: 176–206.

Frankenberg, Ruth. 1993. *White Women, Race Matters: The Social Construction of Whiteness.* Minneapolis: University of Minnesota Press.

Freire, Paulo. 1970. *Pedagogy of the Oppressed.* New York: Continuum International.

Friedman, Milton. 1955. "The Role of Government in Education." In *Economics and the Public Interest,* edited by R. A. Solo, 123–44. New Brunswick, N.J.: Rutgers University Press.

———. 1962. *Capitalism and Freedom.* Chicago: University of Chicago Press.

Frumkin, Peter. 2010. *The Essence of Strategic Giving: A Practical Guide for Donors and Fundraisers.* Chicago: University of Chicago Press.

Gallego, Margaret, and Sandra Hollingsworth. 2000. *What Counts as Literacy: Challenging the School Standard.* New York: Teachers College Press.

Gasman, Marybeth. 2012. "What's New Is Old?" *Phi Delta Kappan* 93, no. 8: 8–11.

Gates, Bill, and Melinda Gates. 2014. *Letter from Bill and Melinda Gates.* Bill and Melinda Gates Foundation. http://www.gatesfoundation.org/Who-We -Are/General-Information/Letter-from-Bill-and-Melinda-Gates.

Gee, James P. 1996. *Social Linguistics and Literacies: Ideology in Discourses.* New York: Routledge/Falmer.

Geertz, Clifford. 1973. *The Interpretation of Cultures.* New York: Basic Books.

Gibbs, Nancy. 2005. "The Good Samaritans." *Time* 166, December 26: cover story.

Giddens, Anthony. 1991. *Modernity and Self-Identity.* Stanford, Calif.: Stanford University Press.

Ginwright, Shawn. 2010. *Black Youth Rising: Activism and Radical Healing in Urban America*. New York: Teachers College Press.

Giroux, Henry. 1996. "Hollywood, Race and the Demonization of Youth: The Kids Are Not Alright." *Educational Researcher* 25, no. 2: 31–35.

———. 2004. *The Terror of Neoliberalism: Authoritarianism and the Eclipse of Democracy*. Boulder, Colo.: Paradigm Publishers.

The Giving Pledge. 2014. http://givingpledge.org/.

Glesne, Corrine. 2011. *Becoming Qualitative Researchers: An Introduction*. Boston: Pearson.

Goffman, Erving. 1959. *The Presentation of Self in Everyday Life*. Garden City, N.Y.: Doubleday.

———. 1961. *Asylums: Essays on the Social Situation of Mental Patients and Other Inmates*. Chicago: Aldine.

———. 1963. *Stigma: Notes on the Management of Spoiled Identity*. New York: Simon & Schuster.

Goldsmith, Stephen, with Gigi Georges and Tim Glynn Burke. 2010. *The Power of Social Innovation: How Civic Entrepreneurs Ignite Community Networks for Good*. San Francisco: Jossey-Bass.

Goode, Judith G., and Edwin Eames. 1996. "An Anthropological Critique of the Culture of Poverty." In *Urban Life: Readings in Urban Anthropology*, edited by G. Gmelch and W. P. Zenner, 405–17. Prospect Heights, Ill.: Waveland Press.

Goulding, Christina. 2005. "Grounded Theory, Ethnography and Phenomenology." *European Journal of Marketing* 39, no. 3/4: 294–308.

Grande, Sandy. 2000. "American Indian Geographies of Identity and Power: At the Crossroads of Indígena and Mestizaje." *Harvard Educational Review* 70, no. 4: 467–98.

Green, Daniel. 2012. "Investing in High School." *Phi Delta Kappan* 93, no. 8: 28–33.

Green, Elizabeth. 2008. "Fewer Blacks, More Whites Are Hired as City Teachers." *New York Sun*, September 25. http://www.nysun.com/new-york /fewer-Blacks-more-Whites-are-hired-as-city/86580/.

Gregory, Steven. 1998. *Black Corona: Race and the Politics of Place in an Urban Community*. Princeton, N.J.: Princeton University Press.

Gruwell, Erin, and the Freedom Writers. 1999. *The Freedom Writers Diary*. New York: Doubleday.

Guggenheim, Davis, dir. 2010. *Waiting for "Superman."* Electric Kinney Films / Participant Media / Walden Media.

Hall, Stuart, and Paul Du Gay, eds. 1996. *Questions of Cultural Identity*. London: Sage.

Haraway, Donna. 1988. "Situated Knowledges: The Science Question in Feminism and the Privilege of Partial Perspective." *Feminist Studies* 14, no. 3: 575–99.

Harrington, Michael. 1997. *The Other America: Poverty in the United States.* New York: Touchstone.

Harris, Angel. 2011. *Kids Don't Want to Fail: Oppositional Culture and the Black–White Achievement Gap.* Cambridge, Mass.: Harvard University Press.

Harrison, Faye. 1992. "The Du Boisian Legacy in Anthropology." *Critique of Anthropology* 12, no. 3: 239–60.

———. 1998. "Introduction: Expanding the Discourse on 'Race.'" *American Anthropologist* 100, no. 3: 609–31.

Hartigan, John. 2005. "Culture against Race: Reworking the Basis for Racial Analysis." *South Atlantic Quarterly* 104, no. 3: 543–60.

———. 2009. "Individuating Obama: Maneuvers through American Racial Discourse." Paper presented at the annual meeting of the American Anthropological Association, Philadelphia.

Hass, Nancy. 2009. "Scholarly Investments." *New York Times,* December 6.

Hay, Iain. 2013. "Questioning Generosity in the Golden Age of Philanthropy." *Progress in Human Geography,* 1–19.

Haymes, Stephen. 1995. *Race, Culture and the City: A Pedagogy for Black Urban Struggle.* Albany: State University of New York Press.

Heath, Shirley Brice. 1983. *Ways with Words: Language, Life and Work in Communities and Classrooms.* Cambridge: Cambridge University Press.

Hebdige, Dick. 1979. *Subculture: The Meaning of Style.* London: Routledge.

Herszenhorn, David M. 2005. "New York City's Big Donors Find New Cause: Public Schools." *New York Times,* December 30.

Hill, Robert A., ed. 1983. *The Marcus Garvey and Universal Negro Improvement Association Papers.* Berkeley: University of California Press.

hooks, bell. 1990. *Yearning: Race, Gender and Cultural Politics.* Boston: South End Press.

———. 1992. *Black Looks: Race and Representation.* Boston: South End Press.

———. 2001. *All about Love: New Visions.* New York: HarperCollins.

———. 2003. *Teaching Community.* New York: Routledge.

HoSang, Daniel. n.d. "The Structural Racism Concept and Its Impact on Philanthropy." In *Moving Forward on Racial Justice Philanthropy.* Philanthropic Initiative for Racial Equity, 23–26. http://racialequity.org/docs/CIF5The%20Structural%20Racism%20Concept%20.pdf.

Hunt, Darek. 2012. "BIA's Impact on Education Is an Education in Bad Education." *Indian Country Today Media Network.* http://indiancountrytodaymedia

network.com/2012/01/30/bias-impact-indian-education-education-bad-edu
cation-75083.

Hursh, David. 2007. "Marketing Education: The Rise of Standardized Testing,
Accountability, Competition, and Markets in Public Education." In *Neolib-
eralism and Education Reform,* edited by E. W. Ross and R. Gibson, 15–34.
Cresskill, N.J.: Hampton Press.

———. 2009. "Beyond the Justice of the Market: Combating Neoliberal Educa-
tional Discourse and Promoting Deliberative Democracy and Economic
Equality." In *Handbook of Social Justice in Education*, edited by W. Ayers,
T. Quinn, and D. Stovall, 152–64. New York: Routledge.

Husock, Howard. 2011. "Disaggregating Public Purposes." *Society* 48: 391–92.

Hyland, Nora E. 2005. "Being a Good Teacher of Black Students? White Teachers and Unintentional Racism." *Curriculum Inquiry* 35, no. 4: 429–59.

IMDb. 2011a. Box office / business for *Dangerous Minds* (motion picture, 1995).
http://www.imdb.com/title/tt0112792/business.

———. 2011b. Box office / business for *Freedom Writers* (motion picture, 2007).
http://www.imdb.com/title/tt0463998/business.

Jackson, John L. 2008. *Racial Paranoia: The Unintended Consequences of Political Correctness*. New York: Basic Civitas.

———. 2013. "Practicing Impolite Conversations: Talking about Race, Reli-
gion, Politics and Everything Else." Paper read at Penn Lightbulb Café,
Philadelphia, September 24, 2013.

Jenkins, Garry. 2011. "Who's Afraid of Philanthrocapitalism?" *Case Western
Reserve Law Review* 61, no. 3: 1–69.

Johnson, LouAnne. 1992. *Dangerous Minds* (originally titled *My Posse Don't
Do Homework*). New York: St. Martin's Press.

Kailin, Julie. 1999. "How White Teachers Perceive the Problem of Racism in
Their Schools: A Case Study in 'Liberal' Lakeview." *Teachers College Record*
1004: 724–50.

Kanter, Rosabeth Moss. 1977. "Some Effects of Proportions on Group Life:
Skewed Sex Ratios and Responses to Token Women." *American Journal of
Sociology* 82 no. 5: 965–90.

Katz, Cindi. 2001. "Vagabond Capitalism and the Necessity of Social Reproduction." *Antipode* 33, no. 4: 709–28.

———. 2004. *Growing Up Global: Economic Restructuring and Children's
Everyday Lives*. Minneapolis: University of Minnesota Press.

Katz, Michael. 2013. *The Undeserving Poor: From the War on Poverty to the
War on Welfare*. 2nd ed. New York: Pantheon Books.

Keehnen, Owen. 1996. "Artist with a Mission: A Conversation with Sapphire."
Owen Keehnen: Interviews. http://www.queerculturalcenter.org/Pages
/Keehnen/Sapphire.html.

Kelley, Robin. 1997. *Yo' Mama's Disfunktional! Fighting the Culture Wars in Urban America*. Boston: Beacon Press.

Kelly, Anthony. 2007. *School Choice and Student Well-Being: Opportunity and Capability in Education*. New York: Palgrave Macmillan.

Kenny, Lorraine D. 2000. *Daughters of Suburbia*. New Brunswick, N.J.: Rutgers University Press.

Keohane, Georgia Levinson. 2013. "Social Entrepreneurship: How Innovative Change-Makers Are Testing New Solutions to Entrenched Social, Economic and Environmental Problems." New York: McGraw Hill Financial Global Institute.

King, Joyce E. 1991. "Dysconscious Racism: Ideology, Identity and the Miseducation of Teachers." *Journal of Negro Education* 60, no. 2: 133–46.

Koyama, Jill. 2010. *Making Failure Pay: For-Profit Tutoring, High-Stakes Testing, and Public Schools*. Chicago: University of Chicago Press.

Koyama, Jill, and Lesley Bartlett. 2011. "Bilingual Education Policy as Political Spectacle: Educating Latino Immigrant Youth in New York City." *International Journal of Bilingual Education and Bilingualism* 14, no. 2: 171–85.

Kozol, Jonathan. 1992. *Savage Inequalities: Children in America's Schools*. New York: HarperPerennial.

Kumashiro, Kevin. 2012. *Bad Teacher! How Blaming Teachers Distorts the Bigger Picture*. New York: Teachers College Press.

Labov, William. 1972. *Language in the Inner City*. Philadelphia: University of Pennsylvania Press.

Ladson-Billings, Gloria. 1995. "Toward a Culturally Relevant Pedagogy." *American Educational Research Journal* 35, no. 3: 465–91.

———. 2006. "From the Achievement Gap to the Education Debt: Understanding Achievement in U.S. Schools." *Educational Researcher* 35, no. 7: 3–12.

LaGravenese, Richard, dir. 2007. *Freedom Writers*. Paramount Pictures.

Landsman, Julie. 2001. *A White Teacher Talks about Race*. Lanham, Md.: The Scarecrow Press.

Lather, Patti. 2004. "This IS Your Father's Paradigm: Governmental Intrusion and the Case of Qualitative Research in Education." *Qualitative Inquiry* 10, no. 1: 15–34.

Leddy, Bruce, David Grossman, and Amanda Bearse, dirs. 2007. *Nice White Lady*. MADtv. Fox Pictures.

Lemov, Doug. 2010. *Teach Like a Champion: 49 Techniques That Put Students on the Path to College*. San Francisco: Jossey-Bass.

Lewin, Tamar. 2010. "School Chief Dismisses 241 Teachers." *New York Times*, July 24.

Lewis, Amanda. 2003. *Race in the Schoolyard: Negotiating the Color Line in Classrooms and Communities*. New Brunswick, N.J.: Rutgers University Press.

Lewis, Oscar. 1959. *Five Families: Mexican Case Studies in the Culture of Poverty*. New York: Basic Books.

Lipman, Pauline. 2004. *High Stakes Education: Inequality, Globalization and Urban School Reform*. New York: RoutledgeFalmer.

———. 2011. *The New Political Economy of Urban Education: Neoliberalism, Race and the Right to the City*. New York: Routledge.

Liss, Julia. 1998. "Diasporic Identities: The Science and Politics of Race in the Work of Franz Boas and W. E. B. Du Bois, 1894–1919." *Cultural Anthropology* 13, no. 2: 127–66.

Little, Sandy. 2003. "The 'Cash' Language: Whose Standard?" *Field Notes* (Massachusetts System for Adult Basic Educational Support) 13, no. 1: 1, 3–4.

Lomawaima, K. Tsianina. 1995. "Educating Native Americans." In *Handbook of Research on Multicultural Education*, edited by J. A. Banks and C. A. M. Banks, 331–47. New York: Macmillan.

Lorenzi, Peter, and Francis Hilton. 2011. "Optimizing Philanthrocapitalism." *Society* 48: 397–402.

Macedo, Stephen. 2003. "Equity and School Choice: How Can We Bridge the Gap between Ideals and Realities?" In *School Choice: The Moral Debate*, edited by A. Wolfe, 51–69. Princeton, N.J.: Princeton University Press.

Macrine, Sheila, Peter McLaren, and Dave Hill, eds. 2009. *Revolutionizing Pedagogy: Education for Social Justice with and beyond Global Neo-Liberalism*. New York: Palgrave Macmillan.

Mandel, Robert, dir. 1996. *The Substitute*. LIVE Entertainment, Orion Pictures.

Marable, Manning. 2000. *How Capitalism Underdeveloped Black America*. Cambridge, Mass.: South End Press.

Marech, Rona. 2003. "'Hip-Hop Lit' Is Full of Grit: New Literary Genre Emerging from Underground Authors." *San Francisco Chronicle*, October 19.

Marx, Sherry. 2006. *Revealing the Invisible: Confronting Passive Racism in Teacher Education*. New York: Routledge.

Maxwell, Joseph A. 2013. *Qualitative Research Design: An Interactive Approach*. 3rd ed. Thousand Oaks, Calif.: Sage.

Medina, Jennifer. 2010a. "Another Rise in City Pupils Graduating in Four Years." *New York Times* online, March 10. http://www.nytimes.com/2010/03/10/nyregion/10graduation.html.

———. 2010b. "Pressed by Charters, Public Schools Try Marketing." *New York Times* online, March 9. http://www.nytimes.com/2010/03/10/education/10marketing.html.

Moll, Luis C., Cathy Amanti, Deborah Neff, and Norma Gonzalez. 1992. "Funds of Knowledge for Teaching: Using a Qualitative Approach to Connect Homes and Classrooms." *Theory into Practice* 31, no. 2: 132–41.

Molnar, Alex. 2005. *School Commercialism: From Democratic Ideal to Market Commodity*. New York: Routledge.

Mora, Richard, and Mary Christianakis. 2011. "Charter Schools, Market Capitalism and Obama's Neoliberal Agenda." *Journal of Inquiry & Action in Education* 4, no. 1: 93–111.

Moynihan, Daniel P. 1965. *The Negro Family: The Case for National Action*. Washington, D.C.: U.S. Department of Labor.

Mulligan, Robert, dir. 1967. *Up the Down Staircase*. Warner Brothers.

Nasaw, David. 2006. "Introduction." In *Andrew Carnegie: The "Gospel of Wealth" Essays and Other Writings*, edited by D. Nasaw, vii–xiii. New York: Penguin Classics.

National Commission on Excellence in Education. 1983. *A Nation at Risk*. Washington, D.C.: U.S. Department of Education.

Naylor, Charlie. 2011. "The Dearth (Or Is It the Death?) of Discourse in the United States: What Does Diane Ravitch Say about Educational Change, and Why Is There So Little Response?" In *BCTF Information Handbook*, 1–15. Vancouver, BC: BC Teachers' Federation.

NeighborhoodLink. 2010. Data mining website. http://www.neighborhood link.com/.

nysed.gov. 2008–9. The New York State School Report Card. Albany, N.Y.: N.Y. State Education Department, Office of Assessment Policy, Development and Administration. https://www.nystart.gov/publicweb.

Obama, Barack. 2011. State of the Union: Winning the Future. http://www .Whitehouse.gov/the-press-office/2011/01/25/remarks-president-state-union -address.

Oliver, Daniel G., Julianne M. Serovich, and Tina L. Mason. 2005. "Constraints and Opportunities with Interview Transcription: Towards Reflection in Qualitative Research." *Social Forces* 84, no. 2: 1273–89.

Omi, Michael, and Howard Winant. 1994. *Racial Formation in the United States: From the 1960s to the 1990s*. New York: Routledge.

Paley, Vivian. 1979. *White Teacher*. Cambridge, Mass.: Harvard University Press.

Payne, Ruby. 1996. *Understanding the Framework of Poverty*. Highlands, Tex.: Ruby K. Payne.

Pedroni, Thomas. 2007. *Market Movements: African American Involvement in School Voucher Reform*. New York: Routledge.

Pérez-Peña, Richard. 2010. "Facebook Founder to Donate $100 Million to Help Remake Newark's Schools." *New York Times*, September 23.

Perry, Pamela. 2002. *Shades of White: White Kids and Racial Identities in High School*. Durham, N.C.: Duke University Press.

Perry, Theresa. 2003. "Achieving in Post-Civil Rights America: The Outline of a Theory." In *Young, Gifted and Black: Promoting High Achievement among*

African American Students, edited by T. Perry and C. Steele, 87–108. Boston: Beacon Press.

Peshkin, Alan. 1988. "In Search of Subjectivity—One's Own." *Educational Researcher* 17, no. 7: 17–21.

Pierre, Jemima. 2004. "Black Immigrants in the United States and the 'Cultural Narratives' of Ethnicity." *Global Studies in Power and Culture* 11, no. 2: 141–70.

Pollock, Mica. 2004. *Colormute.* Princeton, N.J.: Princeton University Press.

———, ed. 2008a. *Everyday Antiracism: Getting Real about Race in School.* New York: The New Press.

———. 2008b. "From Shallow to Deep: Toward a Thorough Cultural Analysis of School Achievement Patterns." *Anthropology and Education Quarterly* 39, no. 4: 369–80.

Popkewitz, Thomas S. 1998. *Struggling for the Soul: The Politics of Schooling and the Construction of the Teacher.* New York: Teachers College Press.

Ravitch, Diane. 2011a. *The Death and Life of the Great American School System.* New York: Teachers College Press.

———. 2011b. "The Myth of Charter Schools." *The New York Review of Books,* January 13.

Rich, Motoko. 2012. "Enrollment Off in Big Districts, Forcing Layoffs." *New York Times,* July 24.

Richey, Lisa A., and Stefano Ponte. 2011. *Brand Aid: Shopping Well to Save the World.* Minneapolis: University of Minnesota Press.

Rickford, John. 1999. *African American Vernacular English.* Oxford: Blackwell.

Riessman, Frank. 1962. *The Culturally Deprived Child.* New York: HarperCollins.

Ritchie, Michael, dir. 1986. *Wildcats.* Sylbert Movie Co., Warner Brothers.

Robin Hood Foundation. 2013. *Robin Hood.* http://www.robinhood.org/.

Robinson, Cedric. 1983. *Black Marxism: The Making of the Black Radical Tradition.* Chapel Hill: University of North Carolina Press.

Rogers, Robin. 2011. "Why Philanthro-Policymaking Matters." *Society* 48: 376–81.

Rose, Tricia. 2008. *The Hip Hop Wars: What We Talk about When We Talk about Hip Hop—and Why It Matters.* Philadelphia: BasicCivitas.

Roska, Josipa, Eric Grodsky, Richard Arum, and Adam Gamoran. 2007. "United States: Changes in Higher Education and Social Stratification." In *Stratification in Higher Education: A Comparative Study,* edited by D. Grusky and P. England, 165–94. Stanford, Calif.: Stanford University Press.

Sackler, Madeleine, dir. 2010. *The Lottery.* Great Curve Films, Gravitas Ventures.

Saltman, Kenneth J. 2010. *The Gift of Education: Public Education and Venture Philanthropy.* New York: Palgrave Macmillan.

———. 2011. "From Carnegie to Gates: The Bill and Melinda Gates Foundation and the Venture Philanthropy Agenda for Public Education." In *The Gates*

Foundation and the Future of U.S. "Public" Schools, edited by P. Kovacs, 1–20. New York: Taylor & Francis.

Sanjek, Roger. 1991. "The Ethnographic Present." *Man* 26, no. 4: 609–28.

Sapphire. 1996. *Push.* New York: Random House.

schools.nyc.gov. 2010. "Cohorts of 2001 through 2005 (Classes of 2005 through 2009) Graduation Outcomes." New York: NYC Department of Education, Graduation and Dropout Reports. http://schools.nyc.gov/Accountability /data/GraduationDropoutReports/default.htm.

Schwartz, Amy, and Leanna Steifel. 2011. "Financing K–12 Education in the Bloomberg Years." In *Education Reform in New York City: Ambitious Change in the Nation's Most Complex School System,* edited by J. O'Day, C. Bitter, and L. Gomez, 55–84. Cambridge, Mass.: Harvard Education Press.

Scott, James. 1985. *Weapons of the Weak: Everyday Forms of Peasant Resistance.* New Haven, Conn.: Yale University Press.

Shiller, Jessica. 2011. "Marketing New Schools for a New Century: An Examination of Neoliberal School Reform in New York City." In *The Gates Foundation and the Future of U.S. "Public" Schools,* edited by P. Kovacs, 53–79. New York: Taylor & Francis.

———. 2012. "Venture Philanthropy's Market Strategies Fail Urban Kids." *Phi Delta Kappan* 93, no. 8: 12–16.

Simon, Cecilia Capuzzi. 2005. "Teaching the Teachers: Those Who Can, and Can't." *New York Times,* July 31.

Singleton, Glenn E., and Cyndie Hays. 2008. "Beginning Courageous Conversations about Race." In *Everyday Antiracism: Getting Real about Race in Schools,* edited by M. Pollock, 18–23. New York: The New Press.

Smith, Adam. (1776) 2010. *The Wealth of Nations.* New York: Simon and Brown.

Smith, John N., dir. 1995. *Dangerous Minds.* Hollywood Pictures.

Smith, Mary. L., Linda Miller-Kahn, Walter Heinecke, and Patricia Jarvis. 2004. *Political Spectacle and the Fate of American Schools.* New York: RoutledgeFalmer.

Smitherman, Geneva. 2001. *Talkin' That Talk: Language, Culture and Education in African America.* New York: Routledge.

Solomon, R. Patrick, John P. Portelli, Beverly-Jean Daniel, and Arlene Campbell. 2005. "The Discourse of Denial: How White Teacher Candidates Construct Race, Racism and 'White Privilege.'" *Race and Ethnicity in Education* 8, no. 2: 147–69.

Souljah, Sister. 1999. *The Coldest Winter Ever.* New York: Pocket Books.

Souto-Manning, Mariana. 2010. *Freire, Teaching and Learning: Cultural Circles across Contexts.* New York: Peter Lang.

Spears-Bunton, Linda, and Rebecca Powell, eds. 2008. *Toward a Literacy of Promise: Joining the African American Struggle.* New York: Routledge.

Speed, Shannon. 2008. "Forged in Dialogue: Toward a Critically Engaged Activist Research." In *Engaging Contradictions: Theory, Politics and Methods of Activist Scholarship*, edited by C. R. Hale, 213–36. Berkeley: University of California Press.

Spencer, Kyle. 2012. "School Choice Is No Cure-All, Harlem Finds." *New York Times*, September 3, A1.

Spindler, George, and Lorie Hammond, eds. 2006. *Innovations in Educational Ethnography: Theory, Methods, and Results*. Mahwah, N.J.: Lawrence Erlbaum Associates.

Spradley, James. 1979. *The Ethnographic Interview*. New York: Holt, Rinehart and Winston.

Stevens, Mitchell. 2007. *Creating a Class: College Admissions and the Education of Elites*. Cambridge, Mass.: Harvard University Press.

Stevens, Sabrina. 2012. "'Bad' Women, Teachers, and Politics." *Huffington Post*, February 24. http://www.huffingtonpost.com/sabrina-stevens-shupe/bad-women-teachers-and-po_b_1299896.html.

Stocking, George. 1974. *A Franz Boas Reader*. Chicago: University of Chicago Press.

Strathern, Marilyn. 1987. "The Limits of Auto-Anthropology." In *Anthropology at Home*, edited by A. Jackson, 16–37. London: Tavistock.

Stuckey, J. Elspeth. 1990. *The Violence of Literacy*. Portsmouth, N.H.: Boynton/Cook.

Sutton, Margaret, and Bradley A. U. Levinson, eds. 2001. *Policy as Practice: Toward a Comparative Sociocultural Analysis of Educational Policy*. Westport, Conn.: Ablex.

Sweeney, Megan. 2010. *Reading Is My Window: Books and the Art of Reading in Women's Prisons*. Chapel Hill: University of North Carolina Press.

Takaki, Ronald. 2000. *Iron Cages: Race and Culture in 19th-Century America*. New York: Oxford University Press.

Thorup, Mikkel. 2013. "Pro Bono? On Philanthrocapitalism as Ideological Answer to Inequality." *ephemera: theory & politics in organization* 13, no. 3: 555–76.

Tickle, Les. 2001. "The Organic Intellectual Educator." *Cambridge Journal of Education* 31, no. 2: 159–78.

Tyson, Karolyn. 2011. *Integration Interrupted: Tracking, Black Students, and Acting White after Brown*. Oxford: Oxford University Press.

Ullman, Char, and Janet Hecsh. 2011. "These American Lives: Becoming a Culturally Responsive Teacher and the Risks of Empathy." *Race, Ethnicity and Education* 14, no. 5: 1–27.

Urrieta, Luis. 2006. "Community Identity Discourse and the Heritage Academy: Colorblind Educational Policy and White Supremacy." *International Journal of Qualitative Studies in Education* 19, no. 4: 455–76.

———. 2009. *Working from Within: Chicana and Chicano Activist Educators in Whitestream Schools*. Tucson: University of Arizona Press.

Valencia, Richard. 1997. *The Evolution of Deficit Thinking: Educational Thought and Practice*. London: RoutledgeFalmer.

———. 2010. *Dismantling Contemporary Deficit Thinking: Educational Thought and Practice*. New York: Routledge.

Valenzuela, Angela. 1999. *Subtractive Schooling: U.S.–Mexican Youth and the Politics of Caring*. Albany: State University of New York Press.

Vargas, João Costa. 2006. *Catching Hell in the City of Angels*. Minneapolis: University of Minnesota Press.

Venkatesh, Sudhir. 2002. "Race and Philanthropy: An Introduction." *Souls: A Critical Journal of Black Politics, Culture and Society* 4, no. 1: 32–34.

Visweswaran, Kamala. 1998. "Race and the Culture of Anthropology." *American Anthropologist* 100, no. 1: 70–83.

Viteritti, Joseph. 2003. "Defining Equity: Politics, Markets, and Public Policy." In *School Choice: The Moral Debate*, edited by A. Wolfe, 13–30. Princeton, N.J.: Princeton University Press.

Watkins, William H. 2001. *The White Architects of Black Education: Ideology and Power in America, 1865–1954*. New York: Teachers College Press.

Weber, Max. 1999. "Ideal-Type Constructs." In *Max Weber: Sociological Writings*, edited by W. Heydebrand, 262–76. New York: Continuum.

Weikart, Lynne E. 2009. *Follow the Money: Who Controls New York City Mayors?* Albany: State University of New York Press.

West, Cornel. 2001. *Race Matters*. New York: Vintage.

Williams, A. Dee. 2009. "The Critical Cultural Cipher: Remaking Paulo Freire's Cultural Circles Using Hip Hop Culture." *International Journal of Critical Pedagogy* 2, no. 1: 1–29.

Williamson, Ben. 2012. "Mediators and Mobilizers of Curriculum Reform: Education Policy Experts of the Third Sector." Paper presented at the School of Education, University of Stirling, Scotland, December 5, 2012.

Willis, Paul. 1977. *Learning to Labour*. Farnborough, England: Saxon House.

Winant, Howard. 2004. *The New Politics of Race: Globalism, Difference, Justice*. Minneapolis: University of Minnesota Press.

Wolfe, Alan. 2003. "The Irony of School Choice: Liberals, Conservatives, and the New Politics of Race." *School Choice: The Moral Debate*, edited by A. Wolfe, 31–51. Princeton, N.J.: Princeton University Press.

Woods, Teri. 2008. *True to the Game III*. New York: Grand Central.

Woodson, Carter G. 1919. *The Education of the Negro Prior to 1861: A History of the Education of the Colored People in the United States from the Beginning of Slavery to the Civil War*. Whitefish, Mont.: Kessinger Publishing.

Yogev, Esther, and Nir Michaeli. 2011. "Teachers as Society-Involved 'Organic Intellectuals': Training Teachers in a Political Context." *Journal of Teacher Education* 62, no. 3: 312–24.

Yoshino, Kenji. 2006. *Covering: The Hidden Assault on Our Civil Rights*. New York: Random House.

Young, Iris M. 1990. *Justice and the Politics of Difference* Princeton, N.J.: Princeton University Press.

Zelkowski, Jeremy. 2011. "Defining the Intensity of High School Mathematics: Distinguishing the Difference between College-Ready and College-Eligible Students." *American Secondary Education* 39, no. 2: 27–54.

Zhang, Yahui, Radhika Gajjala, and Sean Watkins. 2012. "Home of Hope: Voicings, Whiteness and the Technological Gaze." *Journal of Communication Inquiry* 36, no. 3: 202–21.

Zweig, Michael. 2004. "Introduction: The Challenge of Working-Class Studies." In *What's Class Got to Do with It? American Society in the Twenty-First Century*, edited by M. Zweig, 1–18. Ithaca, N.Y.: Cornell University Press.

Index

AMY BROWN is an educational anthropologist and a faculty member in the Critical Writing Program at the University of Pennsylvania.